The Law and Your Business

Business Law for Managers

The Law and Your Business

Business Law for Managers

Editor: Ash Kabi

Quay Publishing
BKT Information Services

Quay Publishing Ltd., Lancaster and **BKT Information Services**, Nottingham

ISBN   1-85642-058-2

British Library Cataloguing-in-Publication Data

The law and your business : business law for managers.
  I. Kabi, Ash, *1939-*
  344.10666
  ISBN   1-85642-058-2

Typeset by **BKT Information Services**, Nottingham, Specialists in Desktop Publishing, Database Development, and Electronic Media Publishing
Printed in Great Britain by
Antony Rowe Ltd, Chippenham, Wiltshire

Preface

The law is an essential component of the environment in which every business operates. Modern managers need to be familiar with an ever-increasing profusion of laws and regulations not only to avoid the many potential pitfalls, but to protect their business interests, and to take advantage of growing number of new opportunities that are created by changes in the law.

The Law and Your Business Business Law for Managers provides an introduction to some aspects of the law which are of crucial significance to the modern manager. Each chapter deals with a particular area of business activities, covering both the relevant UK and EC laws, and has been written by a specialist in the field. The areas covered are: **Competition; Environment and Waste; Health and Safety; Intellectual Property; Business Contracts of Supply, Product Liability, and Negligence;** and **Transport.** Each author outlines the relevant laws and analyzes their implications for industry, pointing out the actions that prudent businesses should take. The authors also examine EC Directives which have been adopted by the Community, but have yet to be enacted in UK law, and point out their ramifications for the business community.

There are many books on business law, but the vast majority of them are written by lawyers for lawyers. This book is written in a straightforward, non-legalistic manner to help the businessman. It is not intended to replace professional advice, but rather to alert the businessman to areas where advice should be sought. It aims to help the modern manager to make an informed decision on business issues affected by the plethora of new laws and regulations.

Because the law is in a continuous state of flux, the picture presented in this book is a 'snapshot' of the state of law at the time of publication. To alert managers to further changes in the law, **BKT Information Services** has created an alerting service, relating to UK and EC business law **Business Legal Information Service (BLIS). BLIS**—which serves as a regular update to *The Law and Your Business*—draws items from official UK Government and EC publications, trade and law journals, and law firms' client briefing materials, and presents them in a concise and readable manner. **BLIS** can be obtained from BKT Information Services, Unit 101, Plessey Business Park, Technology Drive, Beeston, Nottingham NG9 2ND (Tel. 0602 258837, Fax 0602 436548). It is available as a monthly bulletin, a personal computer database, and as a file suitable for loading on computerized information networks.

Ash Kabi

The Authors

The Editor

Ash Kabi

Ash Kabi is currently the General Manager of the Secondary Services Department of the Royal Society of Chemistry. He was also an Associate Professor for Library and Information Transfer Management with the International Management Centre, Buckingham. Besides being a science graduate, he holds a degree in law and has a special interest in the law as it affects the publishing and information business.

Competition Law & Transport

John Hodgson

Senior Lecturer, Nottingham Law School & Consultant, Fraser Brown, Nottingham.

After a number of years in private practice dealing with a substantial volume of road transport prosecutions, he joined Nottingham Law School, where his teaching and research interests include EC law, criminal litigation, and professional discipline and employment issues. He is the author of a number of articles in these fields.

Environment & Waste

Robert Duxbury

Principal Lecturer, Nottingham Law School

Robert Duxbury is a specialist in the field of planning and environmental law. He is legal editor of the *Journal of Property Investment and Valuation* and is examiner in law for Royal Institution of Chartered Surveyors.

Health and Safety

Michael Ellis

Health and Safety Advisor, Senior Lecturer and Consultant in Occupational Safety and Health, Loughborough University of Technology

Michael Ellis was previously employed as a HM Inspector of Factories by the Health and Safety Executive, and before that in the field of engineering design by Rolls Royce and Ruston Gas Turbines Ltd, where he qualified as an engineer. He lectures extensively on health and safety law at Loughborough, and as a visiting lecturer for the Aston University HSE Diploma Programme. He is retained as a consultant by several large employers to provide specialist advice on safety technology, occupational hygiene, and management systems and policies. He has also undertaken considerable work as an expert witness and has been an expert consultant to the Consumers' Association for 14 years.

Intellectual Property

Neil Maybury

Solicitor and Partner, Pinsent & Co, Birmingham: Head of Intellectual Property Unit

Neil Maybury and his unit have a wide-ranging experience in all areas of intellectual property, both contentious and non-contentious. In particular, he has been closely involved with computer-related matters, both professionally and eternally for many years. In 1977, he was responsible, with Dr Steven Castell, for setting up a legal database on Prestel called Infolex. For nine years he was on the Council of the Society for Computers and Law, and for two years Chairman of its Law Committee. During that time he published, with Keith James, a book called *Guide to the Electronic Office*. He serves on many committees including the Birmingham Law Society Information Technology Committee, The Legal Advisory Group of the Federation Against Software Theft, the Birmingham Chamber of Commerce Patents & Technology Committee, and is the Chairman of the AIM Computer Users Association. He also lectures extensively on computer contracts and other areas of intellectual property law. The co-authors of the Chapter on Intellectual Property are Michael Servian and Michael Croft, both members of the Pinsent & Co Intellectual Property Unit.

Business Contracts of Supply, Product Liability, and Negligence

Robert Bradgate

Unit for Commercial Law Studies, Sheffield University

Robert Bradgate obtained a first-class degree in law from Cambridge University in 1979. After qualifying as a solicitor, and working for a time in private legal practice, he was a lecturer at Nottingham Polytechnic from 1986 to 1989, when he moved to his present position. He has written on many aspects of commercial and consumer law: he is the author of *Drafting Standard Terms of Trading* (Longman, 1991) and co-author (with Nigel Savage) of *Commercial Law* (Butterworths, 1991) and *Business Law* (Butterworths, 1987), and (with Geraint Howells and Margaret Griffiths) of *Blackstone's Guide to the Food Safety Act 1990* (Blackstone Press, 1990)

Shane Russell

Senior Lecturer, Nottingham Law School, Nottingham Polytechnic

Shane Russell is a specialist in tort and consumer law. She is a consultant, writer and researcher in the field of product liability and her articles have been published in a wide range of publications, including The Times, the Law Society Gazette, Product Liability International, and the Business Law Review. She is the author of a management report entitled *Product Contamination – An Incident Management Strategy* (Horton Publishing Ltd).

Transport

Paul Fawcett

Senior Lecturer, Manchester College of Arts and Technology

Paul Fawcett is a well-known transport journalist with regular contributions to *Road Law Reports*, *Local Transport Today*, *Coachmart* and other titles, and author of ten published textbooks on transport operations and the law, as well as co-author of Croner's quarterly update, *Coach and Bus Operations*. He provides a transport consultancy service for clients in both the public and private sectors, is a member of the RSA National Committee for Road Transport Education, and a past Chairman of the NW Section of the Chartered Institute of Transport.

Table of Contents

Competition

John Hodgson

Name: Treaty Establishing the European Economic Community

Identity/SI Number: Treaty of Rome

Date effective: 1/1/58 (UK 1/1/73)

Interpretation

Preliminary

The Treaty is the constitution of the EEC. It establishes an institutional framework and defines the sphere of operation of the Community and the basic principles and general policies which are the essence of the Community. The principal institutions are the Council of Ministers which is at once the forum for political discussion and the principal legislative body of the EEC, the Commission, which is the executive and administrative organ (which also has some legislative powers), the European Court of Justice, which is the only authoritative interpreter of the Treaty and Community legislation, and the Parliament. This is primarily a consultative body, although it does have power to veto the budget or dismiss the Commission. The Council can issue directives, which are addressed to member states and require them to take steps to incorporate in national law specified measures to give effect to a Community policy. If a member state fails to do so, or the measures are defective, the state may be brought before the Court for the default. Where the operative date for implementing a directive has passed, the directive acquires additional force, in that compliance with the directive can be pleaded as a defence to an allegation of breach of the national law. The Council and Commission may make regulations. These are immediately and directly binding within the EEC and override any inconsistent domestic law. In general terms also a provision of EEC law (including a relevant binding decision of the Court) will form part of domestic law and take priority over inconsistent provisions of that law. There is provision for a domestic court to obtain a preliminary ruling from the Court in any case involving the application or interpretation of EEC law. Much of the treaty is taken up with the assignment of responsibility as between the various institutions and the provision of procedures for decision-making, review and appeal. There are four subject areas of substantive law (i.e. rules regulating particular activities) which are relevant to this chapter:- competition, common commercial policy, free movement of goods, establishment.

Competition

General

The provisions relating to competition are to be found in the preamble and Part One (Principles) of the Treaty and, in greater detail, in Part Three (Policy of the Community) Title I Chapter 1 (Arts 85-94). At the level of principle the EEC exists to create a supra-national single market, and is concerned that competition in that market should not be distorted. The policy is articulated in three sections relating to undertakings (meaning any business or commercial organisation, whatever its legal status), dumping and state aids.

Undertakings

Article 85

This Article renders void any agreement between undertakings which has for its object or effect the prevention restriction or distortion of competition within the common market. The Article lists types of behaviour which are within its scope, although the list is non-exhaustive.

- Direct or indirect fixing of prices or other trading conditions.
- Limiting or controlling production, markets, technical development or investment.
- Sharing of markets or sources of supply.
- Discriminatory behaviour.
- The imposition of onerous terms of trade.

The behaviour aimed at may be either horizontally or vertically anti-competitive (i.e. involving undertakings at the same stage of the production process, e.g. a producers' cartel, or at different stages, e.g. a manufacturer and his distributors), and in the latter case can operate up or down the chain of distribution. The definition covers:-

- classic cartels
- price rings
- restricted distribution and supply agreements
- joint ventures
- part take-overs
- franchising
- patent and knowhow licensing and analogous situations.

There must be an effect, actual or potential, on the common market, but this requirement has been liberally interpreted so that a single transaction which, taken in isolation, would be insignificant, may be within the scope of the Article if it can be seen as part of a network of similar transactions which collectively have the potential to distort trade within the common market. Although the Article is concerned only with effects on trade within the common market, the undertakings involved need not be established in a common market country. The Article allows for the exemption of agreements which are within the prohibition but which can on balance be justified by reference to stated criteria of improving the production or distribution of goods or promoting technical or economic progress. The EEC Commission (Directorate General IV) is responsible for implementing the Article and for granting exemptions either by individual decision or by a block exemption for a category of agreements. Block exemptions are granted by way of Regulations (summarised in this chapter). The Commission can also grant negative clearance, i.e. a declaration that a particular agreement is outside the scope of the Article. A further function of the Commission is to enforce the application of the Article. It may act of its own motion or as a result of third party complaints. In addition to declaring offending agreements void (i.e. of no legal effect) the Commission can impose substantial fines and make orders restraining future anti-competitive behaviour. There is a right of appeal to the European Court of Justice.

Article 86

This Article prohibits the abuse by an undertaking of a dominant economic position within the EEC or a significant part of it. A dominant position is one where the undertaking is effectively freed from normal competitive constraints because there is no effective competitor. It is necessary to consider size of market share, looking at the market in geographic and product terms. There has been much litigation to establish what is meant by a dominant position. The extent of the geographic market is established by reference to a number of economic factors, including primarily unit costs, transport costs and perishability, the product market by reference to the existence of substitute products acceptable to the consumer. The creation or enjoyment of a dominant position is not prohibited *per se*. Again there is a non-exhaustive list of types of abusive behaviour:-

- Imposition of unfair prices or conditions
- Artificially limiting production or product development
- Discrimination
- Imposition of unusual and onerous terms of trade.

The impact of the abuse may be horizontal (i.e. an attack on competitors) or vertical (in both directions). Behaviour which has been found to be abusive includes:-

- Predatory pricing
- Taking a monopoly profit
- Tying supply of spare parts and consumables
- Refusal to supply
- Failure to implement technological advances
- Mergers (but only when the acquiring enterprise *already* enjoys a dominant position which it is reinforcing).

The application of Art 86 has been affected by the absence of a specific EEC merger control regime; whenever the Commission has wished to regulate mergers it has had recourse to Art 86, although it was not designed for the purpose. The desirability of a particular merger may or may not be a function of the dominance of a market enjoyed by one of the parties to the merger. There is no procedure for exemption, but application may be made to the Commission for negative clearance, either on the basis that the enterprise in question does not hold a dominant position, or on the basis that its proposed activities will not constitute an abuse. In other respects the arrangements for the enforcement of the Article are similar to those for Article 85.

Article 87

This Article confers on the Council of Ministers the power to make regulations to give effect to Arts 85 and 86 including the provision of penalties and establishing the relationship between those Articles and the domestic law and legal systems of the member states.

Article 89

This Article imposes on the Commission a duty to "ensure the application of the principles laid down in Arts 85 and 86," and requires it to investigate suspected infringements.

Article 90

This Article applies the whole of the competition policy to public authorities and undertakings operating revenue-producing monopolies; this will include nationalised industries and public utilities, whether controlled by national or local government, as well as undertakings which are formally independent of the state, but enjoy statutory or contractual monopoly rights. There is a limitation which excludes the application of the competition rules to the extent that this would interfere with the proper performance by these bodies of their functions, but the exception has been narrowly construed. The principle is that such undertakings should not be insulated from market forces or allowed to influence the market unfairly by reason of their status.

Mergers

As indicated above, some use has been made of the powers conferred by Arts 85-86 to control mergers. It is clear that these powers do not provide a merger control code. There is a new Merger Control Regulation (summarised in this chapter).

Dumping

Article 91

This Article deals with dumping within the common market. This is only relevant during the transitional phase of assimilation after accession of a new member state. The Commission may determine that dumping has taken place and require it to cease or allow defensive measures. Once a state is fully assimilated into the common market internal dumping becomes pointless, as the dumped product is regarded as being in free circulation and can be returned to the country of origin, thus undercutting prices on the home market. Dumping by third countries is regulated under the Common Commercial Policy.

State Aids

Article 92

This prohibits as incompatible with the common market aid granted by the member states, directly or indirectly, which tends to distort competition by favouring particular undertakings or products and affects trade between member states. The Article does not apply to disaster relief or individual social aid. There is also provision for aid to promote the economic development of depressed areas, to put into effect "important projects of common European interest" and economic development aid generally where this does not have an unduly adverse effect on trading conditions. In practice this has proved to be an area of difficulty. National governments tend, for a variety of motives, to wish to foster the national economy. There have been many disputes as to whether individual schemes of aid are allowable, particularly in the context of aid to depressed areas.

Article 93

This Article establishes a scheme for the evaluation and control of state aids. The normal procedure is for the Commission to monitor the situation and issue decisions requiring termination or modification of incompatible state aids, subject to a right of appeal to the Court. There is however an emergency procedure under which a state may apply to the Council for a ruling which removes the particular case from the jurisdiction of the Commission

Common Commercial Policy

General

At the level of principle this is expressed as comprising a common external tariff and commercial policy vis a vis other states, together with co-ordination of economic policy generally. In Part Three Title II of the Treaty there is specific reference to economic policy being based on equilibrium of balance of payments, stable currencies and full employment. There is also reference to convergence of monetary and economic policy, introduced by the Single European Act, but this is notoriously an area of political controversy. While these provisions are in some detail they remain statements of principle rather than detailed rules of behaviour for either states or enterprises.

Relations with Third States.

The emphasis is upon a system for ensuring common policies for external trade generally, in relation to tariffs and in relation to trade related development aid. The Commission has responsibility for administering the policy under the guidance of the Council. There is specific provision for anti-dumping measures, and in practice the Commission has been active in this sphere in response to complaints. The usual remedy is the imposition of a duty sufficient to cancel out the unfair price advantage (a counter-vailing duty) where the third state does not respond to the complaint. There is similar machinery to deal with excessive or unreasonable state subsidies.

Free movement of goods (Articles 9-37)

Customs Union

Underlying the common market is a customs union (Arts 11-29). In the formative period of the common market the freezing and progressive abolition of customs duties in intra-community trade was a substantial element of the work of the community institutions. A similar process applies when a new country joins the EEC. The actual customs union is complete for all states other than Spain and Portugal where the transitional measures expire on 31/12/1991 (Act Concerning the Conditions of Accession of the Kingdom of Spain and of the Portuguese Republic). The effect is that goods produced in a member state, and goods from outside the common market which have been imported into a member state and have paid any duty due under the common EEC external customs tariff are treated as being in free circulation throughout the common market (Arts 12-13). Equally there is a Common Customs Tariff for imports from outside the common market which is operated by the customs authorities of the member states with guidance from the Commission in cases of doubt, such as disputed classification of goods. The common market is however wider than a customs union and also prohibits quantitative restrictions on trade between member states, measures having equivalent effect (MHEE) and charges having equivalent effect to customs duties (CHEE). (Arts 30-37 relate to quantitative restrictions and MHEE.)The latter two concepts were originally anti-avoidance provisions, but in the hands of the Court they have taken on a wide significance. Although the rules apply equally to imports and exports, most problems concern imports. In addition the Treaty also prohibits provisions of a state's internal taxation system which discriminate against imported goods.

CHEE

The Court has ruled that any charge or levy, however described, and whether for the direct benefit of the state or payable to some para-statal or authorised private body, which is imposed by reference to the fact that goods have crossed a frontier will be a CHEE unless it represents payment for a service *bona fide* rendered to and for the benefit of the owner of the goods. This ruling has been applied *inter alia* to charges for frontier inspection of meat, fruit and other foodstuffs, levies to cover the cost of preparation of public trade statistics, and contributions to social security funds. All CHEEs are unlawful and void; there is no provision for exemption.

Quantitative restrictions

These comprise quotas and prohibitions on trade in particular commodities.

MHEE

As a result of a series of Court judgments this is now a very extensive and flexible concept. Any measure which may tend to make it more difficult for imported products to be marketed is within the definition. It is not necessary that the measure is not applied to domestic products also, but a measure which is discriminatory in this sense is more likely to be found to be a MHEE. A quality or recipe regulation applying only to imports will almost certainly be a MHEE, but a similar regulation applying also to domestic products may also be so if in practice imports can comply only by extra expense or trouble. Such measures are seen as protectionist, a continuation of tariff barriers by other means. The wide interpretation of MHEE in this field goes hand in hand with the development where appropriate of single European standards, and the recognition of home country standards in all member states in other cases which forms part of the 1992 single market initiative. There is some confusion in the case law as to the distinction between a CHEE and a MHEE. This is significant since, as set out in the next paragraph, exemptions (derogations) from MHEEs are possible. A CHEE must involve a payment. A MHEE need not do so; if it does, the payment must not have been imposed by reference solely to the crossing of a frontier.

Derogations

Art 36 provides for cases where quantitative restrictions and MHEE may be justified by way of exception to the principle of free movement. The permitted justifications are public morality, security or safety, human animal and plant health, protection of the national heritage and protection of intellectual property. Examples of restrictions which have been upheld are those on pornography, works of art and movements restrictions in case of epidemic disease. The Article may not be used to disguise restrictions on trade, and the restrictions proposed must therefore be proportional to the evil being guarded against and applied indiscriminately to domestic products as appropriate. Attempts to protect the German beer and Italian pasta industries from foreign competition by invoking established recipe laws failed. There was no evidence that the altered recipe rendered the product less healthy. Consumer freedom to choose the traditional recipe could be ensured by appropriate labelling regulations.

Discriminatory Internal Taxation (Article 95)

Although separate in the Treaty, this Article is intimately associated with the provisions for free movement of goods. Each member state is free to impose its own system of indirect taxation (subject to general parameters) but may not in so doing discriminate against imports, either by adjusting tax categories and rates to benefit domestic products or by adopting a method of calculation or collection of tax that is discriminatory, examples have included applying a higher rate of car tax to a category of cars selected so as not to contain any domestic models, and imposing tax on imported goods at the imported price (including transport to the border) and on domestic goods at the ex-factory price.

Establishment

Undertakings

Articles 52-58 provide in general terms a right for EEC nationals (including EEC registered companies) to establish themselves in business (including setting up agencies branches and subsidiaries) throughout the EEC. The principal problem of a legal nature is the need to harmonise qualifications, particularly in those cases such as medicine where the possession of a recognised qualification is a necessary prerequisite to establishment. Scientific, engineering and commercial qualifications are generally recognised informally and on their merits. However some member states do restrict the right to set up in business independently in a variety of cases. There are a number of directives amplifying and implementing these provisions of the treaty.

Services

Articles 59-66 relate to the right to provide services in other member states, i.e. to carry out operations without establishing a permanent business. There are special provisions for transport, banking and insurance, and in general the model of the provisions for establish are followed with relevant modifications.

Implications for Industry:

Competition

All enterprises large or small are liable to be affected as villains or victims.

Villains

Trading arrangements may fall foul of Art 85. An application for negative clearance or individual exemption may be required. Compliance with the requirements of a block exemption must be monitored.

Technical departments will be involved in that transactions involving intellectual property are within Art 85, and also because technical improvement is itself a ground for exemption.

Enterprises which are or may be in a dominant position have also to consider their trading practices generally in order to avoid allegations of abuse.

Victims

The activities of suppliers or customers may be in breach of the law. They can be restrained or penalised. This can apply even if the victim is trading entirely domestically, provided the distortion of trade is capable of affecting trade within the market. The potential effect on other enterprises can be taken into account, as can the applicability of block exemptions. If competitors are in receipt of improper state aids this can be challenged.

Common Commercial Policy

This is primarily a matter for action at a political (Governmental) level. Enterprises can apply pressure by lobbying. In concrete terms the only area where specific action can be directly sought is in the field of dumping.

Free Movement of Goods

Any rules of a member state setting standards or prescribing recipes, particularly in areas where there are EEC standards, and any taxation which applies to imports differently to domestic products may justify complaint under Articles 30 and 95 respectively.

Major Impact

All areas of manufacturing industry and distribution.

Name: First Regulation Implementing Articles 85 and 86 of the Treaty [of Rome].

Identity/SI Number Council Regulation 17/62

Date effective: 13/3/62 (UK 1/1/73)

Interpretation

This Regulation provides the machinery which the Commission requires to exercise its powers under Articles 85-86.

The conduct caught by the two Articles is prohibited; no decision is required to achieve this result (Art 1). The Commission may grant a negative clearance (certificate that specified conduct does not infringe the Articles) (Art. 2). Where the Commission finds a breach of the Articles it may require it to be brought to an end. The Commission may be requested to take action by a member state or by anyone with a legitimate interest in the subject matter (Art. 3). All agreements for which exemption is claimed must be notified to the Commission unless they operate solely within one state, are bi-partite resale price maintenance or intellectual property licensing agreements, or are research and development, standardisation or specialisation agreements (and the latter must not affect more than 15% of the relevant market or involve undertakings whose combined turnover exceeds 200M ECU) (Art 4). An exemption must be for a specified period, but is renewable. This can cause difficulties where the agreement is intended to be of a permanent nature. An exemption can be withdrawn if it was improperly obtained, is abused, or there is a material change in circumstances (Art 8). The Commission alone has the power to grant exemptions, but national authorities may apply Art 85(1) and Art 86 provided the Commission is not acting in the case (Art 9). The Commission has power to request information. If this is not supplied, penalties may be imposed (Arts 11, 15). In addition to investigating specific undertakings and alleged contraventions, the Commission has power to carry out general investigations of defined sectors of the economy (Art 12). Officers of the Commission have powers of entry and search, and may take copies of business books and records (Art 14). When a contravention is established a fine of up to 1M ECU or 10% of the previous year's turnover of the undertakings concerned may be levied, supplemented by a daily fine of up to 1000 ECU in respect of a continuing contravention. This will not apply to contraventions arising from an agreement which has been notified for clearance or exemption until the decision of the Commission has been given (Arts 15, 16). The subjects of an enquiry under the Regulation have a right to be heard before a decision is made, and there is a discretion to hear other interested parties (Art 19).

Implications for Industry:

As for the Treaty (Competition)

Major Impact:

Manufacturing industry and distribution

Name: Regulation on the Application of Art 85(3) of the Treaty [of Rome] to Categories of Exclusive Distribution Agreements

Identity/SI Number EEC 1983/83

Date effective: 1/7/83

Interpretation

This Regulation provides a block exemption from Art 85(2) for exclusive distribution agreements (EDAs) which come within its scope, i.e. such agreements will not be void. An EDA is an agreement whereby a manufacturer grants a distributor the exclusive right to distribute his product within a given geographical area.

EDAs which do not come within the terms of the regulation may be made the subject of an application for individual exemption, but cannot benefit from the block exemption. The Regulation is designed to cover the very large number of normal EDAs which are not anti-competitive. It is recognised that an EDA can lead to inter-brand competition because the distributor has the incentive to promote the goods in question, and the existence of dealerships promotes rational and cost-effective distribution. Art 1 states that Art 85(1) of the Treaty of Rome will not apply to EDAs to which there are only two parties, provided the conditions laid down in the rest of the Regulation are satisfied. It is assumed in the Regulation that the two parties are economically independent. Under EEC law an agent, operating wholly on behalf of a supplier is treated, in continental fashion, as an integral part of the supplier's business, not an independent entity. Distributors are running their own business with an establishment and the possibility of flourishing or failing independently of the supplier. Art 2 forbids any restriction on the supplier other than exclusivity of supply, and limits restrictions on the distributor to:

- Non-competition with the contract goods purchase of the contract goods from the supplier only
- Refraining from active marketing outside the contract area.

The distributor may be obliged to handle a complete range, to comply with the suppliers requirements as to sale under a trademark or in specified packaging, to advertise, to maintain a level of stocks and to provide specified levels of technical and after-sales support. These restrictions and obligations represent a maximum. They may be omitted. Art 3 states that Art 1 will not apply where the parties are both manufacturers of similar goods (except for non-reciprocal agreements where at least one party is a small enterprise with a turnover of less than 100M ECU), where there is no alternative source of supply or where there is any active attempt to inhibit parallel imports. These are imports from a third state, and are seen by the Commission as an important means of guaranteeing the existence of effective price competition. Art 6 allows the benefit of the Regulation to be withdrawn where, even though the agreement does not infringe Art 3 there is in fact no effective competition with the contract goods. It is thus possible to prevent an exclusive distributorship where there is no inter-brand competition. The Article also applies where the exclusive distributor abuses his position, and in sundry other cases where there is in fact a significant disruption of access to the contract goods. The Regulation does not apply to agreements relating to the sale of drinks in bars or petrol *solus* agreements.

Implications for Industry

Any enterprise considering entering into an EDA should ensure that it complies with the Regulation. Any enterprise whose interests are damaged by the operation of an EDA should consider whether the EDA is within the protection of the Regulation.

Major Impact

Engineering and technically advanced industry where specialised products and/or small turnover justify the use of exclusive distributors.

Name: Regulation on the Application of Article 85(3) of the Treaty [of Rome] to Categories of Exclusive Purchasing Agreements.

Identity/SI Number: EEC 1984/83

Date effective: 1/7/83

Interpretation

This Regulation provides a block exemption from Art 85(2) for exclusive purchasing agreements (EPAs) which come within its scope, i.e. such agreements will not be void. An EPA is an agreement whereby an undertaking agrees to obtain all its supplies of a given product from one source.

EPAs which do not come within the scope of the Regulation may be made the subject of an application for individual exemption, but cannot benefit from the block exemption. It is recognised that EPAs are not *per se* anti-competitive, in that they allow suppliers to plan production, promote active marketing and ensure regular supplies. There is a separate regime for beer ties and petrol *solus* agreements, which are distinguished by reference to the provision of finance by the supplier to the distributor. The general provisions are contained in Title I of the Regulation. Art 1 exempts EPAs with only two parties from the operation of Art 85(1) subject to the other provisions of the Title. The only restriction which may be imposed on the supplier is one not to compete with the distributor in the distributor's territory and at the same level of distribution (Art 2). The distributor may only be restrained from dealing in competing goods (Art 2). The distributor may be obliged to handle a complete range, to comply with the supplier's requirements as to sale under a trademark or in specified packaging, to advertise, to maintain a level of stocks and to provide specified levels of technical and after-sales service. These restrictions and obligations represent a maximum. They may be omitted. Art 3 disapplies Art 1 where the parties are both manufacturers of similar goods (except for non-reciprocal agreements where at least one party is a small enterprise with a turnover less than 100M ECU). It also applies to agreements for different classes of unconnected goods or where the agreement is capable of lasting for more than five years. Title II contains the special regime for beer EPAs, and Title III that for petrol *solus* agreements. these are to specialised for detailed treatment in this work. Title IV contains miscellaneous provisions, including in Art 14 a power to disapply the relevant provisions of the Regulation where there is in fact no effective competition with the contract goods, access to the market by other suppliers is in fact significantly hindered, or the supplier is guilty of abuse of its position. Art 16 disapplies the Regulation where there is an EPA which is also an exclusive distribution agreement (ie both supplier and distributor are exclusively tied one to the other). Art 17 prohibits the simultaneous operation at one site of agreements under Title I and either Title II or III

Implications for Industry:

Prospective parties to EPAs should ensure that they fall within the block exemption. Where there is an absence of choice because of a local monopoly of tied outlets customers may be able to complain.

Major Impact:

Those industries where it is common to have tied outlets, usually at the retail level.

Name: Regulation on the Application of Article 85(3) of the Treaty [of Rome] to Categories of Research and Development Agreements (RDAs)

Identity/SI Number EEC 418/85

Date effective: 1/3/85

Interpretation

The Regulation proceeds on the basis that R & D generally promotes technical and economic progress, and is to be fostered. RDAs can however be seen as anti-competitive where the parties deprive themselves of the opportunity of independent R & D in the area, or where the RDA extends to the commercial exploitation of the R & D concerned; where the advantages outweigh the disadvantages a block exemption will be available. Art 1 defines RDAs as agreements for R & D only, for R & D followed by joint commercial exploitation of the results, or for the commercial exploitation of the results of a prior R & D only agreement. Art 3 imposes conditions which ensure freedom from restraint in areas outwith the RDA, prevent the creation of a joint sales mechanism and restrict cooperative exploitation to matters covered by specific intellectual property rights or constituting significant knowhow of a commercially exploitable nature. The exemption operates for the R & D period and for the first five years of commercial exploitation, except that where any two parties to the agreement were already competing manufacturers of products capable of being substituted by the products covered by the RDA and having a market share of 20% or more the exemption for exploitation is withdrawn. The exemption can however continue beyond the five year period so long as the combined market share of the parties in contract products and potentially competitive products does not exceed 20%. There is a permissible margin of error of 10% in any two consecutive years and a six month period of grace following the withdrawal of exemption (Art 3). Arts 4 and 5 set out a "white list" of permitted clauses in RDAs:-

- not to compete in R & D in the contract area or related areas, alone or with others
- to procure contract products from parties or others as prescribed in the RDA
- to manufacture only where agreed
- to restrict the application of the results of the R & D to specified fields (except where any parties are competing manufacturers within the meaning of Art 3)
- no active selling in areas of the market reserved to other parties
- to provide feedback on and permit access by other parties to independent developments arising from the RDA
- to disclose patented or non-patented technical knowledge as a necessary basis for the RDA to keep technical knowledge so disclosed by another party confidential and not to use it for unauthorised purposes
- to obtain any appropriate intellectual property rights, and to defend these, and co-operate in defending any belonging to other parties.
- payment of royalties or other consideration to equalise differential costs and benefits from the RDA
- supply of minimum quantities of contract product to other parties
- quality standards

These represent maxima, and similar but less extensive obligations are permitted. Article 6 contains a "black list" of provisions. If any of these apply the agreement does not qualify for exemption, whether they are part of the RDA itself, contained in a separate agreement or arise from a concerted practice of the parties to the RDA:-

- restrictions on unconnected R & D or on contract R & D after the agreement expires
- prohibitions on challenges to the validity of any intellectual property rights relating to the RDA after the RDA has expired
- quantitative restrictions on the exploitation of the contract R & D
- price restrictions
- restrictions on customer selection
- division of the geographical market after expiry of the RDA
- prohibition of third party exploitation of the fruits of the RDA where there is no provision for joint exploitation
- measures designed to protect indirectly a national compartmentalisation of the market by refusal to supply customers or use of intellectual property rights

Art 7 goes on to provide that provisions restrictive of competition which appear on neither the "white list" nor the "black list" are to be subject to the "opposition procedure." Such agreements must be notified, but if the Commission does not oppose exemption within six months it will be deemed granted. The benefit of the Regulation may be withdrawn where there is inadequate scope for others to compete, either at the R & D level or at the product level, or where the parties, without good reason, do not exploit the RDA (Art 10).

Implications for Industry

Joint R & D, especially by means of RDAs is seen as a valuable means to improve the technical qualities of goods. This applies particularly to smaller enterprises, who can only contemplate R & D on a collaborative basis, but also to very large projects which are beyond the reach of even the largest individual enterprise. Care must be taken to avoid the "black list," but there is much scope within the white list, even for co-ordinated commercial exploitation of the fruits of an RDA.

Major Impact

All technologically advanced sectors

Name: Regulation of the Council on the Application of Art 85(3) of the Treaty [of Rome] to Categories of Agreements Decisions and Concerted Practices

Identity/SI Number EEC 2821/71

Date effective: 20/12/71

Interpretation

This is an umbrella Regulation conferring on the Commission powers to grant block exemptions in specified fields, namely standardisation, R & D and specialisation (Art 1). Any such Regulation must be for a specific period and is subject to modification in the light of circumstances (Art 2); it may also be disapplied in particular cases (Art 7).

Implications for Industry

Mainly in relation to the implementing Regulations and the need to ensure input when a Regulation is in draft or being revised.

Major Impact

All sectors affected by the implementing Regulations

Name: Regulation on the Application of Art 85(3) of the Treaty [of Rome] to Categories of Patent Licence Agreements

Identity/SI Number EEC 2349/84

Date effective: 1/1/85

Interpretation

It has been accepted that there is a fundamental incompatibility between the concept of intellectual property, which allows the owner of an idea, process or design to restrict exploitation thereof, and the concept of free competition, which assumes equal access to resources, including intellectual ones. The Regulation recognises the contribution made by the existence of patent protection to the desire of inventors to invest time and money in projects and the benefit to the consumer of technical innovation. The Regulation relates to bilateral agreements, which are exempted from Art 85 under Art 85(3) and which are either pure patent licensing agreements, or combine patent licensing and the transfer of non-patented knowhow. There is a "white list" of permitted obligations in Arts 1 and 2:-

- exclusivity
- non-competition by either party against the other or by the licensee against other licensees in defined reserved areas so long as patent protection subsists
- prevention of active sales to customers outside the licensed area and any marketing outside the licensed area for the five year period commencing with the first commercial exploitation of the patent within the common market so long as parallel patent protection subsists
- use of the licensor's trademarks and getup (style of presentation)
- procurement of components or services from the licensor or his nominee, where justified on technical grounds
- minimum royalties or production minima
- restrictions on the fields of exploitation of the patent
- an obligation of confidentiality and a restraint on post-termination exploitation of the patent
- restraint on sub-licences or assignment
- marking the product to indicate the patent protection
- cooperation in restraining infringement
- qualitative controls relevant to ensuring compliance with the patent specification
- mutual feedback coupled with the right to a non-exclusive licence to exploit improvements

---

- a most favoured licensee clause

There is also provision for exemption of similar but less extensive provisions.

Art 3 contains a "black list" of prohibited provisions, the presence of which means that the agreement will not qualify for block exemption:-

- prohibition of a challenge by the licensee of the validity of the licensor's intellectual property rights
- automatic prolongation of the licence by the inclusion of subsequent patents (subject to exemptions and the right to claim royalties on knowhow for so long as it remains confidential)
- restrictions on competition other than those specifically cleared by Art 1
- royalties which do not relate specifically to current patents or confidential knowhow
- quantitative maxima
- price controls
- restrictions on customers who may be supplied
- compulsory assignment to the licensor of patents for new applications or improvements devised by the licensee
- inducements to accept additional unwanted and irrelevant licences
- extensions to the permitted restraint on marketing in other parts of the common market
- measures against parallel importers designed to block their access to supplies of goods

In the last two cases a concerted practice to the same effect is also prohibited. Art 4 applies the opposition procedure where an agreement contains provisions which are on neither the "white list" nor the "black list." Such agreements must be notified, but if the Commission does not oppose them within six months they are deemed to be exempted. The Regulation does not apply to patent pools, arrangements relating to a joint venture, reciprocal agreements between competing enterprises or plant breeder's rights (Art 5). Exemption may be withdrawn where there are unacceptable anti-competitive effects, eg absence of effective competition, a long term exclusive licence is not being effectively exploited or evidence of action which has the effect of dividing the market geographically, in particular the use of intellectual property rights to prevent parallel imports (Art 9).

Implications for Industry

The Regulation applies to all patent licensing agreements which operate at a significant level within the EEC. Black listed clauses are fatal. Non white listed clauses may or may not be acceptable; they should be used only when commercially necessary, and the agreement notified. Negotiation is possible within the opposition procedure.

Major Impact

All sectors where patent protection is available.

Name: Regulation of the Council on the Application of Art 85(3) of the Treaty [of Rome] to Categories of Agreements and Concerted Practices

Identity/SI Number EEC 19/65

Date effective: 2/3/65

Interpretation

This is an umbrella Regulation conferring on the Commission powers to grant block exemptions in specified fields, namely exclusive purchasing, exclusive supply and mutual agreements involving both Art 1). Any such Regulation must be for a specific period and is subject to modification in the light of circumstances (Art 2); it may also be disapplied in particular cases (Art 7).

Implications for Industry

Mainly in relation to the implementing Regulations and the need to ensure input when a Regulation is in draft or being revised.

Major Impact

All sectors affected by the implementing Regulations

Name: Regulation on the Application of Art 85(3) of the Treaty [of Rome] to Categories of Knowhow Agreements

Identity/SI Number EEC 556/89

Date effective: 1/4/89

Interpretation

The Regulation relates to bilateral agreements, which are exempted from Art 85 under Art 85(3) and which are either pure knowhow agreements, or combine patent licensing and the transfer of non-patented knowhow in a manner which is outside the scope of Reg (EEC) 2349/84. Knowhow is defined as technical information that is secret, substantial and can be identified in some specific formulation There is a "white list" of permitted obligations in Arts 1 and 2:-

- exclusivity
- non-competition by either party against the other or by the licensee against other licensees in defined reserved areas
- prevention of active sales to customers outside the licensed area and any marketing in the common market but outside the licensed area for a five year period
- use of the licensor's trademarks and getup
- limitation of production to the amount necessary to satisfy the licensee's own requirements
- minimum royalties or production minima

- restrictions on the fields of exploitation of the knowhow
- an obligation of confidentiality and a restraint on post termination exploitation of the knowhow
- restraint on sub-licences or assignment
- cooperation in restraining infringement
- qualitative controls relevant to ensuring compliance with the knowhow specification
- mutual feedback coupled with the right to a non-exclusive licence to exploit improvements
- a most favoured licensee clause

There is also provision for exemption of similar but less extensive provisions. Except as noted the protection extends for a maximum of ten years. There are special rules for the patent elements of mixed patent/knowhow agreements. Art 3 contains a "black list" of prohibited provisions:-

- prohibition of a challenge by the licensee of the validity of the licensor's intellectual property rights or the secrecy of the knowhow
- automatic prolongation of the licence by the supply of subsequent knowhow (subject to exemptions and the right to claim royalties on knowhow for so long as it remains confidential)
- restrictions on competition other than those specifically cleared by Art 1
- royalties which do not relate specifically to current patents or confidential knowhow
- quantitative maxima
- price controls
- restrictions on customers who may be supplied
- compulsory assignment to the licensor of patents for or other rights over new applications or improvements devised by the licensee
- inducements to accept additional unwanted and irrelevant licences
- extensions to the permitted restraint on marketing in other parts of the common market
- measures against parallel importers designed to block their access to supplies of goods

In the last two cases a concerted practice to the same effect is also prohibited. Art 4 applies the opposition procedure where an agreement contains provisions which are on neither the "white list" nor the "black list." Such agreements must be notified, but if the Commission does not oppose them within six months they are deemed to be exempted. The Regulation does not apply to patent or knowhow pools, arrangements relating to a joint venture, reciprocal agreements between competing enterprises or plant breeder's rights (Art 5). Exemption may be withdrawn where there are unacceptable anti-competitive effects, eg absence of effective competition, a long term exclusive licence is not being effectively exploited or evidence of action which has the effect of dividing the market geographically, in particular the use of intellectual property rights to prevent parallel imports (Art 9).

Implications for Industry

The Regulation applies to all patent licensing agreements which operate at a significant level within the EEC. Black listed clauses are fatal. Non white listed clauses may or may not be acceptable; they should be used only when commercially necessary, and the agreement notified. Negotiation is possible within the opposition procedure.

Major Impact

All sectors where patent protection is available.

Name: Regulation on the Application of Art 85(3) of the Treaty [of Rome] to Categories of Franchise Agreements.

Identity/SI Number EEC 4087/88

Date effective: 1/2/89

Interpretation

The Regulation relates to franchise agreements (FAs). These are essentially licences to use various forms of intellectual property, typically trade marks and know-how, coupled with restrictions related to the supply or purchase of goods to be used in connexion with the franchised operation.

FAs typically create a limited number of outlets for the franchised product or service. They are however regarded favourably as the franchise format enables the franchiser to expand the outlets for his product or service in conjunction with the franchisee, who will supply capital and management, while the franchiser can ensure quality control. FAs typically operate in areas where there is active competition from other similar products, and the restriction on the number of franchised outlets does not impair overall consumer choice. By Art 1 of the Regulation a block exemption under Art 85 (3) is granted in respect of FAs which comply with the other provisions of the Regulation. Art 2 specifies the restrictions which the parties may accept; the franchiser may undertake not to compete with the franchisee, while the franchisee may undertake

- To operate only from specified premises
- Not to seek customers outside the franchise area
- Not to manufacture or deal in competing goods (other than spare parts or accessories)

Art 3 contains a list of permissible restrictions on the franchisee, some where it is necessary to protect the franchiser's intellectual property rights or to maintain the integrity of the franchise network:-

- Abiding by quality specifications
- Using the franchiser's approved product
- Non-competition with the franchised operation
- Not to have a controlling stake in any competitor
- To sell goods only to end users or to fellow franchisees
- To achieve minimum levels of sales and follow a business plan
- To meet advertising costs

Others are not subject to the above limitation:-

- Confidentiality in relation to knowhow
- Communication of, and permission to exploit, improvements in knowhow
- To notify and/or pursue infringements
- Not to use knowhow for other purposes
- To participate in training programmes
- To adopt the franchiser's commercial methods
- To comply with the franchiser's standards
- To permit inspections
- Not to relocate without consent
- Not to transfer the franchise without consent

The franchisee must be free to obtain goods from any proper source, must honour all guarantees given on franchised goods within the EC and must make his status as an independent undertaking clear. Art 5 contains a "black list" of provisions , the inclusion of any of which will prevent the block exemption from applying.

- FAs between existing competitors
- Restrictions on obtaining goods other than those specifically permitted
- Prohibition on using knowhow after termination where that knowhow is now in the public domain
- Control of prices by the franchiser
- Restrictions on supply to end users by reference to residence

There is provision for agreements containing provisions which are not referred to in the Regulation to be notified to the Commission. If there is no objection within six months the block exemption will apply (The opposition procedure).

Implications for Industry

Franchising presently operates primarily in the field of services (printing) and catering. It can apply to retailing, particularly of a specialised kind.

Major Impact

Food industries, retailing generally.

Name: Regulation on the Control of Concentrations between Undertakings

Identity/SI Number EEC 4064/89

Date effective: 21/9/90

Interpretation

The Treaty of Rome contained no express powers to regulate mergers and takeovers. For many years there were major differences between the member states as to the need for the Commission to have such powers, and the scope of any powers they should have. The present Regulation is aimed only at concentrations (mergers or takeovers) having a significant EC dimension.

Art 1 defines the EC dimension. The aggregate turnover of the undertakings concerned must exceed 5,000 million ECU.

Furthermore, both the following criteria must be satisfied

- At least two of the undertakings must each have aggregate turnover within the EC of over 250 million ECU
- The undertakings must not all achieve at least two-thirds of their aggregate EC turnover within one and the same member state

The combined effect of these provisions is to exclude those concentrations which are too small to matter at EC level, those which affect the EC only incidentally and those which operate within a single national economy. There is however power in Art 22 to apply the rules laid down in the Regulation at the request of a member state to a concentration which does not qualify, but which is likely to have serious anti-competitive effects within that state.

Art 3 defines concentrations for the purpose of the Regulation. A concentration will arise where:-

- Two or more previously independent undertakings merge
- An undertaking, or those controlling it, acquire control of another undertaking, directly or indirectly
- Undertakings create a joint subsidiary on a permanent basis

Control is very widely defined. It includes practical as well as legal control.

In practical terms the definition covers the following common situations

- A true merger
- A true takeover, whether agreed or contested
- Absorption of part of another undertaking
- Bringing two undertakings under common control
- A part merger bringing parts of two undertakings together in a jointly owned undertaking

Concentrations possibly having an EC dimension must be notified to the Commission within a week. The Commission must investigate without delay. Following the initial investigation it may:-

- Declare that the concentration is outside the scope of the Regulation
- Declare that the concentration is not incompatible with the aims of the common market and may proceed
- Commence a full investigation

In order to prevent the disadvantages that might arise from delay, aspects of a concentration may be allowed to proceed on an interim basis (e.g. where one undertaking is being rescued from insolvency).

The purpose of the investigation is to establish whether the concentration is or is not compatible with the common market according to criteria laid down in Art 2:-

- The need to secure effective competition within the EC having regard inter alia to possible competition from non-EC undertakings
- The market position of the parties to the concentration, the conditions in the market for their products and similar products, technical and economic progress and economic factors generally

The remaining articles contain supplemental and procedural provisions, and provide for penalties for failure to notify and for failure to co-operate with the Commission, either in the course of an investigation or in implementing a decision.

Implications for Industry

Will only directly affect large enterprises considering mergers or takeovers. Smaller companies considering foreign links will need to consider whether these rules will be applied in the foreign state under Art 22.

UK Primary and Secondary Legislation

When considering the UK legislation it is important to note that the Government have made proposals for substantial changes. These have been the subject of a White Paper. If implemented, these proposals will align UK and EC competition law to a great extent by the use of a common set of concepts. The intention is to assimilate UK rules to the EC ones, and to apply them to situations where the EC rules do not apply because the necessary international dimension is not present.

Name: Fair Trading Act 1973

Identity/SI Number 1973 c 41

Date effective: Various dates in 1970s

Interpretation

This Act is the principal UK legislation regulating the creation and operation of monopolies. It also amends the Restrictive Practices Act (see page 20) and contains other provisions which are outside the scope of this chapter.

The Act creates the Office of Director General of Fair Trading (DGFT) (S1) and confers on him far-ranging powers to keep under review the practices of the market in relation to the interests of consumers. This extends to interests in relation to health and safety as well as purely economic questions relating to terms of trade etc (S2(1)). There are similar powers in relation to *'the carrying on of commercial activities in the UK'* in relation specifically to monopolies and uncompetitive practices (S2(2)). The DGFT reports to the Secretary of State for Trade and Industry.

The Act also creates the Monopolies and Mergers Commission (MMC) (S4), and gives it the function of investigating monopoly situations and problematical mergers referred to them under the provisions of the act and to issue reports for the guidance of the Secretary of State. A monopoly in relation to the supply of goods is defined in the Act (S6 (1)), as arising when 25% of goods of that description are supplied either by or to a single supplier, the members of a group of companies under common control, or the members of a group acting in concert so as in any way to prevent restrict or distort competition. This part of the definition is deliberately wide so as to catch these groups irrespective of their structure and method of functioning. A closer definition would tempt those wishing to exploit loopholes. There is a very similar definition of a monopoly in relation to services (S7 (1)). There is a slightly modified definition of a monopoly in relation to exports (S8). The basic premise is still that a monopoly exists where 25% of the market is affected, but the types of agreement that can amount to a monopoly are extended to cover agreements that operate primarily in the foreign market, and to which UK exporters are party. The geographic area in which a monopoly may be investigated may be limited to a part of the UK (S9).

Initial investigation of the possible existence of a monopoly is carried out by the DGFT (S44(1)). In order to carry out this function he may require information from undertakings as to the value and amount of goods or services of the relevant description which they produce, their production capacity and available workforce (S44(2)). Where the monopoly is a "complex" one (i.e where it arises from the operation of an agreement between independent undertakings) the DGFT may also require information about any such agreement (S45). Failure to supply information lawfully required, or the supply of false information, is a criminal offence (S46).

Where the DGFT (S50) or the Secretary of State for Trade and Industry (S51) considers that a monopoly situation does or may exist he may refer the matter to the MMC. The reference must be specific as to the goods or services concerned (S47 (1)), and may be limited to a consideration of agreements creating a complex monopoly (S47(2)). The reference may be limited to an enquiry as to whether a monopoly situation exists (a reference limited to the facts) (S48), or may require the MMC to further report on whether any monopoly found to exist operates or may operate against the public interest (S49). The terms of a reference may be altered by the authority which made the reference (S52). References must be publicised to give those affected the opportunity of responding (S53). The report of the MMC is made to the Secretary of State (S54(1)). It must include definite conclusions and reasons for these together with a sufficient account of the factual background (S54(2)), and, where appropriate, recommendations for remedying any anti-competitive effects found to exist (S54(3)), either by governmental action or by action by the persons concerned (S54(4)). The appropriate minister may, on receipt of a report which identifies anti-competitive practices make a variety of orders declaring a particular practice or agreement unlawful, preventing refusal to supply or unfair trading conditions, regulating prices and division of monopolistic companies (S56 and Sched 8).

The Secretary of State may refer to the MMC any merger (or proposed merger (S75)) where at least one of the parties is, or is controlled by, a UK registered company, the value of the assets taken over exceeds £30M and the result of the merger is to create or strengthen a monopoly situation (defined in the same way as 25% of the relevant market) in respect to any category of goods and services within the UK (S64). A merger is defined as two companies coming under common control (including *de facto* control) or one company ceasing trading and ceding its business to another (S65). The reference may be limited to certain aspects of the merger (S69(4)). The MMC must produce a report within not more than six months (S70), and this must contain conclusions, reasons and an account of the factual background (S72(1)). Where the conclusion is that the merger will operate against the public interest, the report must deal with the action necessary to remedy this, and may make recommendations (S72(2)). There is power for the Secretary of State to prevent a merger being put into effect pending a report (S74). Once a report has been made, the Secretary of State may (but is not bound to) make any of the orders which may be made in relation to a monopoly report (S73(2) and Sched 8). There is a general power to refer other anticompetitive trade practices or restrictive labour practices to the MMC (Ss78-79).

All MMC reports are laid before Parliament and published except where this would be against the public interest (S83).

Where the MMC is obliged to consider whether actions are against the public interest they must in particular have regard to (S84(1)):

- maintaining effective competition;
- promoting the interests of consumers in relation to the price, quality and variety of goods and services;
- promoting technical development and the growth of new markets and manufacturers;
- promoting the balanced distribution of industry and employment within the UK; and
- promoting active export competitiveness of UK companies.

Implications for Industry

Where a company, alone or in concert with others has 25% or more of a market, or where it is involved in a merger of those dimensions, the Act will apply, and if the effect is against the public interest enforcement action may follow.

Major Impact

All areas of manufacturing and service industry

Name: The Restrictive Trade Practices Act 1976

Identity/SI Number 1976 c 34

Date effective: 1970s

Interpretation

The Act applies to agreements operative in the UK between two or more undertakings which regulate any of the following (S6):

- the price to be charged or quoted to third parties for goods or work on goods
- recommended resale prices
- terms and conditions of supply to third parties
- quantity or type of goods to be supplied to third parties what work is to be done to goods to or from whom or where goods are to be supplied
- provide for the exchange of information on any of the above matters (S7)
- regulate any of the above matters *mutatis mutandis* in relation to categories of services controlled by the Act (S11)
- provide for the exchange of information on any of the above matters (S12)

All such agreements must be registered in a register maintained by the Director General of Fair Trading (DGFT). If an agreement is not duly registered it is void and it is unlawful to implement it (S35).

The DGFT may refer any registered agreement to the Restrictive Practices Court (RPC) which is part of the High Court for a ruling as to whether its provisions are contrary to the public interest (S2). If they are ruled to be contrary to the public interest the agreement is void, and the RPC may restrain parties to it from giving effect to it or entering into any similar agreement (S3). The Act operates concurrently with the equivalent EC rules (Art 85), but the RPC may decline to act or postpone its action in the light of the situation under EC law (S5). The DGFT may also defer action on similar grounds (S21).There is a general presumption that such agreements operate contrary to the public interest, and it is for the parties to the agreement to prove the contrary by establishing (S10 in relation to goods, S19 in relation to services is to like effect):-

- that the restriction is necessary to protect the public against injury to person or property from the goods
- that removal of the restriction would deny the public substantial benefits which they derive from it
- the restriction is necessary to defend the parties against the anti-competitive or monopolistic behaviour of a third party
- that removal of the restriction would significantly increase unemployment
- that removal of the restriction would seriously and adversely affect exports
- that the restriction is merely ancillary to another acceptable restriction
- that the restriction does not affect competition

There is power to exempt agreements of national significance (S29), and agreements designed only to reduce or moderate prices (S30). There are various provisions applying to special cases and machinery for operating the register and, conducting investigations and prosecuting infringements.

Implications for Industry

Any form of resale price maintenance, collusion over terms of supply or market sharing agreement is caught. There is no lower limit of turnover or otherwise. It is very unlikely that an agreement will be upheld by the DGFT or the RPC but provisional validity can be obtained by registering, and there may be a substantial delay before the agreement is considered. The interrelationship with the EC rules must always be considered.

Major Impact

All sectors of industry

Name: The Resale Prices Act 1976

Identity/SI Number 1976 c 53

Date effective: 1970s

Interpretation

The Act deals with resale price maintenance (RPM). There are separate provisions for collective RPM and individual RPM. Collective RPM is unlawful. It arises (S1) where two or more suppliers agree to:-

- refuse to supply dealers who have broken a price maintenance clause
- discriminate against such dealers
- supply only wholesale dealers who will apply collective RPM in relation to their retailer customers
- recover penalties from dealers who infringe a price maintenance clause

It also arises (S2) where dealers agree to boycott or discriminate against suppliers who refuse to enforce price maintenance. Furthermore, a recommendation to act in any of the above ways is equated to an agreement so to do (S3), and trade associations are equated to traders (S4). As the agreement is unlawful, the courts will take no account of it, and therefore even other innocuous terms cannot be enforced.

Individual RPM arises where a contract for sale by a supplier to a dealer or any associated agreement establishes a minimum resale price (S9(1)). Any such term is void, and its inclusion unlawful, but the rest of the contract remains enforceable (S9(2)). It is also unlawful to issue a price list stating minimum resale prices, but it is permissible to issue a list of recommended resale prices (*ibid*). There are special arrangements which permit the owner of a patent from regulating in a patent licence or assignment the price at which the licensee or assignee may sell the patented product (S10). It is also unlawful for a supplier to withhold supplies from a dealer on the ground that he has infringed or is likely to infringe a minimum resale price established by the supplier and also to cause or procure any other supplier to withhold supplies for the same reason (S11). Withholding of supplies comprises (S12(1)):-

- refusal or failure to supply altogether
- significant discrimination in terms of trade

However a withholding which is justifiable on grounds other than RPM is permissible (S12(2)), although the presumption is that where the supplier is aware of a breach or threatened breach of RPM within the last six months any withholding from an established customer is presumed to be on that ground (S12(3)).

Where goods have been used by a dealer as loss leaders (i.e. sold not in order to obtain a profit but to attract customers into the store) then withholding is lawful (S13).

There is provision for goods to be exempted from the provisions of the Act by an order of the Restrictive Practices Court (RPC) (S14). Application may be made by the Director General of Fair Trading, by a supplier or by a suppliers' trade association (S15). The RPC must be satisfied that the detriment to consumers arising from RPM is outweighed in the particular case by the benefit to consumers conferred by any of the following factors (S14(2)):-

- quality and variety of goods available
- number of outlets
- long-term level of price
- health and safety hazards from "unqualified" dealers
- quality and availability of after-sales and other ancillary services

In practice successful applications are very rare.

The primary remedy for breach of the Act is by way of an application for an injunction on the part of the Crown (S25(2)), but anyone injured by a breach may bring an action for damages for breach of statutory duty (S25(3)).

Implications for Industry

It is in practice impossible to operate a system of RPM, whether collective or individual, and whether formal or informal. Those who seek to do so are acting unlawfully and may be liable in damages to anyone injured thereby.

Major Impact

All manufacturing and distribution sectors of the economy

Name: The Competition Act 1980

Identity/SI Number 1980 c 21

Date effective: April-May 1980

Interpretation

The Act deals in part with the control of anti-competitive practices which are defined (S2(1)) as a course of conduct by a person or associated persons intended or likely to have the effect restricting distorting or preventing competition within the UK in connection with the production supply or acquisition of goods or services except to the extent that the course of conduct corresponds to a provision of an agreement registered or registrable under the Restrictive Trade Practices Act (S2(2)). Initial investigation is carried out by the Director General of Fair Trading (DGFT) (S3(1)), subject to a reserve power vested in the Secretary of State for Trade and Industry to discontinue an investigation (S3(5)). The DGFT has power to compel the production of documents and information (S3(7)). When the investigation is complete the DGFT will publish a report; if there is a case to answer he must consider whether to refer the case to the Monopolies and Mergers Commission (MMC) (S3(10)). He may however accept an undertaking to refrain from the anti-competitive behaviour in question in lieu of a formal reference (S4). The MMC must investigate where a reference has been made and report to the Secretary of State. If the report concludes that anti-competitive behaviour has occurred they may make recommendations for preventing continuance or recurrence (S8). On receipt of the report the Secretary of State may either request the DGFT to obtain an undertaking (S9), or make an order prohibiting the practice and/or exercising any of his powers under Sched 8 PartI of the Fair Trading Act 1973 (see above) (S10). There is also power to refer the activities of nationalised industries and similar bodies to the MMC for a report on their efficiency and costs, quality of service and possible abuse of a monopoly situation (S11), and to require the DGFT to carry out an enquiry into any price of significance to consumers which is also of major public concern (S13).

Implications for Industry

The Act increases the flexibility of the powers conferred by the Fair Trading Act, and is best seen as an extension of that Act

Major Impact

As for Fair Trading Act

Name: The Anti-Competitive Practices (Exclusions) Order 1980

Identity/SI Number:SI 1980/979

Date effective: 12/8/80

Interpretation

The Order provides a series of exclusions which operate to prevent a course of conduct from being capable of being an anti-competitive practice for the purposes of the Competition Act 1980. The Director General of Fair Trading's powers to obtain information under the Competition Act are modified so as to allow him to ascertain whether the criteria for exemption are met (Reg 3)

The exclusions are:

- agreements relating solely to exports
- agreements relating to international carriage by air or sea
- the activities of building societies
- various activities in pursuance of agreements regulated under the Restrictive Trade Practices Act (all Sched I)
- the activities of undertakings which (alone or as part of a group both (Reg 2) have a turnover of less than £5M, and enjoy less than one quarter of a relevant market

Implications for Industry

Remove the threat of investigation from small enterprises which are not dominant in their specialised market

---

Competition

Major Impact

Small enterprises generally

Name: The Registration of Restrictive Trading Agreements Order 1984

Identity/SI Number: SI 1984/392

Date effective: 18/4/94

Interpretation

The Order provides the detailed rules for the registration of agreements under the Restrictive Trade Practices Act 1976 in order to obtain the benefit of provisional validity, and also provides for public inspection of the register.

Implications for Industry

Must be complied with by any enterprise wishing to register an agreement

Major Impact

Generally applicable

Environment and Waste

Robert Duxbury

EEC LEGISLATION

Name: Treaty establishing the European Economic Community

Identity: Treaty of Rome

Date effective: 1/1/58 (UK 1/1/73)

Interpretation:

Preliminary

The task of the European Community as laid down by the Treaty of Rome consists partly of the promotion of an harmonious development of economic activities and a continuous and balanced expansion. The Council of Ministers has stated that this is something the achievement of which "cannot not be imagined in the absence of an effective campaign to combat pollution and nuisances or of an improvement in the quality of life and the protection of the environment." Accordingly, starting in 1973, the Community has adopted several consecutive Action Programmes for the Environment. The most recent updating of the Action Programme covers the period 1987–1992. It sets out the Community's aims for the environment as:

(i) the prevention, reduction and elimination of pollution and nuisances;

(ii) the maintenance of a satisfactory ecological balance and protection of the biosphere;

(iii) the sound management of natural resources;

(iv) the importance of good environmental planning with regard to working and living conditions;

(v) participation in appropriate action at international level.

Two further underlying principles appear in the Action Programme, ie the principle that prevention is better than cure and that the "polluter pays."

When the 1973 Action Programme was first adopted there was no provision in the Treaty of Rome providing expressly for an environmental policy. The measures adopted under the 1973 Action programme were based on Article 100 or Article 235 of the Treaty (or both).

Article 100 empowers the institutions to "issue directives for the approximation of such provisions laid down by law, regulation or administrative action in member states as directly effect the establishment or functioning of the Common Market." This has been used, eg to harmonise exhaust standards of motor vehicles.

Article 235 provides that "if action by the Community should prove necessary to attain, in the course of the operation of the Common Market, one of the objectives of the Community, and this Treaty has not provided the necessary powers" . . . then the Community may take "appropriate measures."

However, the 1986 Single European Act provides an addendum to the Treaty of Rome (in Articles 130R-130T) providing for an EC environmental policy. As a result measures adopted since the Single Act came into force (in July 1987) refer to the new articles instead. These are as follows:

Article 130R

1. Action by the Community relating to the environment shall have the following objectives:

    - to preserve, protect and improve the quality of the environment,
    - to contribute towards protecting human health,
    - to ensure a prudent and rational utilisation of natural resources.

2. Action by the Community relating to the environment shall be based on the principles that preventive action should be taken, that environmental damage should as a priority be rectified at source, and that the polluter should pay. Environmental protection requirements shall be a component of the Community's other policies.

3. In preparing its action relating to the environment, the Community shall take account of:

    - available scientific and technical data,
    - environmental conditions in the various regions of the Community,
    - the potential benefits and costs of action or of lack of action,

    the economic and social development of the Community as a whole and the balanced development of its regions.

4. The Community shall take action relating to the environment to the extent of which the objectives referred to in paragraph 1 can be attained better at Community level than at the level of the individual Member States. Without prejudice to certain measures of a Community nature, the Member States shall finance and implement the other measures.

5. Within their respective spheres of competence, the Community and the Member States shall co-operate with third countries and with the relevant international organisations. The arrangements for Community co-operation may be the subject of agreements between the Community and the third parties concerned, which shall be negotiated and concluded in accordance with Article 228.

The previous paragraphs shall be without prejudice to Member States' competence to negotiate in international bodies and to conclude international agreements.

Article 130S

The Council, acting unanimously on a proposal from the Commission and after consulting the European Parliament and the Economic and Social Committee, shall decide what action is to be taken by the Community.

The Council shall, under the conditions laid down in the preceding sub-paragraph, define those matters on which decisions are to be taken by a qualified majority.

Article 130T

The protective measures adopted in common pursuant to Article 130S shall not prevent any Member State from maintaining or introducing more stringent protective measures compatible with this Treaty.

Most of the measures adopted so far have been directives which are not normally enforceable in the UK courts, although exceptionally they may be directly effective under the European Communities Act. Directives are however binding as to the result to be achieved but leave to national authorities in member states the choice of form and methods. In the UK implementation may be by statute, by delegated legislation or by administrative action. EEC regulations have effect as law in member states without the need for governmental action. Only one regulation (on CFC's) has so far been adopted under the environmental policy (see later). Recommendations are not legally binding at all.

EEC legislation on the environment will be dealt with under the following heads: air pollution; noise pollution; inland water pollution; dangerous substances etc; waste; environmental impact assessment.

Air pollution

EEC measures against air pollution have concentrated upon pollution by motor vehicles, CFC's, smoke pollution, sulphur dioxide emissions, nitrogen oxide emissions and pollution from asbestos.

1970 Council Directive on Air Pollution by Motor Vehicles (70/220/EEC)

This sets standards as to the emission of gaseous pollutants (carbon monoxide, hydrocarbons, nitrogen oxides) for the construction of petrol and diesel engine motor vehicles. The directive applies to cars and light vehicles up to three and a half tonnes. A further directive (in 1987) similarly applies limits to gaseous pollutants from diesel engines over three and a half tonnes (ie HGV's). The effect of the directives is that member states must not impose stricter standards on vehicles being imported from other parts of the EEC. They are not required to ensure that all vehicles within their territory comply with the directive's standards.

1980 Council Decision on Chlorofluorocarbons (CFC's) in the Environment (80/372/EEC)

1982 Council Decision on Precautionary Measures concerning CFC's in the Environment (82/795/EEC)

The 1980 decision required member states to take all appropriate measures to ensure that industry did not increase its capacity for producing CFC's. The 1982 decision repeats the 1980 ban on production, but gives a reference figure for total EEC capacity. CFCs, which are non-flammable gases, are used mainly as aerosol propellants in air-conditioning, refrigeration and the manufacture of polyurethane foam. The 1980 and 1982 decisions led to the 1988 Regulation on Certain CFC's and Halons which deplete the Ozone Layer. The regulation controls the importation, production and consumption of a listed group of CFC's and halons. Permitted importations are subject to licences issued by member states. Limits are set on the production of such substances within the EEC and upon their consumption, with a freeze being imposed at 1986 levels of production and consumption. Production and consumption is to be reduced to 80% of the 1986 levels by 1993 and 50% of those levels by July 1998.

1980 Council Directive on Air Quality Limit Values for Sulphur Dioxide and Suspended Particulates (80/779/EEC)

This directive sets "limit" and "guide" values for sulphur dioxide and suspended particulates (ie smoke) concentrations in the atmosphere. Similarly, the 1985 Directive on Air Quality Standards for Nitrogen Dioxide (85/203/EEC) requires member states to take necessary measures to ensure that by July 1st 1987 the concentrations of nitrogen dioxide in the atmosphere in their territories do not exceed the limit values specified in the directive. In addition the 1988 Council Directive on the Limitation of Emissions of Certain Pollutants into the Air from Large Combustion Plants (88/609/EEC) provides for the reduction in overall emissions of sulphur dioxide from existing combustion plants in three stages by 1993, 1998 and 2003.

1987 Council Directive on the Prevention and Reduction of Environmental Pollution by Asbestos (87/217/EEC)

This requires member states to take the measures necessary to ensure that asbestos emissions into the air, asbestos discharges into aquatic environment and solid asbestos waste are, as far as reasonably practicable, reduced at source and prevented.

Noise pollution

Directives have been issued controlling noise pollution from a number of sources, including construction plant and equipment.

1978 Council Directive on Noise from Construction Plant and Equipment (79/113/EEC)

This directive indicates standards and procedures for testing emissions from construction plant and equipment generally. This was followed by directives on Compressors (84/533/EEC); Tower Cranes (84/534/EEC); Welding Generators (84/535/EEC); Power Generators (84/536/EEC); Powered Concrete-Breakers and Picks (84/537/EEC); Excavators and Loaders (86/662/EEC).

Inland water pollution

It is in this area that the EEC has been active with regard to the issue of directives. Directives have been adopted, inter alia, on the discharge of dangerous substances into water and water quality.

1976 Council Directive on Pollution caused by the Discharge of Dangerous Substances into the Aquatic Environment (76/464/EEC)

This lists certain substances and families of substances (eg mercury, persistent mineral oils and persistent synthetic substances) the discharge of which must be licensed by member states and regulated by them in accordance with emission standards to be set by the EEC Council in later directives for particular substances. Directives have been issued in respect of discharges of titanium oxide waste (78/176/EEC and 82/883/EEC), of mercury by the chloralkali electrolysis industry (84/156/EEC) of cadmium (85/513/EEC), of hexachlorocyclohexane (84/491/EEC), and of carbon tetrachloride, DDT and pentachlorophenol (86/280/EEC).

Dangerous substances

The most significant initiative in this area is the 1982 Council Directive on the Major Accident Hazards of Certain Industrial Activities (84/501/EEC) prompted by the Seveso disaster when dioxin dust escaped from a factory and caused serious pollution. It controls certain industrial activities involving the use or presence of dangerous substances. The installations and substances concerned are listed in the directive and include chemical manufacturing and processing and the storage of dangerous substances. Member states are required to adopt the measures necessary to ensure that the manufacturer is obliged to take all the measures necessary to prevent major accidents and to limit their consequences for man and the environment. The directive was amended in 1988 to extend its scope so as to include all storage of dangerous chemicals, packaged or loose, on whatever site.

1987 Council Regulation on Maximum Permitted Levels of Radioactive Contamination of Foodstuffs following a Nuclear Accident (Euratom No 3954/87)

This regulation (which has immediate legal effect in the member states) contains maximum permitted levels of contamination in foodstuffs and feedstuffs. It also establishes procedures by which the EEC will respond to any nuclear accident to enforce these levels. The regulation was a response to the Chernobyl disaster.

Waste

1975 Council Directive on Waste (75/442/EEC)

This is the basic EEC measure in this area. "Waste" is defined as "any substance or object which the holder disposes of or is required to dispose of by national law. Member states are required to establish waste disposal authorities to manage waste disposal although the directive incorporates the "polluter pays" principle so that the cost of the disposal must fall on the holder of the waste. The 1975 directive was a "framework directive" under which a number of subsequent directives have been made disposing of particular types of waste, including Polychlorinated Biphenyls and Polychlorinated Terphenyls (PCB's).

1984 Council Directive on the Supervision and Control within the EC of the Transfrontier Shipment of Hazardous Waste (84/631/EEC)

This concerns the transport by road, water or air of hazardous waste across national boundaries. When such waste is transported directly or indirectly from the territory of one member state to that of another, the holder of the waste must notify the competent authorities of the member state whose territory is to be entered. The shipment may only take place following acknowledgement of the notification and after any objections by the receiving state have been resolved satisfactorily. The directive contains certain conditions as to packaging etc, of the shipment.

Environmental Impact Assessment

1985 Council Directive on the Assessment of the Effects of Certain Public and Private Projects on the Environment (85/337/EEC)

The 1985 directive obliges member states to ensure that the effect of certain proposed development projects on human beings, fauna, flora and other aspects of the environment is considered before permission for them is given. The obligation applies to a list of projects including the construction of oil refineries, power stations, steelworks, asbestos and chemical works, motorways, airports, ports and places for the disposal of radioactive and other dangerous waste.

In the case of other projects (listed in the directive) which include various agricultural and industrial projects prima facie less environmentally harmful, an environmental impact assessment must be undertaken "where member states consider that their characteristics so require."

The assessment procedure involves the applicant giving details as to his project and its likely environmental effect and the public and interested public authorities being given an opportunity to comment. The comments must be taken into account when the decision on the application is given. The directive has been incorporated into English planning law and local planning authorities can require an environmental impact assessment in accordance with the directive.

Implications for industry

The implications of the foregoing for industry will be self-evident. It should be noted that most of the EEC legislation is in the form of directives which have become part of UK law by virtue of UK environmental legislation. This is considered later in the chapter

TOWN AND COUNTRY PLANNING

Name: Town and Country Planning Act 1971

Identity: c.78

Date effective: 28/10/71

Interpretation:

Preliminary

This Act, which governs Town and Country Planning in England and Wales, has been amended by reference by the following Acts;

- Town and Country Planning (Amendment) Act 1972
- Town and Country Amenities Act 1974
- Town and Country Planning (Amendment) Act 1977
- Local Government, Planning and Land Act 1980
- Local Government and Planning (Amendment) Act 1981
- Town and Country Planning (Minerals) Act 1981
- Town and Country Planning Act 1984
- Town and Country Planning (Compensation) Act 1985
- Housing and Planning Act 1986

The amendments are incorporated into the original text of the Act of 1971. However, it should be noted that in early 1990, the government published bills to consolidate the legislation relating to town and country planning which were expected to receive the Royal Assent in July 1990 and to come into force within three months of being passed. The bills are;

- Town and Country Planning Bill
- Planning (Listed Buildings and Conservation Areas) Bill
- Planning (Hazardous Substances) Bill
- Planning (Consequential Provisions) Bill

Administrative framework of Town and Country Planning

In order to understand the planning system established by the Act of 1971, and how it affects industry, it is necessary to examine the administrative framework created by the Act. The basic scheme of the Act is to require local authorities to make development plans for their area and to require planning permission for all development of land.

Administratively there are two main tiers, central government and local government. Centrally, the Secretary of State for the Environment is charged with the duty of securing consistency and continuity in the framing and execution of a national policy with respect to the use and development of land throughout England and Wales. The Department of the Environment issues circulars to local planning authorities containing policy and advice on various planning matters. These circulars are very influential in planning (eg in planning appeals) although they do not have the force of law.

At the local level, the county council is the county planning authority for their area and the district council is the district planning authority for their area. In the London boroughs and metropolitan district councils all planning functions are carried out by the district planning authority. In the non-metropolitan areas planning functions are divided between the county planning authority and the district planning authority.

It is the duty of every planning authority to prepare a development plan. In the non-metropolitan areas this will consist of a structure plan and any local plans currently in force. These plans may be consulted in order to assess the likelihood of obtaining planning permission for some proposed development, eg to relocate a factory, however it should be noted that they are for guidance only and will not necessarily be followed by the local authority.

The structure plan is prepared by the county planning authority and must be approved by the Secretary of State for the Environment. It is essentially a long-range "strategic" plan consisting of a written statement of policies and the reasons for the policies supplemented by diagrams.

Local plans are usually made by the district planning authority and must conform with the structure plan for the area. There may be, and invariably are, several local plans for a particular district. A local plan may deal with land use and development over the whole or most of the district or deal with a particular type of development. They may also deal with particular subjects, eg the reclamation of derelict land. Local plans are normally based on ordinance survey maps and do not require the approval of the Secretary of State in order to be adopted.

In the London boroughs and metropolitan districts all development plans will eventually be replaced by single-tier "unitary" development plans.

The need for planning permission

The basis of the planning system is the need for planning permission, which is required for the carrying out of any development of land.

"Development" is therefore a key concept and is defined by the Act as "the carrying out of building, engineering, mining or other operations in, on, over or under land, or the making of any material change in the use of any buildings or other land."

It will be seen that the above definition consists of two branches, (a) operational development and (b) material changes of use. These will be examined in turn.

(a) Operations

This consists of building, engineering, mining and other operations and the courts have held that an "operation" is something that changes the physical characteristics of the land.

(i) **Building operations** are further defined as including rebuilding operations, structural alterations of, or additions to, buildings, and other operations normally undertaken by builders. "Building" is defined as including any structure or erection or part of a building, as so defined but not including plant/machinery inside a building.

The effect of the above is that the introduction of any structure (unless very small indeed) on land in the open air which has some degree of permanence and is not freely or easily moveable may constitute a building operation. This means that many things not normally thought of as buildings will be regarded as such for the purpose of the Act, eg fences, walls, masts, aerials and even tree-houses and model villages have been held to be buildings. Note that some small operations are automatically granted planning permission by the General Development Order (see later). However, if an object is freely moveable it will probably not constitute a building, eg the stationing of a caravan, although to use a caravan residentially may involve a material change of use.

It should be noted that certain building operations are expressly stated by the Act to not be development, ie works for the maintenance, improvement or other alteration of a building which affect only the interior or do not materially affect the exterior. Thus internal rearranging of partitions etc does not require consent. However, the provision of additional space below ground is outside the exemption.

(ii) **Engineering operations.** These are defined by the Act as including the formation or laying out of means of access to highways. The words "engineering operation" are to be given their ordinary meaning and will therefore include the construction and maintenance of roads, bridges, drainage works etc and any major earth-removal works.

(iii) **Mining operations.** This includes the recovery of all minerals and substances in or under land of a kind ordinarily worked for removal by underground or surface working. It has also been extended (in 1981) to the recovery of material originally extracted from the land and then deposited on it such as coal from slag heaps.

(iv) **Other operations.** This will cover any other operation which changes the physical character of the land but does not fall within (i), (ii) or (iii) above. Thus the installation of a protective grille over a shop window and door has been held to fall under this head.

It is not clear whether demolition is included under this head. The position seems to be that whereas the total demolition of a building is not development, the demolition of a part of a building is development if it materially affects the external appearance. Also, some demolition will fall under the heading of engineering operations. However, the demolition of buildings in conservation areas (see later) generally requires consent.

(b) Material change of use

A material change of use is a change in the purpose to which land is devoted which is significant from a planning viewpoint. What is required is a change in the character of the use of the particular unit of land in question, eg a change from a warehouse to a factory. Whether a change of use is material or not is said to be a matter of fact on degree and is often a difficult question.

The law on material change of use is somewhat technical but may be summarised as follows. Within a unit of land there may be one main use (the "dominant" or "primary" use) to which all other uses are merely incidental or ancillary. Eg a factory may have a suite of offices, a storage area, a handling depot and an area where there are some incidental retail sales. As long as these uses serve the main use they are permitted. If, say, the retailing use intensifies and includes goods not manufactured at the factory but elsewhere there may occur a material change of use.

It is, of course, possible for a unit to have more than one primary use in which case it is usually referred to as a "mixed" or "composite" use. A material change in the proportion of blend of such uses may itself constitute a material change of use.

Excluded uses

The Act makes it clear that certain matters do not involve a material change of use and these include the use of the land for agriculture (but this does not authorise "agri-business" uses) and also changes of use within the Use Classes Order 1987.

The Use Classes Order is a statutory instrument made by the Secretary of State and is of vital importance as it prescribes that many everyday changes of use do not involve development and therefore do not require planning permission.

The Order divides uses into some sixteen use classes and prescribes that any change within a class does not constitute development. Changes of use from one class to another do not automatically constitute development but will probably do so in the majority of cases as they will involve a material change in the character of the use.

The 16 Classes are as follows - (NB Part B is in summary form only).

Part A

Class A1: Shops

Use for all or any of the following purposes –

(a) for the retail sale of goods other than hot food,

(b) as a post office,

(c) for the sale of tickets or as a travel agency,

(d) for the sale of sandwiches or other cold foods for consumption off the premises,

(e) for hairdressing,

(f) for the direction of funerals,

(g) for the display of goods for sale,

(h) for the hiring out of domestic or personal goods or services,

(i) for the reception of goods to be washed, cleaned or repaired,

where the sale, display or service is to visiting members of the public.

Class A2: Financial and Professional Services

Use for the provision of –

(a) financial services, or

(b) professional services (other than health or medical services), or

(c) any other services (including use as a betting office) which it is appropriate to provide in a shopping area,

where the services are provided principally to visiting members of the public.

Class A3: Food and Drink

Use for the sale of food or drink for consumption on the premises or of hot food for consumption off the premises.

Part B

Class B1: Business

Use for all or any of the following purposes –

(a) as an office other than a use within Class A2,

(b) for research and development of products or processes,

(c) for any industrial process,

being a use which can be carried out in any residential area without detriment to the amenity of that area by reason of noise, vibration, smell, fumes, smoke, soot, ash, dust or grit.

Class B2: General Industrial (ie those not in B1 or B3-B7)

Class B3-B7: Various Special Industrial Uses

Class B8: Use for storage or as a distribution centre

Part C

Class C1: Hotels and hostels

Use as a hotel, boarding or guest house or as a hostel where, in each case, no significant element of care is provided.

Class C2: Residential Institutions

Use for the provision of residential accommodation and care to people in need of care (other than a use within Class C3).

Use as a hospital or nursing home.

Use as a residential school, college or training centre.

Class C3: Dwellinghouses

Use as a dwellinghouse (whether or not as a sole or main residence) -

(a) By a single person or by people living together as a family, or

(b) by not more than 6 residents living together as a single household (including a household where care is provided for residents).

Part D

Class D2: Non-residential institutions

(a) for the provision of any medical or health services, except the use of premises attached to the residence of the consultant or practitioner,

(b) as a creche, day nursery or day centre,

(c) for the provision of education,

(d) for the display of works of art (otherwise than for sale or hire),

(e) as a museum,

(f)   as a public library or public reading room,

(g)   as a public hall or exhibition hall,

(h)   for, or in connection with, public worship or religious instruction.

Class D2: Assembly and leisure

Use as -

(a)   a cinema,

(b)   a concert hall,

(c)   a bingo hall or casino,

(d)   a dance hall,

(e)   a swimming bath, skating rink, gymnasium or area for other indoor or outdoor sports or recreation, not involving motorised vehicles or firearms.

The following points should be noted in connection with the Use Classes Order:

(a)   The Order does not comprise an exhaustive list of land uses. Some uses are outside the Order and are called "sui generis" uses (eg an artist's studio). The order specifically identifies a number of uses not included in any class of the order. These are the use of buildings or other land:

    (i)   as a theatre,

    (ii)   as an amusement arcade or centre, or a funfair,

    (iii) for the washing or cleaning of clothes or fabrics in coin-operated machines or on premises at which the goods to be cleaned are received direct from the visiting public,

    (iv)   for the sale of fuel for motor vehicles,

    (v)   for the sale or display for sale of motor vehicles,

    (vi)   for a taxi business or business for the hire of motor vehicles,

    (vii) as a scrapyard, or a yard for the storage or distribution of minerals or the breaking of motor vehicles.

It follows that a change of use from any of the above to any use specified in the use classes (or vice versa) is a material change of use.

(b)   The Use Classes Order is given even greater flexibility by Part 3 of the General Development Order (see later), which grants planning permission for certain changes of use from one class to another.

(c)   The local planning authority can impose a condition on a planning permission (see later) restricting a change of use within a class. Thus a planning permission for office premises could expressly prohibit a change to light industry.

(d)   It is permissible to subdivide premises relying on the Use Classes Order. Thus a factory may be subdivided into two or more workshop units in separate occupation.

(e)   The premises must be in use (ie not redundant/derelict) in order to be able to rely on the Use Classes Order.

(f)   Classes B3-B7 contain a large number of very specialised industrial uses. The Use Classes Order should be consulted as to this but it should be noted that these use classes are under review by the government as they require updating.

Established uses

A use which began before 1 January 1964 without planning permission and which has continued ever since is referred to as the "established" use of the land and is immune from the enforcement provisions of the Act (see later). This means that the use can be carried on with impunity.

Situations of doubt

The Act provides that any person who proposes to carry out any operation or make a change of use may apply to the local planning authority for a determination whether the proposed activity would constitute development. If they decide that the works would not constitute development and grant a certificate to that effect then this is as good as a planning permission.

Implications for industry

Planning permission will be required for building etc operations and for some changes of use. However, many changes of use in the business sphere are deemed not to involve development by virtue of the Use Classes Order. When premises are acquired, it is vital to ascertain the planning status of the land, ie what it can be used for. This task is usually carried out by solicitors acting for the purchaser.

How is planning permission obtained?

1. Planning permission is normally obtained by submitting an application to the local planning authority. However a number of exceptions to this requirement should be noted:

    (a) Planning permission is automatically granted for some 28 classes of development specified by the General Development Order 1988 (as amended by Amendment Orders in 1988 and 1989). The classes of development include:

        (i) Sundry minor operations, including the erection of fences, walls etc subject to certain limitations (Part 2, GDO)

        (ii) Certain changes of use in the Use Classes Order, ie

        - From A3, or sale of motor vehicles to A1
        - A3 to A2
        - B2 to B1
        - Premises within A2 with display windows at ground floor level to A1

            Provided that the change of use does not relate to more than 235 square metres of floor space in the building, B8 to B1; B1 or B2 to B8.

        (iii) Temporary uses

    (b) Where a temporary planning permission expires, a grant of planning permission is not required to resume the previous normal authorised use of the land.

    (c) Where the land is situated in an Enterprise Zone or Simplified Planning Zone. In these cases planning permission is normally automatically granted for development or classes of development specified in the scheme.

2. Applications for planning permission. Application is made to the local planning authority for the area in which the land is situated. Any person can apply for planning permission in respect of any land and it is not necessary to obtain the consent of the owner. However, where the applicant is not the owner, the owner must be notified of the application and a certificate to that effect submitted with the application.

The decision. Once the local planning authority have considered the application, they may:

(a) grant permission unconditionally (rare);

(b) grant permission subject to such conditions as they think fit;

(c) refuse planning permission;

(d) refer the application to the Secretary of State if directed to do so - a "called-in" application.

The local planning authority must notify the applicant in writing of their decision within 8 weeks. In the case of refusal or conditional grant clear reasons must be given. If notification does not take place within the proper time the applicant can appeal to the Secretary of State "as if" his application had been refused.

Planning permission may be full or outline. Outline permissions are granted only in respect of the erection of a building and are subject to a condition that application to the local planning authority for subsequent approval of reserved matters must be made within three years of the permission or any other period stipulated by the authority.

The reserved matters are siting, design, external appearances, access and landscaping.

Appeal. The applicant may appeal to the Secretary of State against the decision of the local planning authority (or their failure to give a decision within the time-limit) within six months of receipt of notice of the decision. Most appeals today are decided by inspectors appointed by the Secretary of State and are conducted by way of written representations, but there is provision for the holding of a public local inquiry if the appellant wishes. The decision of the Secretary of State or his inspector on a planning appeal can be challenged in the High Court on a point of law within six weeks of the date of the decision by any person aggrieved by it.

The legal effect of planning permission

As a general rule planning permission attaches to the land and therefore endures for the benefit of subsequent owners and occupiers. Every planning permission is subject to a condition that the development must begin within five years of the grant or it will lapse. In the case of outline planning permissions, the development must be begun within five years of the date on which outline planning permission was given or within two years of the final approval of reserved matters whichever the later. In both cases the authority may impose different periods.

The Act lays down what will constitute a commencement of the development for the purpose of the above rules; eg laying of cables, roads, digging of foundation trenches etc.

Conditions. We have seen that the local planning authority may impose such conditions on a grant of planning permission as they think fit. However their powers are not unlimited and the courts have held that such conditions should:

(i) be imposed for a planning purpose and not some ulterior motive,

(ii) be fairly and reasonably related to the permitted development, and

(iii) not be unreasonable.

If the applicant feels that a condition falls foul of one or more of these requirements then the condition may be invalid and discharged on appeal. As an alternative to appealing against a condition to the Secretary of State, it is possible to submit a subsequent application for planning permission to carry out the development without complying with conditions attached to a previous grant.

By way of example, suppose XYZ plc wish to build a factory. The proposed site adjoins a busy road. The local planning authority grant planning permission but subject to a condition that an ancillary or service road be built across the frontage of the site, at the developer's expense. This would ultimately join up with similar roads on the adjoining sites so as to provide a safe access. In fact such a condition is unreasonable as it requires the developer to build a road at his own expense and dedicate it to the public. (A more proper course would be for the highway authority to purchase the necessary land for the road and pay compensation). XYZ could appeal against the condition in which case it could be discharged. However if the condition were regarded as fundamental to the permission, XYZ might lose the whole permission as it would be invalid. A better course of action from their point of view would be to submit a subsequent application asking for the condition to be discharged or modified. If this procedure is followed the planning permission would not be lost.

Planning agreements

The Act provides for any person with an interest in land to enter into a planning agreement with the local authority. Such agreements are very common in practice and usually accompany a planning permission. They provide a means of imposing obligations upon developers which could not legally be imposed by the use of conditions attached to planning permission. They are used to require the developer to make a contribution towards the cost of, eg off-street parking, sewers, roads and other infrastructure connected with the development.

The consequences of carrying out development without planning permission

1. The carrying out of development without planning permission (or breach of conditions attached to planning permission) is not in itself a criminal offence. However, where such development takes place the local planning authority is empowered to issue an enforcement notice to remedy the situation. If the enforcement notice is not complied with, then, and only then is a criminal offence committed.

2. In certain cases unauthorised development becomes immune from enforcement after a period of four years. These are:

    (a) operational development without planning permission;

    (b) failure to comply with conditions attached to (a);

    (c) change of use without permission of any building to use a single dwellinghouse or the failure to comply with a condition having that effect.

    Apart from the above (and an established use) a material change of use is not subject to any time limit with regard to enforcement.

3. There are technical rules as to the content and service of enforcement notices which have to be followed by the local planning authority. If you are served with an enforcement notice, there is always a chance that it might be defective in relation to these requirements. If so, you will have a right of appeal to the Secretary of State (see later).

    The technical rules referred to above may be outlined as follows:

    (i) The enforcement notice must be served on the owner and occupier of the land.

    (ii) The contents of the notice must comply with the statutory requirements laid down by the Act. Although there is no prescribed form of notice, the enforcement notice must specify certain matters, ie

      (a) the alleged breach of planning control must be described clearly and accurately

      (b) the steps to be taken to remedy the breach must be drafted so as to enable the persons served to know what they have to do to comply with the notice

      (c) the date on which the enforcement notice is to take effect must be specified and also a reasonable period for compliance must be stated

      (d) the planning reasons for the issue of the enforcement notice must be stated and the precise boundaries of the land must be specified whether by a plan or otherwise.

Nullity and invalidity. Defective enforcement notices are either a nullity or merely invalid. A notice will be a nullity where it is misleading or ambiguous or, say, where the date upon which the enforcement notice is to take effect is not specified. For example, an enforcement notice requiring a market to cease trading "in summer-time" was held to be a nullity as the period could not be precisely determined. An enforcement notice that is a nullity is of no effect and can theoretically be ignored although in practice it is advisable to obtain a court declaration that it is a nullity.

A notice that is invalid is one that is defective (eg it may contain a factual error) but the defect is not so serious as above. An invalid notice can only be challenged by way of appeal to the Secretary of State. The Act gives the Secretary of State a wide power to correct any informality, defect or error or to vary the terms of the notice providing this can be done without injustice either to the appellant or the local planning authority.

Enforcement appeals. An appeal to the Secretary of State may be lodged at any time after service but must be before the date on which the enforcement notice takes effect. If the appeal is out of time, it is lost as the Secretary of State has no power to extend the time. Once proceedings are instituted, the enforcement notice is of no effect pending the final determination of the appeal (or withdrawal of the enforcement notice).

Under the Act a right of appeal is granted to any person with an interest in the land, whether or not he has been served with an enforcement notice, and also to any person who is an occupier by virtue of a licence in writing.

The ground of appeal in the Act are:

(a) that planning permission ought to be granted for the development to which the notice relates, or as the case may be, that a condition or limitation alleged in the enforcement notice not to have been complied with ought to be discharged; [Whether or not it is expressly made a ground of appeal, there is a deemed application for planning permission on the lodging of the notice of appeal];

(b) that the matters alleged in the notice do not constitute a breach of planning control;

(c) that the breach of planning control alleged in the notice has not taken place;

(d) in cases where the four-year rule applies, that the four years has elapsed at the date of issue;

(e) in any other case, that the alleged breach of planning control occurred before the beginning of 1964;

(f) that copies of the enforcement notice were not served as required by the Act;

(g) that the steps required to be taken by the notice exceed what is necessary to remedy any breach of planning control or for making the development comply with the terms of the planning permission or for removing or alleviating any injury to amenity;

(h) that the period specified in the enforcement notice for complying with the notice is unreasonably short.

The appeal may be determined by either a public local enquiry, or if all parties agree, by way of written representations. The Secretary of State may uphold, quash or, as we have seen, vary the enforcement notice. The Secretary of State is also empowered to grant planning permission for the development to which the enforcement notice relates, discharge any condition and determine any purpose for which the land may lawfully be used. The Secretary of State's decision on any point of law may be challenged in the High Court.

Non-compliance with the enforcement notice. If the enforcement notice is not complied with, then prosecution may follow. The offence carries a fine of an unlimited amount if convicted or indictment in the Crown Court. Continuation after conviction is a further offence, subject to a daily fine. In certain circumstances the local planning authority may enter the land and carry out works at the owner's expense. If these penalties do not have the desired effect the authority may resort to obtaining an injunction, ie a court order compelling compliance on pain of imprisonment for contempt of court.

Stop-notice. Appeal against an enforcement notice automatically suspends the operation of the notice. There is therefore normally nothing to prevent the developer from carrying on with the unlawful development pending the determination of the appeal, which might be some 9-15 months.

To deal with this situation, the local planning authority is empowered to serve a stop-notice. The notice prohibits any activity which is alleged in the enforcement notice to constitute a breach of planning control. However, a stop notice may not be used to prohibit any activity which was begun to be carried out more than 12 months earlier unless the activity is, or is incidental to, operations or is the deposit of refuse or waste materials. There is no appeal against a stop notice as such and prosecution will follow contravention. However if the enforcement is itself a nullity or is invalid then so too is the stop notice.

Specific planning controls

In addition to the general planning controls already described there are specific controls over certain types of development, ie historic buildings and conservation areas; outdoor advertisements; protection of trees; minerals and hazardous substances.

1. Historic buildings

Under the Act the Secretary of State may compile a list of buildings considered to be of "special architectural or historic interest." At present there are just under half a million listed buildings.

Any building can be listed but certain buildings are exempt from the effects of listing, ie crown property, ecclesiastical buildings in use as such and scheduled ancient monuments. The word "building" bears its ordinary meaning in the planning legislation (see earlier) and the control extends not only to the building itself but also to any object or structure fixed to the building (including interior fixtures) and any ancillary structure within the grounds.

(i) **Criteria for listing**. The main factor is age but other relevant factors are economic or social history, historical association or "group value" (the contribution a building makes to a group of buildings eg a terrace of properties).

There are three grades of listed building:

- Grade I - buildings of exceptional interest.
- Grade II.
- Grade II* - particular fine grade II buildings.

The grading has no legal significance. It may, however, be relevant in determining whether listed building consent will be given or whether grants may be available.

(ii) **Consequences of listing.** The main consequence is that listed building consent is required for the demolition of a listed building or for its alteration or extension in a manner which would affect its character as a building of special architectural or historic interest. The procedure relating to listed building consent is very similar to that relating to planning permission. Where proposed works to a listed building also involve development, planning permission will be required in addition to listed building consent.

The execution of works requiring listed building consent without such consent is a criminal offence. It is an offence of strict liability (ie you can be convicted whether or not you know the building is listed) and any fine can take into account any financial benefit to the defendant.

There is an appeal against a refusal of listed building consent and the local planning authority may issue and serve a listed building enforcement notice, against which there is also a right of appeal.

(iii) **Repairs to listed buildings**. Under the Act, the local planning authority have the power to execute any repairs which are urgently necessary for the preservation of listed buildings. They may also serve a repairs notice on the owner requiring the owner to carry out works considered reasonably necessary for the proper preservation of the building. If not carried out, the local planning authority may proceed to compulsorily purchase the building after a period of two months. Where the building has deliberately been allowed to fall into disrepair, the authority may make a direction for minimum compensation. This will result in compensation below market value in most cases.

2. Conservation Areas

Under the Act every local planning authority must examine its area periodically to determine whether (a) any parts of their area are of special architectural or historic interest, **and** (b) whether the character or appearance of these areas is such that it is desirable to preserve or enhance them. Such areas will be designated as conservation areas. In 1987 there were 5,558 conservation areas in England and Wales. A conservation area need not necessarily consist of buildings, it can be eg village greens, open space, trees.

Notice of designation must be published in the local press. There is no individual notification of owners and occupiers who have no right to object.

The legal consequences of designation are:

(i) **Control of demolition.** Whereas some of the buildings in a conservation area may be listed in their own right, prohibits the demolition (but not alteration etc) of any building in a conservation area without listed building consent (called "conservation area consent"). Certain classes of small buildings are exempt.

In making a decision as to whether consent for demolition (or a development proposal) should be granted, the Act states that "special attention shall be paid to the desirability of preserving or enhancing its character or appearance." It has been held that in complying with the duty imposed by this subsection, the Secretary of State has to do more than merely satisfy that harm will not be caused to the conservation area (see later).

(ii) **Trees.** Trees not already subject to a tree preservation order are protected. Any person wishing to cut down etc a tree in a conservation area must notify the local planning authority who then have six weeks in which to make a tree preservation order.

(iii) **Advertisements.** There is more stringent control than usual here. The local planning authority may submit to the Secretary of State for his approval an order designating a conservation area in need of special control of advertisements.

(iv) **Planning applications.** Where an application for planning permission is for development which in the opinion of the local planning authority would affect the character or appearance of a conservation area, the local authority must publish notice in the local press and allow 21 days for the making of representations.

(v) **Permitted Development in the General Development Order.** Limits of permitted development may differ in conservation areas.

3. Control of advertisements

The Act gives the Secretary of State powers to control outdoor advertisements. This is achieved by regulations made by the Secretary of State and the powers can only be exercised in the interests of amenity and public safety, and not as an instrument of censorship.

The Act contains provisions relating to enforcement - any person who displays an advertisement in contravention of the regulations is guilty of an offence punishable by a fine.

The regulations widely define advertisements so as to include any word, letter, model, sign, placard, board, notice, device or representation displayed for the purpose of advertisement, announcement or direction and includes hoardings and similar structures and balloons used for this purpose. There are, however, a number of advertisements over which the regulations exercise no control, including advertisements on enclosed land, indoor advertisements not visible from outside, advertisements displayed on a vehicle, advertisements on balloons at a height of more than 60 metres. Detailed consultation of the regulations will be required in most cases.

Under the regulations, consent is deemed in many cases, eg announcements of elections, functional advertisements of local authorities, professional name-plates and others. In most cases, the regulation contained detailed provisions regulating the size and position of such deemed consent advertisements.

Unless an advertisement has deemed consent for its display, then express consent is required. Application for express consent is made to the local planning authority, who may refuse or grant consent subject to certain standard conditions and such additional conditions as they think fit. The standard conditions require the advertisements to be kept clean and tidy and in a safe condition. Grants of consent last for (usually) a period of five years. If consent is refused the applicant may appeal to the Secretary of State.

Where the display of advertisements in accordance with the regulations involves development, the Act provides that planning permission for that development shall be deemed to be granted.

3. Trees

If it appears to the local planning authority that it is necessary to protect trees or woodland, they may make a tree preservation order with respect to such trees, groups of trees or woodlands as may be specified in the order.

A tree preservation order prohibits the cutting down, topping, lopping, uprooting, wilful damage or wilful destruction of trees, except with the consent of the local planning authority. There is an exception for trees which are dying or dead or have become dangerous or where it is necessary to abate a nuisance.

It is an offence to cut down etc, a tree which is subject to a tree preservation order. Conviction carries a fine which may reflect the financial benefit to the defendant of the offence. It is an offence of strict liability thus it is irrelevant whether or not the defendant knew that the tree in question was subject to an order.

4. Minerals

Special controls are considered necessary to control the environmental effects of mineral development, which may be outlined as follows.

County councils are to act as mineral planning authorities to be responsible for all planning control over mineral working, including the service of enforcement and stop notices.

The Act authorises the mineral planning authority when granting planning permission for mineral working, to impose both "restoration" and "aftercare" conditions on the land in question. Planning permissions for mineral working are to last for 60 years or any other time-limit the mineral planning authority may impose.

5. Hazardous substances

The essence of the control is that a hazardous substances consent from the hazardous substances authority is required for the presence of a hazardous substance in excess of the controlled quantity on, over or under land either at one installation, or aggregated at all structures or installations controlled by the same person within 500 m. of each other.

As a general rule the authority responsible for administering hazardous substances control will be the local (district) planning authority. At present, hazardous substances are defined by regulations and consist of various liquid and gaseous substances. However the regulations do not apply to installations handling radioactive substances or (generally) explosives, to certain types of pipe-line, or to premises used for the disposal of hazardous wastes, which are subject to other statutory controls.

The framework of controls over hazardous substances closely parallels general planning and enforcement provisions. However one important difference is that where there has been a breach of hazardous substances control, any person causing or permitting the breach is guilty of an offence.

Implications for industry

The specific planning controls raise a number of points to note. The amount of listed buildings is on the increase and some consideration should be given before buying listed commercial, office or industrial premises. The possibility of extending or adapting the premises may be rather limited and it may not be possible to realise the full potential of the building in terms of value. However it should be noted that alterations to listed buildings are not subject to VAT if the works have listed building consent. It remains payable on all works which do not require listed building consent. Nevertheless grants may be available under certain statutes - information concerning this may be obtained from English Heritage.

With regard to signs and advertisements, most outdoor signage will require consent, and this will be particularly so in the case of conservation areas, many of which are areas of more stringent control. It should also be borne in mind that individual trees or groups of trees subject to tree preservation orders may inhibit development.

ENVIRONMENT LAW

Name: Public Health Act 1936

Identity: C.49

Date effective: 31/7/36

Interpretation:

Preliminary

The Act embodies the concept of the statutory nuisance and allows local authorities and aggrieved individuals to take action in respect of such nuisances.

Part III

Part III of the Act deals with nuisances and offensive trades. It imposes a general duty on local authorities to inspect their areas for the detection of "statutory nuisances." This concept is defined by the Act which provides that certain matters "prejudicial to health or a nuisance" shall be statutory nuisances.

The matters are:

(i) any premises (including land) whose condition is so serious as to give rise to a real risk to health or a deterioration in those already sick

(ii) any animal kept in such a way as to give rise to a health hazard

(iii) accumulations of rubbish or putrefying matter (but not inert matter)

(iv) any dust or effluvia caused by any trade, business, manufacture or process and injurious, or likely to injure the public health or a nuisance and any workplace which is not provided with sufficient ventilation, not kept clean or free from noxious effluvia or which is so over-crowded as to be prejudicial to health.

The Act states that other matters may be declared to be statutory nuisances. It seems that smells alone do not constitute statutory nuisances but the premises that are the source of the smell could be so insanitary as to constitute one. Note that the Act expressly excludes most mining and smelting processes.

Procedure

Both local authorities and private individuals may take action in respect of statutory nuisances. Where proceedings are brought by local authorities, the procedure is to serve an abatement notice on the party responsible giving reasonable time for compliance. If the notice is disregarded, the local authority may bring proceedings in the magistrates' court. If the nuisance is not abated the court must issue a nuisance order requiring the defendant to comply with the abatement notice. There is an appeal to the Crown Court and fines for contravention.

Where nuisances are likely to recur, a prohibition notice may be served (under the Public Health (Recurring Nuisances) Act 1969) and this procedure can be used even though the alleged nuisance is not actually existing at the time.

A private citizen may initiate proceedings in respect of a statutory nuisance by making a complaint to a Justice of the Peace.

Offensive Trades

The Act also delineates certain "offensive trades" including blood and bone boiling, fat extraction, glue making etc, (this list is not exhaustive - the Act itself should be consulted). It is an offence, punishable by fines, to establish an offensive trade without the consent of the local authority. They may impose a time-limit but no other conditions.

Implications for industry

Although derived from nineteenth century public health legislation, the concept of the statutory nuisance remains one of the most effective ways that local nuisances endangering health can be dealt with. This should be borne in mind, particularly where it is sought to locate industrial premises near residential areas.

Name: Control of Pollution Act 1974

Identity: c.40

Date effective: 31/7/74

Interpretation:

Preliminary

Despite the title of the Act this is not a comprehensive code of environmental law imposing a general environmental standard. It is, rather, a piecemeal provision which in some instances overlaps with other provisions (eg Town and Country Planning Act, Health and Safety at Work Act). The Act does not in general deal with pollution by radioactive materials (where alternative powers exist under the Radioactive Substances Act), with Crown premises although property belonging to public corporations (except NHS) is subject to the Act. Enforcement and administration of Parts I and III of the Act is the concern of local authorities. Part II is the concern of water authorities.

Part I

Part I of the Act deals with the disposal of controlled waste.

"Waste" includes scrap metal, effluents or other unwanted surpluses and any substances/articles requiring disposal as being broken, worn out, contaminated or spoiled (other than substances falling within the Explosives Act 1875).

"Controlled waste" means household, industrial and commercial waste and any such waste as defined above. There are a number of detailed exceptions to the Act and the delegated legislation made under it should be consulted - in particular mineral, agricultural waste and some sewage are not controlled.

Under the Act, persons may not either deposit controlled waste on land or use any equipment for the disposing of such waste, unless the relevant land is occupied by the holder of a waste disposal licence. It is an offence to contravene this control.

In the case of poisonous, noxious and polluting wastes causing an environmental hazard where the manner of its deposit indicates abandonment, there is provision for imprisonment for up to 5 years. However, there must be a material risk of death, injury or impairment of health, or a threat to water supplies. The Act provides a variety of defences against such a prosecution, eg the defendant acted under instructions from an employer and did not realise the nature of the contravention.

Waste disposal licences may be applied for in writing to the relevant local authority. Before a licence is issued the authority must consult the relevant water authority. Conditions may be attached to licences, eg as to the supervision of disposals, duration, hours of site-working and so forth. There is a right of appeal against the refusal of a licence (or the imposition of conditions) to the Secretary of State.

Where controlled waste is deposited without licence, the authority may serve on the occupier of the affected land a notice requiring him to remove the waste within a specified period. There is an appeal to the magistrates against such a notice.

Regulations may be made under the Act by the Secretary of State in the case of the disposal of special waste. This is controlled waste so dangerous and difficult to dispose of that special provision for disposal is required. Special wastes include acids and alkalis, asbestos, arsenic, biocides and other substances dangerous to life. There are codes of practice to deal with specific wastes (eg PCB's).

Non-controlled waste. The Act makes it an offence to deposit waste other than controlled waste where if the waste were controlled an offence would be committed. Thus non-controlled waste cannot be deposited where it is poisonous, noxious or polluting and its presence would be likely to give rise to an environmental hazard.

Part II

This part of the Act deals with the pollution of water.

Under the Act it is an offence to cause or knowingly permit any poisonous, noxious or polluting matter to enter (generally) any fresh water such as streams or rivers. (There is a rather complex exception here to cover mineral or quarry waste.) If the pollutant is deliberately poured down a drain which eventually finds its way into a stream, an offence will be committed even though the polluter is unaware of the system of drainage. It is however possible for the Secretary of State or relevant water authority to grant a disposal licence and disposal may also be permitted by local legislation and by a number of other means outlined by the Act.

Similar controls also exist in respect of trade or sewage effluent. Discharges into sewers prior to discharge into water is also controlled by the Public Health Act 1936 which prohibits the discharge of chemical waste and other matters. However certain trade effluents may be discharged with consent under the Public Health (Drainage of Trade Premises) Act 1937. These are defined as liquids, with or without suspended particles, produced in the course of trade or industry at trade premises.

Part III

Under this part of the Act, where a local authority conclude that noise amounting to a nuisance is present in their area, they are required to serve an abatement notice on the person responsible.

The notice may require abatement or the taking of such steps as may be necessary to prevent recurrence. There is a right of appeal to the magistrates' court. One of the grounds of appeal is that the noise arises from the course of a trade or business and the best practicable means have been used to counteract it.

It is an offence to contravene an abatement notice. A number of defences are available against such a prosecution including one that the defendant had "reasonable excuse" and where the noise arose in the course of a trade or business, that the best practicable means were used to counteract it.

In addition, where an occupier of premises is aggrieved by noise amounting to a nuisance in his capacity as occupier, he may make a complaint to the magistrates, who may make an abatement order.

Construction site noises are specifically dealt with by the Act. Where the local authority conclude that such works are, or will be, carried out on any premises, they may serve a notice imposing requirements as to the manner of doing the works. This may deal with, eg permitted noise levels. Again there is an appeal to the magistrates. It is an offence to contravene such a notice. It is possible to pre-empt the above notice by the developer applying to the local authority for consent specifying details of the proposed works.

The Act also deals with street noise. It is an offence to operate a loudspeaker in a street between 9 pm and 8 am for any purpose, and at any other time for the purpose of advertising any entertainment, trade or business. There are exceptions to cover, eg the emergency services.

Noise abatement zones

The Act allows local authorities to designated noise abatement zones. It is possible for owners and occupiers of affected premises to object to the proposal to designate, and such objections must be considered by the local authority before making the order. The authority must then measure and record in the "noise level register" the level of noise emanating from premises within the zone. A copy of the recorded measurement must be served on the owner and occupier of the premises in question and there is then a right of appeal to the Secretary of State. The noise level in the register may not be exceeded except with the written consent of the local authority which may be given subject to conditions. There is again a right of appeal to the Secretary of State.

To exceed the registered noise level is an offence. The local authority may serve a noise reduction order and, again, there is a right of appeal against such an order. Under the Act the Secretary of State has power to approve codes of practice containing guidance on noise.

Disclosure of information

The Act prohibits the disclosure of any information relating to a trade secret obtained by virtue of the Act.

Implications for industry

The impact of the above provisions will be self-evident. It should not, however, be forgotten that there is usually a right of appeal either to the local authority or the Secretary of State against most of the enforcement decisions made under the Act.

Name: Clean Air Act 1956 and 1968

Identity: c.52; c.62

Date effective: 5/7/56; 25/10/68

Interpretation:

Preliminary

The Acts control the emission of smoke and also grit and dust.

1. Scope of Acts. "Smoke" is defined as including soot, ash, grit and gritty particles emitted as smoke.

    The Act of 1956 prohibits the emission of dark smoke from a chimney of any building. The Act defines dark smoke but, in practice, environmental health officers usually rely on their experience as to what constitutes dark smoke. Where dark smoke is emitted the occupier of the building in question is guilty of an offence. There are a number of detailed defences, eg the contravention was due to lighting up a cold furnace and that all practicable steps had been taken to prevent or minimise emissions.

    Emissions of dark smoke from industrial and trade premises other than via chimneys are generally controlled by the Clean Air Act of 1968. The Act also contains detailed controls with regard to furnaces in buildings and chimneys.

2. Procedure under Acts. Under the Act of 1956, any local authority may, by order declare all or part of its district a smoke control area, thus making it an offence to emit any smoke. Control extends to industrial chimneys as well as chimneys of buildings.

    Under the Act of 1968, it is also an offence to acquire any solid fuel, other than an authorised fuel, for use in a smoke control area. The enforcement of these provisions is the responsibility of local authorities who have powers of entry. There is, however, a duty to notify the occupier of contravening premises both in relation to the emission of dark smoke and smoke control areas. In prosecutions it will be a defence to prove the obligation to notify has not been complied with. It should be noted here that there are supplementary powers in the Act of 1974 (Control of Pollution Act) under which the Secretary of State is empowered to make regulations as to the composition and content of fuel used in motor vehicles and to make further regulations as to the sulphur content of fuel oils.

Name: Radioactive Substances Act 1960

Identity: c.34

Date effective: 2/6/60

Interpretation:

Preliminary

Radioactive substances are the subject of special legislation.

Scope of Act. The basic provision is that no person may, on any premises, keep or use radioactive material for the purpose of any undertaking unless registered under the Act or exempted by the Act itself. The Act defines "radioactive material" in scientific and very technical terms.

The Act further provides that no person may, except as authorised, dispose of radioactive waste or cause or permit disposal from the premises of his undertaking. "Disposal" includes removal, deposit, destruction, discharge into water, air, sewers, drains and burial. Accumulations with a view to subsequent disposal are also prohibited.

Exemptions to the above provisions are granted to sites licensed under the Nuclear Installations Act 1965 and sites operated by the United Kingdom Atomic Energy Authority. Under the 1965 Act, no person, other than UKAEA, may use sites for installing or operating nuclear reactors for the production or use of atomic energy or for storing, processing etc of nuclear fuels/radioactive by-products unless a nuclear site licence has been granted by the Health and Safety Executive.

Health and Safety

Michael Ellis

Name: Health and Safety at Work etc. Act 1974 (HSW Act),

Date Effective: April 1975

Interpretation:

Preliminary – General Review And Synopsis

The HSW Act applies to all places of employment within Great Britain and imposes responsibilities upon employers, the self employed, managers, employees, manufacturers, designers and suppliers of articles and substances for use at work. The Act establishes a duty on employers to provide and maintain a healthy and safe environment and adequate welfare facilities. The HSW Act is an enabling Act, incorporating provision for making regulations and Approved Codes of Practice (ACOP).

Employers are required to prepare a written statement of Health and Safety policy, detailing the organisational and administrative arrangements to ensure that health and safety is effectively managed.

Personal responsibilities also devolve upon managers, employees and other persons.

The HSW Act supplements the requirements of the Factories Act 1961 (F. Act) which applies to manufacturing activities only; this will gradually be replaced by EEC initiated health and safety laws.

The philosophy behind health and safety legislation is one of self regulation and companies must establish a commitment at the highest level to achieve the minimum objective of meeting statutory duties and the requirements set in the Policy.

Failure to comply with the above may lead to the imposition of fines of up to £20,000 by magistrates courts, and unlimited fines and imprisonment on indictment. Improvement and prohibition enforcement notices may also be served by Enforcing Authorities.

Management of Health and Safety

Policy and Organisation – HSW Act Section 2(3)

Companies employing more than five persons must produce a written statement of Health and Safety Policy including organisational arrangements established to achieve the objectives of the Policy. The core of the Policy document should be a statement of intent and commitment, signed by the Chief Executive. The means of achieving these objectives must be detailed in subsidiary parts of the document, explaining individual duties and responsibilities by explicitly outlining management key roles within the organisation and specialist support facilities available to managers. Guidance for preparing policies has been issued by the HSE (see Bibliography); whilst each Policy will be unique to a company, a suggested format and structure is as follows:-

Part 1 – General Policy

This is a statement of intent, outlining the Company's commitment, and forming the first section of the document, it should be signed by the Chief Executive, regularly updated and communicated to the workforce.

Part 2 – Organisation

The second section of the Policy should detail:

- organisational arrangements necessary to achieve the Policy objectives
- key functions and responsibilities and include safety in job descriptions
- committee structures and terms of reference, and standard procedures relevant to the Health and Safety issues, for example the placing of contracts, engagement of contractors and ordering new plant and substances.

Part 3 – Arrangements

The final part of the Policy should list arrangements for implementation, including information and training; procedures for preparing and revising safe systems of working, operational procedures and codes of practice; arrangements for environmental monitoring, noise assessments and other aspects of occupational hygiene; occupational health and facilities for medicals and first aid; plant and machinery safety; safe access/place of work; fire and emergency procedures including evacuation; testing and maintenance of plant and ventilation systems; finally, arrangements for monitoring compliance, including audits, inspections, incident reports and follow-up investigations.

Policy statements must be revised and updated to meet new legislation, changes in organisations and risk. The Policy should be drawn to the attention of all employees; this can be achieved by issuing individual copies if the policy is concise; larger, more complex, organisations may issue the policy in summary form, for example via a Health and Safety handbook, cross-referencing this with the main Policy document.

General Duties of Employers to Employees

HSW Act section 2(1) & (2)

Section 2(1) imposes a duty on employers to ensure, so far as is *reasonably practicable* (see *Edwards v. National Coal Board*), the health, safety and welfare of employees. These duties are further elaborated in Section 2(2) which requires, so far as is reasonably practicable

- the provision and maintenance of plant and systems of work that are safe and without risk to health
- the establishment of arrangements to ensure that substances and articles can be used, handled, stored and transported in a way that is safe and without risk to health
- the provision of information, instruction, training and supervision so as to ensure the health, safety and welfare of those employed
- the maintenance of the workplace in a healthy and safe condition and the need to ensure and maintain safe access and egress
- a safe and healthy working environment and adequate welfare facilities

These general requirements must be read in conjunction with specific duties appearing in complementary legislation, for example, the obligations relating to health at work included in the Control of Substances Hazardous to Health Regulations (COSHH) and stricter duties set by the Factories Act 1961 in respect of issues such as cleanliness and machinery guarding, which impose absolute duties overriding Section 2 of the HSW Act.

Safe Systems of Working Section 2(2a)

The failure to provide a safe system of working is a contributory factor in the majority of workplace accidents; thus the provision of a safe system of work is particularly important. The term is not defined within the Act, but has been the focus of attention by the courts. Employers must assess every health and safety implication of work and plan to eliminate or reduce risks to an acceptable level by implementing the systematic organisation of tasks, utilising safety devices and protective equipment, when appropriate. The planning and sequence of work for high risk operations often necessitates a formal approach, using for example written procedures and permit to work systems. All systems must be monitored and accompanied by adequate training and effective communications.

Duties of Employers and the Self-employed to Others

HSW ACT – SECTION 3

Section 3(1)

Employers must so far as is reasonably practicable, ensure that their work activity does not put at risk the health and safety of persons not in his employment including contractors, other companies' employees working on or near the site, and the public.

Work activities involving several employers must be looked at critically by all concerned. The principal occupier must take the leading role in co-ordinating site safety to ensure that the risks at the overlap between activities are identified and controlled. Demarcation of work and safety arrangements for activities involving several organisations, for example servicing, maintenance and installation work, must be carefully considered by the occupier exercising overall control of the site, who must play a co-ordinating role, and ensure that contractors are informed about inherent risks, monitor work overlaps and check contractors' competence. The *Regina v Swan Hunter* judgement emphasised the occupier's strict duties to contractors and to meet these written procedures and formally recorded systems should be encouraged, together with joint agreement upon key aspects of health and safety.

Employers must consider risks that work activities pose for visitors and members of the public; care must be paid at the perimeter of sites to ensure that the public are adequately safeguarded from plant and substance hazards and visitors must be protected.

Section 3(2)

The self-employed must conduct their undertakings so as to ensure that neither their safety, nor that of others, is put at risk.

Premises Used for Employment

Section 4

Persons in control of premises used for employment purposes by persons not directly in their employment must, so far as is reasonably practicable, ensure safe access and egress to common parts of premises and safety of fixed plant and services. These obligations may be transferred to tenants by contractual agreement on matters relating to maintenance and access.

Duties Of Suppliers, Importers, Designers and Manufacturers of Articles And Substances for Use at Work

HSW Act Section 6

Section 6, amended by the Consumer Protection Act 1987, imposes obligations on suppliers, designers, manufacturers and importers of articles and substances for use at work, and articles of fairground equipment, to ensure that the products are, as far as is reasonably practicable, safe and without risk to health. Secondhand and leased or hired articles are included.

The amendment arose from Section 36 (Schedule 3) of the Consumer Protection Act 1987 and came into force on 1 March 1988. The change in the law was necessary as the original Section 6 was ineffective due to ambiguities which had been challenged at Magistrates and Crown Court level.

The principal obligations are as follows:

Articles – Section 6(2) & 6(3)

Articles and fairground equipment should be designed and constructed to be safe and without risk to health when being set, used, cleaned or maintained by persons at work. Articles should be safely erected and installed. In the case of fairground equipment used for public entertainment this duty extends to the public.

Tests and examinations should be undertaken to ensure that the above duties are met. Adequate information must be provided to achieve safe operation and use without risk to health; this information should take the form of instruction manuals, training schedules and operational details for normal use, maintenance and setting, and emergencies.

Product information becoming evident subsequent to supply indicating a serious risk should be issued to users as revised information by the supplier.

Substances – Section 6(4) & 6(5)

Substances should, so far as is reasonably practicable, be safe and without risk to health when used, handled, processed, stored and transported by persons at work; tests and examinations should be undertaken to ensure safe use.

Manufacturers of substances should undertake research aimed at discovering health and safety hazards inherent in the substance and eliminating or minimizing risk to health and safety which foreseeable use gives rise to.

Adequate information about the risks, conditions of safe use, results of tests and research, should be provided to users, including revisions if serious risks to health are subsequently identified.

Companies supplying and manufacturing substances should prepare health and safety data sheets as a means of providing Section 6 information. The following checklist provides guidance upon substance data sheet content and format, based upon the HSE publication '*Substances for use at Work Provision of Information*'.

- Product name
- Intended uses
- Composition
- Physical and chemical properties

- Health hazards
- Occupational Exposure Standards
- Fire hazards
- Storage precautions
- Transport precautions
- Handling/use precautions (including advice on personal protective equipment)
- Emergency action
  - Fire, spillage, first aid
  - Ecological hazards
  - Waste disposal and relevant regulations
  - Advice to occupational medical officers
- References
- Name, address and telephone number of supplier
- Issue number, date of issue/revision

Disclaimers, exclusion or exemption clauses – Section 6(8)

Designers, suppliers and importers cannot relieve themselves of obligations by using disclaimers or release clauses and may only relinquish their duties if the client accepts this duty by preparing a release letter stating the steps he will take to meet these duties in lieu of the ostensible supplier.

In general the use of release letters should be discouraged as those best equipped to meet Section 6 are designers and manufacturers.

Responsibilities of Employees, Other Persons and Executive Managers

HSW Act Sections 7, 8 and 37

Section 7 – Employees

Employees should:-

- take reasonable care of their health and safety and that of others who may be affected by their acts or omissions
- co-operate with the employer to ensure that the employer can comply with statutory obligations.

Section 8 – Other Persons (Non-employees)

No person should intentionally and recklessly misuse or interfere with anything provided under H & S legislation in the interests of health, safety and welfare.

Section 37(1) – Executive Managers Personal Liability and Duties

If an offence is committed by a body corporate with the consent of the directors, executives, managers and company secretaries, or is due to their neglect, or is a result of their connivance, they are deemed guilty of the offence and will be proceeded against and punished accordingly.

There has been little 'reported' case law following prosecutions under the Section, with the exception of *Armour v Skeen*, which emphasised that directors and managers are personally under a duty to ensure that a company's statutory duties are performed; failure to do so renders executives open to personal prosecution.

Joint Consultation – Safety Representatives and Committees

Name: The Regulations on Safety Representatives & Safety Committees 1978

SI Number: SI 1977 no. 500

Date Effective: 1 October 1978

The regulations should be read in conjunction with the Approved Codes of Practice, Safety Representatives and Time off for the Training of Safety Representatives. They apply to all workplaces with Recognised Trade Unions and provide a framework to reach agreement on the appointment of Safety Representatives and establishment of Safety Committees to ensure a dialogue on key aspects of health and safety.

Safety Representatives are Trade Union appointed; the appointment can only be revoked by the Trade Union, or if the Representative resigns or leaves.

The function of the Safety Representative is to represent members in consultation with employers on matters of health, safety and welfare. Furthermore, the Safety Representative inherits specific rights following his appointment in writing, including the investigation of accidents, dangerous occurrences, complaints, and routine safety inspections once every three months (more frequently if the employer agrees); inspections can be repeated whenever there has been a significant change in working conditions or risk.

The Safety Representative has the right to represent employees in consultations with employers and Inspectors of the Enforcing Authority and to receive information from Inspectors in accordance with Section 28 (8) of the HSW Act.

Where Safety Committees have been formed the Safety Representatives may attend.

Employers should allow Safety Representatives time off with pay during working hours to perform their functions and undergo reasonable training.

There are no rigid ratios relating to the numbers of appointed Safety Representatives; this depends upon the size of the workplace and workforce, pattern of work, e.g. shifts, nature of the process and associated risks.

Two or more Safety Representatives can request employers to establish a Safety Committee, the composition and terms of reference of which should be jointly agreed.

Dependent upon the terms of reference and mode of operation, Safety Committees can either become counter productive vehicles for cataloguing long lists of complaints, or proactive positive catalysts for vigorous discussion and debate, acting in a promotional and monitoring role to ensure the effectiveness of safety arrangements and development of safety awareness.

Safety Representatives do not inherit additional liabilities by accepting the role, but must abide by the general duties of the HSW Act. The Regulations are overseen by the Enforcing Authority but Safety Representatives may present complaints to ACAS and also Industrial Tribunals if employers fail to permit time off with pay to fulfil the stated functions or receive training.

The Regulations do not apply when there is no Recognised Trade Union but do form a model for joint consultation upon health and safety for all forward thinking companies, whether or not they recognise trade unions. All companies are advised to promote a joint approach via employee Safety Representatives and forming effective Safety Committees to help achieve the commitment of the workforce, effective communication of information and development of safety awareness.

EMPLOYMENT OF YOUNG PERSONS, TRAINEES AND WOMEN

Name: Health & Safety (Training for Employment) Regulations 1990

SI No.: 1990/1380

Date Effective: 8/8/90

Synopsis

The legislation extends the definition of employee, for the purposes of the HSW Act, to include YTS trainees, school age pupils undergoing on the job training and college students on "sandwich" courses ; thus the same standards of protection are required for such persons as that given to employees under Section 2 of the HSW Act.

Name: Employment Act 1989, Sex Discrimination Act 1986 – Hours of employment

Synopsis

From the 27th February 1987 the Sex Discrimination Act 1986 removed the restrictions on women's hours of employment set under the Factories Act 1961 and essentially, limitations upon women's hours of work and nightwork are now repealed. The Employment Act 1989 amended legislation discriminating between men and women in employment, with the exception of legislation retained to protect women during pregnancy.

The hours of employment of young persons, (persons not 18 years old) is controlled by legislation set by the Factories Act 1961 and associated Orders, including restrictions on starting and finishing times, the length of the working day, restriction of maximum working hours to 48 per week; prohibition of night shift working and requirements in respect of overtime. A Government Discussion Document repealing all restrictions on the employment of young people represents the Government's current proposals to remove restricting legislation on young persons' hours of work, and widespread revocation of existing legislation is proposed.

Reporting of injuries, diseases and dangerous occurrences

Name: The Reporting of Injuries, Diseases and Dangerous Occurrences Regulations 1985 (RIDDOR)

SI: 1985 No. 2023

Date effective: 1st April 1986

Synopsis

RIDDOR requires the reporting of three broad categories of incident arising from workplace activities to the Enforcing Authority, namely specified types of physical injury and death, dangerous occurrences and diseases linked to work activity.

Accidents   Reportable events include death, specified major injuries (amputations, serious fractures, etc.) and conditions leading to an absence over three days from work. For employees, the employer should submit a return to the Enforcing Authority on statutory form F2508. Similar requirements apply to those receiving training for employment and the self-employed. Those providing training should submit reports for trainees. The person in control of premises where self employed persons work is responsible for reporting, although self employed persons themselves must report injury if they are in sole control.

All injuries   must be entered in the D.S.S. Accident Book B1 510 which must be kept available in a prominent position within every workplaces.

Seventeen **Dangerous Occurrences** appear in Schedule 1, Part 1 of RIDDOR; these include incidents such as cranes overturning, scaffolding collapsing and fires and explosions, all must be recorded and reported on Form 2508 in line with the above procedures, whether or not injury has occurred.

Diseases   RIDDOR specifies 28 diseases linked to work activities, including pneumoconiosis, occupational asthma, vibration white finger, occupational cancers and some infectious diseases linked to work activities; the list in RIDDOR does not cover every occupationally linked illness, however.

Cases of Disease in employees must be reported when a written diagnosis has been received from a doctor. The responsibilities for reporting are as listed for accidents; all reports should be sent to the Enforcing Authority on Form F 2508 A.

Registers and Records

Health and Safety legislation requires various records and registers to be maintained, particularly in pursuance of the Factories Act 1961 and attendant regulations; the principal ones are as follows:

Notifications

Notification to Enforcing Authority:

(1) Occupation of a Factory Form 9

(2) Occupation of an Office Form OSR 3

(3) Occupation of Construction or Building Operation Form 10

(4) Injury and Dangerous Occurrence Form 2508

(5) Occupational Disease Form 2508 A.

Registers and Abstracts

(1) Factories General Register Form 31

(2) Reports of inspection of scaffolds, excavations and lifting appliances in the construction industry Form 91 Parts 1 & 2

In addition to the above, employers must keep a register recording all reported injuries, diseases and dangerous occurrences.

Abstracts of special regulations enacted under the Factories Act must be displayed in premises to which they apply.

Name: Health and Safety (Information for Employees) Regulations

SI No: 1989/682

Date effective: 18/10/89

The Regulations require employers to display a statutory notice listing the key points of health and safety legislation and details of the Enforcing Authority and Employment Medical Advisory Service; alternatively, employers may issue the leaflet, "Health and Safety Law What You Should Know", to every employee.

Safety Signs

Name: Safety Signs Regulations 1980

S.I. 1980 No. 1471

Date Effective: 1/1/81 for new signs, 1/1/86 for all signs

Synopsis

All safety signs must comply with the regulations. A safety sign combines geometrical shape, colour and pictorial symbol to provide specific health or safety information or instructions (whether or not any text is necessary.) Safety signs (including any colours) giving health and safety information or instructions to employees must comply with BS 5378: Part 1: 1980 *"Safety signs and colours Part 1: Specification for colour and design"*. Part 2 of BS 5378 concerns colorimetric properties and dimensions. Part 3 gives specifications for additional signs. The basic requirements for signs are:-

Prohibition signs

Round with white background, red border and cross bar. Symbols must be black and placed centrally on the background without obliterating the cross bar. The sign means that something must not be done.

Warning signs

Triangular with a yellow background and a black border. The symbol, placed centrally, must be black. This sign warns of a hazard.

Mandatory signs

Round with a blue background and white symbol. This sign states what protective equipment must be worn.

Emergency signs

Square or oblong with white symbols on green background. This sign indicates safe conditions such as first-aid or emergency routes.

FACTORIES

Name: Factories Act 1961

Date effective: April 1962

Interpretation:

Preliminary

The Factories Act 1961 (F. Act) is complementary to, rather than in substitution for, the HSW Act 1974. It applies to premises designated as factories in Section 175 of that Act, which defines as factories premises with a curtilage, close or boundary in which persons are employed in manual labour in processes for, or incidental to -

manufacture of articles, altering, repair, ornamenting, finishing, cleaning, washing, breaking or adapting of articles, adaption for sale of articles, slaughtering of animals and associated activities.

The term factory includes the notional factory activities of docks and shipyards; packaging; laundries; construction and repair of locomotives, vehicles and other plant used for transport; printing; workshops manufacturing of scenery and costumes for theatres; building operations and works of engineering construction.

The Enforcing Authority must be notified one month prior to the occupation of factory premises on statutory Form 9; separate notification requirements relate to construction work liable to exceed six weeks when Form 10 must be submitted.

Parts of the Factories Act are gradually being repealed and replaced by more up-to-date regulations and Approved Codes of Practice applying to all work activities, based mainly upon EC Directives. Contrasting with the general duties of the HSW Act, which emphasises a systems and organisational approach, the F. Act is prescriptive, specifying standards applicable to machinery, boilers, cranes, general welfare, cleanliness and safe access and imposing strict duties, many of which are absolute. The principal requirements are as follows.

Welfare and Health

General Cleanliness – Section 1

Employers must keep factories clean and free from noxious odour. Accumulations of dirt and refuse must be removed daily and floors washed or swept weekly.

Internal walls must be painted or colour washed, unless finished with a smooth impervious surface capable of being effectively cleaned and washed. Walls and ceilings painted with oil bound paint and varnish must be thoroughly washed with hot water and soap once every fourteen months and redecorated once every seven years. Colourwashed walls incapable of being washed effectively should be redecorated once every fourteen months.

The duties relating to cleanliness are prescriptive and the periods specified are without prejudice to overall compliance, cleaning frequencies must be increased if standards deteriorate within the above timescales.

Overcrowding – Section 2

A factory should not be so overcrowded as to be injurious to the health of employees. Without prejudice to this the volume of space per person should not be less than 400 cubic feet; in calculating the volume no space shall be taken into consideration above a height of 14 ft from the floor.

Temperature – Section 3

Effective provision should be made for securing and maintaining a reasonable temperature in work rooms. Guidelines upon a "reasonable temperature" for specific activities are published by the Chartered Institute of Building Services (CIBS).

Where work is of a sedentary nature, a minimum temperature of 16°C (60°F), must be achieved after the first hour.

Heating appliances should not allow the escape of fumes which are offensive or injurious. Processes which are artificially humidified are also subject to Section 68 of the F. Act.

General Ventilation – Section 4

So far as is practicable, effective and suitable provision is necessary to secure and maintain adequate ventilation by circulating fresh air. The number of air changes per hour to achieve adequate ventilation depends on the volume of the room, processes, numbers employed and environmental factors including air movement, humidity and temperature. The CIBS provides guidance upon ventilation standards.

This section was amended by the COSHH Regulations from 1st October 1988 when the requirement to render harmless pollutants in the atmosphere was repealed together with Section 63, (Local Exhaust Ventilation).

Lighting – Section 5

Effective provision to secure and maintain sufficient and suitable lighting is required for areas where persons work or pass. CIBS publishes guidance for workplaces which, if achieved, satisfy the requirements of the Section.

Drainage of Floors – Section 6

Effective drainage should be provided and maintained where wet processes are undertaken.

Sanitary Conveniences – Section 7

Sufficient and suitable sanitary conveniences should be provided, maintained and kept clean in accordance with the Sanitary Accommodation Regulations 1938 (SR & O 1938, No. 611). This requirement is enforced by Local Authority Environmental Health Departments.

Drinking Water – Section 57

An adequate supply of wholesome drinking water, from the public main or some other source approved in writing by the local authority should be provided and maintained at convenient points accessible to all employees.

Washing Facilities – Section 58

Washing facilities, including a supply of running hot and cold water, soap and clean towels or other means of cleaning and drying should be provided and maintained.

Accommodation for Clothing – Section 59

Accommodation for clothing not worn during working hours should be provided and maintained and such arrangements which are reasonably practicable made for drying clothing.

Sitting Facilities – Section 60

Where work is capable of being undertaken from the sitting position without detriment, suitable facilities for sitting should be provided and maintained.

Underground Rooms – Section 69

The Enforcing Authority may certify underground rooms as being unsuitable for work.

Lifting Excessive Weights – Section 72

A person should not be employed to lift, carry or move any load so heavy to be likely to cause injury.

The section does not specify maximum loads and requires each case to be considered on merit, taking into account the physique, age and sex of the individual, the volume and weight of the load, the height and distance over which the load is to be moved. This duty will eventually be superseded by a European Directive on lifting loads. (See European Law.)

Homeworkers – Section 133

If outworkers are employed in work specified in the Homework Order, 10 April 1911 (SR & O 1911 No. 394) a list showing the names and addresses of employees undertaking work must be kept and submitted to the Local Authority.

Safety – Part II F. Act 1961

The F. Act sets absolute duties for the safeguarding of machinery, use of lifting machinery, cranes, hoists and lifts, safe access to work places, work in confined spaces and on plant containing explosive or inflammable materials.

Introductory Note: Machinery – Sections 12–16

The sections requiring the guarding of dangerous parts of machinery have received much judicial consideration by criminal and civil courts and the duty to securely fence parts of machinery specified in Sections 12, 13 and 14 is absolute, unless the parts are safe by position or construction. (*John Summers v Frost.*)

Prime Movers – Section 12

Prime movers, the head and tail race of waterwheels and water turbines, electrical rotating machines and associated flywheels must be securely fenced unless safe by position.

Transmission Machinery – Section 13

Transmission machinery, defined in Section 176 of the F. Act is required to be securely fenced unless safe by position or construction. Devices to promptly isolate transmission machinery from the power supply are required.

Other Dangerous Parts of Machinery – Section 14

All other dangerous parts of machinery not covered by Sections 12 and 13 should be securely fenced, unless safe by position or construction.

If dangerous parts cannot be protected by fixed guards, Section 14 requirements are deemed to have been met if a device is provided to automatically prevent the operative from coming into contact with the dangerous part.

Stock bars projecting back from the head stock of lathes must be securely fenced.

Construction use and Maintenance of Fencing and Other Safeguards – Section 16

The section qualifies Sections 12, 13 and 14, requiring guards to be substantially constructed, constantly maintained and to be kept in position whilst the parts are in motion or use, unless necessarily exposed for examination, lubrication or adjustment shown to be immediately necessary, in which case the requirements of the Operations at Unfenced and Machinery Regulations 1938 (SR & O 1938 No. 641 amended by SR & O 1946 No. 156) must be met. **This does not provide a blanket exemption for setters and maintenance personnel to operate machinery with guards removed.** The only instance when it is permissible to operate with no guards is when there is *absolutely no alternative means* of undertaking the examination, lubrication or adjustment, in which case Machinery Attendants must be appointed under the Regulation. Usually work can be safely undertaken by the use of secondary temporary guards if the primary guarding renders the work impossible; alternatively machines may be operated at a slow inching or crawl speed or barred over by hand to facilitate slow, safe movement for setting and adjustment.

All duties relating to the use, construction, and maintenance of safeguards are absolute, and no account is taken of the additional time or cost to achieve compliance.

Technical Guarding Standards – BS 5304

Technical guidance relating to the identification of dangerous parts and the development of effective safeguards is contained in British Standard Code of Practice for Safety of Machinery 5304: 1988. This provides advice upon the assessment of machinery hazards and the selection of appropriate safety devices. Fixed guards are the most preferable having no moving parts. Interlocked guards are necessary in circumstances where regular access is required, using electrical, mechanical, hydraulic or pneumatic interlocking circuits operating on principles of failing to safety, positive operation and defeat proof design. Technical specifications for interlocking are influenced by the degree of risk, taking into consideration the injury potential and frequency of access. Other guards appropriate to protect against danger are trip guards, which BS 5304 identifies as including photo-electric and infrared systems, pressure mats and trip wires and automatic guards operating in sequence with the dangerous parts to physically move the operative from danger.

Self Acting Machines – Section 19

If machines are self acting, no traversing part or material carried should be allowed to run within 18 inches of adjacent fixed structures.

Cleaning of Machinery by Women and Young Persons – Section 20

Women and persons under 18 are not allowed to clean prime movers, transmission machinery and other dangerous parts of machinery when in motion.

Training and Supervision of Young Persons Working Dangerous Machines – Section 21

Young persons are prohibited from working upon machines specified in the Dangerous Machines (Training of Young Persons) Order 1954 (SI 1954 No. 921) unless they have received sufficient training or are under the adequate supervision of an experienced person. Many machines specified by the Order are no longer in current use but it does include baking and meat mincing machines, engineering milling machines, power presses and printing equipment. Notwithstanding this duty, there is a broader based duty relating to training and supervision imposed by Section 2 of the HSW Act which applies to all potentially hazardous activities.

Hoists and Lifts – Sections 22 and 23

Hoists and lifts must be of good mechanical construction, sound material, adequate strength and properly maintained. The equipment must be thoroughly examined by a Competent Person usually an engineer surveyor from the insurers, once every six months; he will issue a report on the statutory Form F54. The maximum working load must be specified and displayed within the lift. The lift shaft and car should be enclosed and protected by interlocked access gates.

Chains, Ropes and Lifting Tackle – Section 26

Lifting equipment should be of good construction, sound material, adequate strength, free from patent defect when used for raising or lowering persons, goods or materials. Manufacturers' test certificates should be obtained and lifting tackle thoroughly examined by a Competent Person at least every six months, he will report on the prescribed register, Form 88.

A table showing the safe working loads of every kind and size of chain, rope or lifting tackle must be displayed in the lifting tackle store adjacent to the point of use together with the safe working load for different leg angles of multiple slings.

Cranes and Lifting Machines – Section 27

Cranes and lifting machines, whether fixed or moveable, and including anchoring and fixing appliances, should be of good construction, sound material, adequate strength and free from patent defect. There is a requirement to ensure that all equipment is properly maintained and it should be thoroughly examined by a Competent Person at least once every fourteen months and a report issued on Register, Form 88.

Safe working loads of lifting machines must be clearly displayed. No lifting equipment, except for the purposes of testing, should be loaded beyond the safe working load. Test certificates must be issued for new equipment, specifying the safe working load.

Where work adjacent to wheeled overhead crane tracks takes place and there is a risk of persons being struck by the crane, effective measures should be taken to ensure that the crane does not approach within 20 feet of workplaces; steps should also be taken to warn of the approach of the crane if there is a risk of individuals being stuck by the load.

Floors, Passages and Stairs Safe Access – Sections 28 & 29

Floors, steps, stairs, passages and gangways should be of sound construction, properly maintained, and so far as is reasonably practicable, kept free from obstructions and substances liable to cause persons to slip. Staircases must be provided with handrails and lower rails.

Openings in floors should be securely fenced, except where the nature of the work renders it impracticable.

Ladders must be soundly constructed and properly maintained.

So far is as reasonably practicable, safe access and a safe place of work should be provided and maintained throughout the factory. Where work occurs at a height from which a person is liable to fall a distance of more than 6 ft. 6 in. then, unless this affords secure foothold and secure handhold, all reasonably practicable means, by fencing or otherwise, should be provided to ensure safety.

Fixed vessels, structures, sumps and pits the edge of which is less than 3 ft. above the ground, or platform from which a person might fall shall, if containing scalding, corrosive or poisonous liquids be covered or securely fenced to a height of at least 3 ft.; means of access used above or across vessels must be at least 18 in. wide and securely fenced to a height of 3 ft. on both sides.

Dangerous Fumes and Lack of Oxygen – Section 30

Work in confined spaces such as tanks and pits should only be undertaken if there is adequate egress. Where there is liable to be a lack of oxygen or dangerous fumes, entry shall not occur until formally authorized by a responsible person and no-one should enter unless wearing breathing apparatus and where practicable a safety belt and rope. A second person should keep watch on the outside to effect rescue and resuscitation equipment be readily available.

Confined spaces may be tested and then certified as safe for entry for specified periods without breathing apparatus provided that effective steps have been taken to prevent the ingress of fumes, sludge and deposits liable to give off dangerous emissions removed, and spaces adequately ventilated. The most effective way to ensure that these conditions are met is to restrict entry under a strictly enforced permit to work system as set out in the Health and Safety Executive's Guidance Note *'GS5. Work in Confined Spaces'*.

Precautions with regard to explosive inflammable dust gases and vapours – Section 31

Where operations produce dust of such character and extent as to be liable to explode on ignition, all practicable steps should be taken to restrict the spread and effects of an explosion by the provision of chokes, baffles and vents or similarly effective devices.

Plant containing explosive or inflammable gases or vapours under pressure greater than atmospheric must not be opened unless the flow of gas or vapour is effectively prevented. Before removing the fastenings of joints and connections all practicable steps should be taken to reduce the pressure to atmospheric pressure and no explosive gas or vapour should be allowed to enter the pipe unless all connections are secured.

Tanks and vessels containing flammable substances must not be subject to welding and similar operations unless steps have been taken to remove the substance and fumes or to render them non explosive/non inflammable. Explosive and flammable substances must not be allowed to re-enter plant until it is sufficiently cooled to prevent the risk of ignition.

OFFICES

Name: Offices, Shops and Railway Premises Act 1963

Date effective: February 1964

Synopsis

The act makes strict provision for securing the health, safety and welfare of persons employed in offices, shops, some railway premises and premises selling food and drink to be consumed in public. The Act follows the pattern of the F. Act 1961 and imposes parallel requirements. Offices are also subject to all legislation enacted under the HSW Act.

CONSTRUCTION

Construction and building work, including building maintenance, cleaning structures and all works of engineering construction, are defined in Section 176 of the F. Act 1961 and are subject to the following special Regulations.

Name: The Construction (General Provisions) Regulations 1961

SI No: 1961 No. 1580 amended by SI 1966 94 and SI 1974 1681

Date effective: 1st March 1962

Synopsis

The General Provisions Regulations impose a basic obligation to appoint site safety supervisors on construction sites. Detailed requirements are also imposed in relation to the protection of employees whilst working in or adjacent to excavations, safety of mechanically propelled vehicles, demolition safety, the guarding of dangerous machinery, protection from falling materials and safeguarding from projecting nails in timber and other materials and the lifting of excessive weights. There is also a requirement to provide adequate lighting where lifting appliances are used adjacent to dangerous openings.

Name: The Construction (Lifting Operations) Regulations 1961

SI No. 1961 No 1581

Date effective: 1st March 1962

Synopsis

The Regulations impose stringent requirements regarding the use of cranes, lifting machines and hoists and require testing, maintenance and statutory registers.

Name: Construction (Working Places) Regulations 1966

SI No. 1966 No. 94

Date effective: 1/5/66

Synopsis

Stringent standards are set to ensure safe access to construction operations. These include the safe use of ladders and specific standards regarding work at heights in excess of 6 ft 6 in. which principally should be undertaken from scaffolding with toe boards and guard rails. Roof work at heights in excess of 6 ft 6 in. requires protection when there is a risk of falling through fragile materials, from the edge or from sloping roofs; this protection includes the use of toe boards, guardrails and working platforms.

Name: Construction (Health & Welfare) Regulations 1966

SI No. 1966 no 95 amended by SI 1974 no 209 and SI 1981 No 917

Date effective:

Synopsis

The regulations lay down welfare standards for construction and building sites with particular emphasis upon the provision of washing facilities, toilet accommodation, protective clothing and sheltered accommodation for clothing and taking meals.

PRESSURE VESSELS AND ASSOCIATED SYSTEMS

Name: The Pressure Systems and Transportable Gas Containers Regulations 1989

SI No. S.I. 1989 No. 2169

Date Effective: Phased in over period 1st July 1990 to 1st July 1994

The first phase of these Regulations came into force on 1st July 1990. The Regulations apply to pressure systems containing gases (including liquified gas) and steam operating at pressures greater than 0.5 bar (approximately 7 psi) above atmospheric where pressure x volume of the largest vessels in the system exceeds 250 bar litres.

The duties will be phased in over a four year transitional period, becoming fully operative on 1st July 1994 to repeal the Factories Act requirements relating to steam plant and air receivers contained in Sections 32-39 of that Act. Requirements relating to the supply of information for new plant, the safe installation of plant and the establishment of safe operating limits on existing plant apply from 1st July 1990. The duties relating to the safe manufacture and maintenance of transportable gas cylinders apply to suppliers, importers, fillers and owners from 1st January 1991.

Basically, users should set safe operating limits of pressure and temperature, draw up certified schemes of examination and testing, provide adequate operating safety instructions relating to normal use and emergencies and ensure adequate records are kept. Competent persons must be appointed to complete the above functions. The underlying theme throughout places greater responsibility upon systems' users. Insurance companies will normally be in a position to provide guidance upon the practical implementation of the Regulations which are supported by an A.CoP.

ELECTRICAL SAFETY

Name: Electricity at Work Regulations 1989

S.I. 1989 No. 635

Date Effective: 1st April 1990

Preliminary

The purpose of the Regulations is to require precautions to be taken against the risk of death or personal injury from electricity in work activities. The Regulations replace the Electricity Regulations 1908, made under the F. Act which only applied to factory activities. The new Regulations cover all workplaces and should be read in conjunction with the *Memorandum of Guidance on the Electricity at Work Regulations 1989* (HMSO). The Regulations should be considered in parallel with the Institution of Electrical Engineers Regulations for Electrical Installations (the IEE Wiring Regulations). The IEE Regulations are non-statutory regulations providing guidance upon the design, selection, erection, inspection and testing of electrical installations; compliance with the IEE Regulations is likely to achieve compliance with the Electricity at Work Regulations within the context of protection against electrical injuries associated with shock, burns, fires, arcing and explosions. The principal duties apply to the employer and there are also responsibilities upon employed persons and the self employed.

Synopsis of Regulations

The main duty is to ensure that electrical systems are constructed to prevent danger, and of adequate strength and capacity to ensure safe operation. The equipment should be protected against adverse or hazardous environments, mechanical or chemical damage, the effects of weather, pressure or temperature and risks associated with the ignition of flammable or explosive substances. Electrical conductors should be insulated or placed in a safe position to prevent danger and conductors earthed. Protection against excess current must be achieved and isolators fitted to cut off the supply.

The Regulations impose conditions to implement safe systems of working, in particular the need to ensure that circuits have been made dead whilst working on the equipment and emphasise that work upon live conductors should only be undertaken as a last resort, when there is no alternative, and such work restricted to authorised competent persons.

Adequate working space, safe access and lighting must be provided at electrical installations to ensure safe working.

OCCUPATIONAL HEALTH

Name: Control of Substances Hazardous to Health Regulations 1988

S.I. 1988 No. 1657

Date Effective: 1 October 1989

Preliminary

The Control of Substances Hazardous to Health Regulations 1988 ('COSHH') represents the most significant development in the field of workplace health and safety since the enactment of the HSW Act 1974. The regulations impose an obligation upon all employers to undertake an assessment of health risk for activities associated with substances hazardous to health used at work and in parallel to assess the effectiveness of existing control systems such as exhaust ventilation and respiratory protective equipment. Regulation 17 incorporates transitional provisions which allowed a three month lead in period for risk assessments to be completed by 1st January 1990. The essence of the regulations, which incorporate the essential principles of occupational health and hygiene, is to ensure a proactive approach to the assessment and prevention or control of exposure. COSHH makes provision for air monitoring within the workplace, health surveillance and information, instruction and training for persons who may be exposed to substances hazardous to health. The continuing theme throughout COSHH is the need to adopt a formalised approach, thus written records of assessments, air monitoring, health surveillance, testing and maintenance of control systems must be established.

The regulations should be read in conjunction with the Approved Codes of Practice, Control of Substances Hazardous to Health and Control of Carcinogenic Substances.

Duties

The principal obligations and duties devolve upon the employer to protect employees. Employers should, so far as is reasonably practicable, also apply COSHH to other persons, whether at work or not, who may be affected by the employer's work.

Prohibitions – Regulation 4

Schedule 2 imposes prohibitions upon certain uses of specified substances; for example, sand and materials containing free silica are prohibited from use as abrasives for the blasting of articles.

Application and Exemptions – Regulation 5

Some substances, including lead and asbestos, are exempt from COSHH as they fall under the scope of existing comprehensive legislation. Furthermore, risks solely related to radioactive, explosive or flammable properties, fire or pressure are exempt.

'Substance hazardous to health' is defined as substances listed in Part 1A of the Classification, Packaging and Labelling of Dangerous Substances Regulations 1984 for which the nature of risk is specified as very toxic, toxic, harmful, corrosive or irritant. Also included are substances having Maximum Exposure Limits (MEL), specified in Schedule 1 of COSHH, and Occupational Exposure Standards (OES); dust of any kind which is present in substantial concentrations and micro-organisms are included.

Assessment of Health Risks – Regulation 6

An employer should not carry out work liable to expose employees to substances hazardous to health unless he has made a suitable and sufficient assessment of risk to health and the steps needed to meet the requirements of the COSHH Regulations.

To achieve compliance employers should appoint COSHH Assessors, or assessment teams, with collective expertise to undertake assessments of risk and control systems and identify the necessity for environmental monitoring. The first stage is to prepare an inventory of substances/processes to which the regulations apply and then determine the extent of exposures via the inhalation, ingestion or skin absorption routes. This involves a careful consideration of substance toxicity and suppliers' data sheets. The degree of risk is determined by reviewing work methods, the form of the substance, the volume, frequency and periods of use. Details of the assessment together with associated conclusions and actions must be formally recorded.

Regulation 6(2) requires the assessment to be reviewed if there is reason to suspect it is no longer valid or there has been a significant change in the work.

On completion of the assessment, the assessors must conclude whether a risk exists and determined the effectiveness of existing control systems. The conclusions of the initial assessment should include recommendations in respect of the prevention or control of exposures, the necessity for air monitoring and need for additional controls.

Control of Risk, Use of Control Measures and Maintenance – Regulations 7, 8 & 9

Regulation 7 requires employers to ensure that exposures of employees to substances hazardous to health is prevented, or where this is not reasonably practicable, adequately controlled. Prevention and control should be achieved as far as is reasonably practicable without reliance being placed on personal protective equipment. Thus enclosure of processes, exhaust ventilation systems, safer substitute materials, elimination of harmful processes and development of safe operational procedures must be considered within the context of controlling or eliminating risk. As a last resort, if the foregoing precautions are not reasonably practicable, personal protective equipment appropriate to the risk should be issued, this includes respiratory protection, gloves and other types of protective clothing .

There are obligations upon employers and employees to ensure that control measures are properly and effectively used, as specified by Regulation 8 of COSHH. Maintenance, examination and testing of control measures must be formally undertaken, in accordance with Regulation 9; this includes testing air flows and implementing the maker's specified maintenance requirements.

The emphasis in Regulations 7, 8 and 9 is to eliminate or prevent exposure and validate the effectiveness of control measures to ensure that the OES and MEL are not exceeded; if theMEL is exceeded, the Regulations are deemed not to have been met. Exposures should be reduced to the lowest level which is reasonably practicable below the MEL for substances listed in Schedule 1.

Monitoring exposure – Regulation 10

Air monitoring to identify the concentration and composition of airborne substances should be undertaken in many cases as part of the initial risk assessment and also wherever significant levels of exposure are anticipated. Routine monitoring of exposure should also be completed to validate the effectiveness of control systems.

Health surveillance – Regulation 11

Employees exposed to substances hazardous to health may require health surveillance where valid surveillance techniques exist to detect exposures and validate that adequate protection is achieved.

COSHH records

Formal records of assessments, thorough examination, maintenance and testing, air monitoring and health surveillance must be maintained by all employers subject to COSHH.

Name: Classification, Packaging, Labelling of Dangerous Substances Regulations 1984, 1986 and 1988 (CPL Regs)

SI No. 1244 Amendments 1922 & 766

Date Effective: 12th September 1984

Synopsis

The Regulations implement EC Directives and apply to the supply, conveyance by road and packaging and labelling of dangerous substances classified in Schedule 1; this includes substances which are explosive, oxidising, highly flammable, toxic, harmful, corrosive and irritant. Standards of packaging and hazard warning labels and symbols are defined in the regulations which also specify requirements for supply and carriage.

Name: Notification of New Substances Regulations 1982

S.I. No. 1496

Date effective: 26 November 1982

Synopsis:

The regulations implement various EC Directives and require manufacturers or importers to notify the HS Executive of new substances where total quantities of one tonne or more are supplied in any period of twelve months. The information should include a technical dossier evaluating foreseeable risks, a declaration concerning hazardous effects of substances with respect to usages envisaged and a declaration as to whether the substance is dangerous in accordance with classifications set within European Council Directive No. 67/548/EEC. (See also European Law EINECS Scheme.)

Name: Dangerous Substances (Notification and Marking of Sites) Regulations 1990

S.I. 1993 04

Date Effective: 1/9/90

Synopsis

The regulations apply to sites storing 25 tonnes or more of dangerous substances as specified under the Classification, Packaging and Labelling of Dangerous Substances Regulations 1984. The requirement is for persons in control of sites to notify the enforcing authority of the following information, unless notification to the enforcing authority has already occurred via the existing legislation, Notification of Installations handling Hazardous Substances Regulations 1982 or Control of Industrial Major Accidents Hazards Regulations 1984 -

1. Persons in control are required to notify the enforcing authority of basic information relating to total quantity and nature of substances stored; the information must be in a form meeting the criteria published by the enforcing authorities. This information must also be submitted to the fire authority.

2. Hazard warning signs indicating the nature of the site must be clearly displayed at all site entrances.

NOISE

Name: Noise at Work Regulations 1989

Date Effective: 1st January 1990

Synopsis

The Regulations require employers to prevent damage to the hearing of workers from excessive noise at work and are based upon a European Community Directive requiring similar laws throughout the Community. Employers, and in some cases the self- employed, are required to initiate assessments of risk by undertaking noise surveys under the control of a competent person. The assessment should be undertaken within the context of three Action Levels:

- the first Action Level daily personal noise dose exposure $L_{EP,d}$ 85 dB(A).
- the second Action Level daily personal noise exposure $L_{EP,d}$ 90 dB(A)
- Peak Action Level peak sound pressure of 200 pascals (140 dB re 20 uPa.)

The survey should identify noisy plant, processes and employees liable to be exposed to doses approaching the First, Second and Peak Action Levels.

Exposures above the first Action Level dictate that hearing protection be made available to the workforce.

Exposures in excess of Action Level 2 impose mandatory requirements to reduce the risk of hearing damage and exposure. In the first instance, the duty is elimination or control of noise at source; only when this is not reasonably practicable can reliance be placed upon the use of hearing protection. Where the initial survey identifies work with variable exposures, this should be taken into account in prescribing control measures and establishing ear protection zones identified by the display of warning notices.

Employees should be informed of risks and precautions necessary to prevent hearing damage.

The Regulations also impose a duty upon manufacturers to provide information if their products for use at work are liable to emit noise exceeding the Action Levels.

FIRST AID

Name: Health & Safety (First Aid) Regulations 1981

SI Number: 1981 No. 917

Date Effective: 1 July 1982

Synopsis

The Regulations and associated ACoP require all employers to appoint trained first aid personnel or establish equally effective arrangements via occupational health centres. First aiders must be formally trained and hold a First Aid at Work Certificate which should be renewed every three years. The Regulations also require First Aid boxes stocked in accordance with the standards specified and supplementary specialist first aid expertise and facilities to cover occupationally related hazards.

EUROPEAN SAFETY LAW

Implications of Council of European Communities Directives (EC Directives) on Health and Safety

Recently enacted Statutes relating to occupational noise, the control of substances hazardous to health, the notification of new substances and packaging, transport and labelling of substances align with EC directives. Future directives will significantly influence the evolution and development of health and safety law within the United Kingdom, as harmonisation of standards for health and safety is required by Article 118A. The Article encourages improvements for the health and safety of workers, especially the working environment and recommends that Directives shall avoid imposing administrative, financial and legal constraints which would hold back the creation and development of small and medium sized undertakings.

The following Directives were submitted to Council in the first half of 1988 and subsequently adopted The Framework Directive; Workplaces; The use of machines, equipment and installations; The use of personal protective equipment; Work with Visual Display Units; and Handling heavy loads where there is a risk of back injury; Carcinogens and Biological Agents. Further Directives, covering areas excluded from the Workplace Directive will follow, these include Construction, Extractive Industries, (oil, gas, mining and quarrying), Transport and Fishing.

The main features of the principle directives are described later. The directives are based on five common principles and themes for employers, set out in Article 6(2) of the Framework Directive, these are to:

- avoid risks
- evaluate the risks which cannot be avoided;
- combat risks at source;
- replace the dangerous by the non-dangerous or the less dangerous
- give collective protective measures priority over individual protective measures

These principles form the approach adopted in all the directives. Other common themes include the need to give full information, instruction and training to employees.

The practical impact will not be to add additional requirements but rather to make explicit what is already implicit in the HSW Act. Firms which follow existing good practice will have no problems with the directives.

All Member States are required to translate the adopted directives into national law by the end of 1992. The directives are of major significance to UK health and safety law. In considering the implementation of the directives, the Health and Safety Commission has laid down two guiding principles:

- that the existing legislative framework should not be disrupted
- where appropriate, advantage should be taken of opportunities presented by the directives to reform and rationalise pre-1974 legislation

The Health and Safety Executive is actively considering how best to implement the directives and consultation documents will be produced setting out proposals for the implementation of each directive. The requirements of impending directives are reviewed below.

Name: Directive on the introduction of measures to encourage improvements in the safety and health of workers at the workplace

Ref: 89/392/EEC

Date adopted: 12/6/89

Implementation: 31/12/92

Synopsis

The directive applies to all workplaces and workers therein and employers are obligated to take the necessary measures for the protection of safety and health of workers, including prevention of occupational risks. Employers should develop a coherent policy of prevention by combating risks at source, adapting the work to man and to technical progress, replacing the dangerous by the non-dangerous or less dangerous and developing an overall prevention policy based on technology, organisation of work, working conditions and human relationships. Safety measures must be integrated into the undertaking at all hierarchical levels.

Employers must ensure consideration is given to ergonomic principles, in particular the design of workplaces, choice of plant and equipment and choice of working methods and must also take measures to permit workers to organise their work in accordance with their capabilities where reasonably practicable. Special consideration should be given to planning and organising work of a monotonous to repetitive nature and close cooperation is required with the planning and introduction of new technologies.

Employers are required to designate supervisory staff with regard to health and safety and make arrangements regarding first aid, fire fighting, the evacuation of workers and similar emergency arrangements.

An analysis of risks to health and safety is required with the commensurate establishment of protective measures. A list of occupational accidents and diseases must be maintained together with an analysis of causes and the measures to be taken to prevent recurrences.

The directive requires the provision of information, consultation and training for workers and imposes a duty upon each worker to take reasonable care of his safety and health and that of others.

Effectively much of the above mirrors the general duties imposed by Section 2 of the HSW Act.

Name: Minimum Health and Safety Requirements for the Workplace

Date submitted: 11/3/88

Ref: 89/654/EEC

Date adopted: 30/11/89

Implementation: 31/12/92

Synopsis

The directive requires member States to take measures to ensure that workplaces (except transport and temporary or mobile work sites) when used as intended and properly maintained, cannot adversely affect the safety and health of workers or other persons present.

The minimum requirements for workplaces are detailed in Annex 1 and relate to the need for structural stability; safe electrical installations; emergency exists; fire detection and fire fighting; ventilation; room temperatures; natural and artificial room lighting; the structure of floors, walls and ceilings of rooms; the provision of safe traffic routes for personnel; the provision of rest rooms and sanitary equipment including changing areas, washrooms and toilets; the organisation of workplaces to take into account handicapped workers. New workplaces require windows and skylights, and bays/ramps for loading purposes.

Name: Council Directive concerning the minimum safety and health requirements for the use of machines, equipment and installations

Date submitted: 11/3/88

Ref: 89/655/EEC

Date adopted: 30/11/89

Implementation: 31/12/92

Synopsis

This directive, influenced by the harmonisation and standardisation requirements of Article 108, seeks to remove conflicts caused by different technical specifications and standards which in turn lead to different levels of safety and health and distort competition.

Employers must ensure that the following principles are implemented.

- work equipment is suitable, properly adapted and can be used without risks to health or safety, and is adequately maintained;
- where specific hazards are likely to be involved, access to the equipment is restricted to those employees given the task of using it;
- where work equipment cannot be made totally safe, measures should be taken to minimise the risks.

Annex 1 establishes minimum standards relating to machine controls and emergency isolation; risks relating to objects falling or being ejected; the anchoring and securing of machinery; the protection of moving parts to prevent contact with the workers; the provision of adequate lighting; protection against high or very low temperatures; provision of clear and conspicuous warning indicators and a basic requirement establishing that machines should not be used for operations or conditions for which they were not designed or are unsuitable and the necessity for proper maintenance to ensure safe operation. Also, maintenance should be carried out outside danger zones or during machine shutdown where technically possible.

Annex 2 reproduces non-exhaustive guidelines upon which compliance with Annex 1 can be based and establishes ergonomic principles concerning machines with regard to the presentation of health and safety information, control functions, mental stress and fatigue and physical fatigue.

Name: Directive concerning the minimum health and safety requirements for the use by workers of personal protective equipment

Ref: 89/656/EEC

Date adopted: 30/11/89

Implementation: 31/12/92

Synopsis

The objective of the Directive is the protection of workers by use of Personal Protective Equipment (PPE) when risks cannot be avoided or overcome, by built-in protection, organisational measures, work methods or procedures. Employers must assess the risks and select PPE which is appropriate, adapted or adaptable to individual workers, and corresponds to work conditions, taking into account ergonomic requirements and the workers' state of health. Where the presence of several risks makes it necessary to wear more than one item of PPE, equipment must be compatible. Conditions of use must be determined by the seriousness of risk and frequency of exposures.

Annex 1 of the Directive provides a specimen risk assessment table, upon which compliance strategies can be built and **Annex 2** provides a non-exhaustive list of items falling within the scope of definition of PPE. **Annex 3** specifies criteria for evaluating PPE and in particular the risks covered. **Annex 4** lists the activities to be taken into account by Members States in establishing regulations; and covers head protection, foot protection, eye or face protection, respiratory protection, hearing protection, body, arm and hand protection; weather proof clothing, reflective clothing, safety helmets; safety ropes; and skin protection.

Name: Directive concerning the minimum safety and health requirements at work with visual display units

Date adopted: 29/5/90

Implementation: 31/12/92

Synopsis

The directive applies to work stations equipped with VDUs except drivers' cabs or control cabs for vehicles and machinery. The directive lays down general duties to ensure that VDU work cannot compromise the safety or health of workers and requires employers to perform an analysis of work stations to evaluate the safety and health risks and take remedial measures to eliminate risks and provide periodic breaks or changes in activity.

Work stations coming into service after December 1992 must comply with the minimum requirements of the Annex; this includes the work station design (screen, keyboard, desk, adjustable chairs, space and layout and environmental factors such as glare, lighting, noise and humidity). Work stations already in service must also comply to similar requirements within four years of the directive coming into force. The directive requires adequate training and establishes a duty to consult the workforce. Ophthalmological examinations are required prior to commencing VDU work, if workers report visual discomforts and on a routine basis. The provision of special glasses is required if eye examinations shows they are required and that glasses intended for normal purposes cannot be used.

Name: Council Directive on the minimum health and safety requirements for handling heavy loads where there is a risk of back injury for workers

Ref: 90/269/EEC

Date adopted: 29/5/90

Implementation: 31/12/90

Synopsis

The directive establishes the principle that employers should, as far as possible, take steps to avoid the need to manually handle heavy loads without mechanical assistance. Where manual handling of heavy loads cannot be avoided, employers must assess in advance the physical effort required and characteristics of the loads. These characteristics are examined in Annex 1, which identifies the key factors in preventing back injuries as being loads which are too heavy, too large, unwieldy, difficult to grasp, unbalanced or unstable. The directive affirms that employers must take into account individual characteristics of workers when organising manual handling at work and in particular the physical characteristics, including the health of the worker, size, dress and training. Workers should be properly trained and informed and employers are required to take into account physical and organisational factors such as headroom, working space, conditions of floors and the frequencies and distances of lifting, lowering, or carrying.

The directive places emphasis upon work organisation, training and systems, as summarised above, as opposed to quoting maximum weights.

Name: Carcinogens Directive

Date adopted: 9/90

Implementation: by 31/12/92

Synopsis

The provisions are applied to substances labelled R45 "May cause cancer" and also substances and processes specified in Annex 1 to the directive. The directive sets out a framework of protection for workers exposed to carcinogens requiring -

- an assessment of risk
- dependent on the outcome of the assessment, replacement by harmless or less dangerous substances or failing this, use within an enclosed system. Where enclosure is not possible, the duty is to reduce exposures to as low a level as possible
- procedures for situations where abnormal or exposure in emergency conditions occurs
- monitoring and health surveillance appropriate to the type of substance and exposure
- adequate information, training, information and instruction about risks and precautions and results of health surveillance are required.

Name: Proposed Directive Protection of workers from risks associated to biological agents at work

Date: Approved by Social Affairs Council – Subject to scrutiny by European Parliament – likely to be adopted late 1990

Synopsis

The proposal is one of three EC directives in the broad area of microbiology and biotechnology safety. The others relating to microorganisms and genetically modified organisms were adopted in April 1990. The directive applies to all work activities where workers are exposed to biological agents and discriminates between activities where there is a conscious decision to work with them, for example microbiological laboratory work, and those where exposure could be incidental to work activities, for example health care and farming. The directive will require a risk assessment by employers as a pre-requisite to the prevention or reduction of risks of exposure. The common themes of information, instruction and training are incorporated into the directive, which also requires lists of exposed workers to be kept.

The containment principles embodied in the Directive are broadly in line with those presently incorporated into guidance already published within the U.K.

Name: European Inventory of existing commercial chemical substances (EINECS)

Date effective: 15/12/90

The EINECS inventory is published by the European Commission and lists substances commercially available in the EEC between 1st January 1971 and 18th September 1981, a total in excess of 100,000. Excluded from the inventory are medicinal products, narcotics, radioactive substances, foodstuffs or wastes. The purpose of EINECS is to distinguish between new and existing substances within the EEC, and substances not appearing in the Register will be defined as new and should be notified under the Notification of New Substances Regulations 1982. Companies supplying or importing substances not listed in EINECS and not already notified as "new substances" should contact the Health and Safety Executive's Data Appraisal Unit, as should companies planning to supply or import substances, before embarking upon test programmes. The contact number for the Unit is: (051) 951 4000.

Selected List of Current Health and Safety Statutes

Acts

Factories Act 1961

Health and Safety at Work etc. Act 1974

Offices, Shops and Railway Premises Act 1963

Radioactive Substances Act 1960

Social Security Act 1975

Social Security Act 1986

Regulations

Regulation/Order S.R. & O., S.I., Subsequent Amendment

Abrasive Wheels Regulations 1970 1970/535

Asbestos (Licensing) Regulations 1983 1983/1649 1986/392

Asbestos Products (Safety) Regulations 1985 1985/2042

Asbestos (Prohibitions) (Amendment) 1988/711 Regulations 1988

Classification, Packaging and Labelling of Dangerous Substances Regulations 1984 1984/1244 1986/1922 1988/766

Classification, Packaging and Labelling of Dangerous Substances (Amendment) Regulations 1986 1986/1922

Classification, Packaging and Labelling of Dangerous Substances (Amendment) Regulations 1988 1988/766

Construction (General Provisions) Regulations 1961 1961/1580 1966/94 1974/1681 1984/1593

Construction (General Provisions) Reports Order 1962 1962/224

Construction (Health and Welfare) Regulations 1966 1966/95 1980/1248 1981/917

Construction (Lifting Operations) Regulations 1961 1961/1581 1984/1593

Control of Asbestos at Work Regulations 1987 1987/2115

Control of Industrial Major Accident Hazards 1984/1902 Regulations 1984

Control of Lead at Work Regulations 1980 1980/1248

Control of Substances Hazardous to Health Regulations 1988 1988/1657

Dangerous Machines (Training of Young Persons) Order 1954 1954/921

Dangerous Substances (Conveyance by Road in Road Tankers and Tank Containers) Regulations 1981 1985/1333 1985/2023 1985/1951

Electricity at Work Regulations 1989 1989/635

Foundries (Protective Footwear and Gaiters) Regulations 1971 1971/476

Grinding of Metals (Miscellaneous Industries Regulations 1925 1925/904 1949/2225 1950/688 1981/1486

Health and Safety (Enforcing Authority) Regulations 1977 1977/746 1980/1744 1985/1107 1986/294

Health and Safety (Enforcing Authority) (Amendment) Regulations 1980 1980/1744

Health and Safety (Enforcing Authority) (Amendment) Regulations 1985 1985/1107

Health and Safety (First-Aid) Regulations 1981 1981/917

Health and Safety (Training for Employment) Regulations 1990 SI 1990/1380

Highly Flammable Liquids and Liquefied Petroleum Gases Regulations 1972 1972/917

Horizontal Milling Machines Regulations 1928 1928/548 1934/207

Ionising Radiations Regulations 1985 1985/1333 1986/392

Iron and Steel Foundries Regulations 1953 1953/1464 1974/1681

Noise at Work Regulations 1989

Non-Ferrous Metals (Melting and Founding) Regulations 1962 1962/1667 1974/1681 1981/1332

Notification of Installations Handling Hazardous Substances Regulations 1982 1982/1357 1984/1244

Notification of New Substances Regulations 1982 1982/1496 1985/1333

Notification of New Substances (Amendment) Regulations 1986 1986/890

Operations at Unfenced Machinery Regulations 1938 1938/641 1946/156 1976/955

Protection of Eyes Regulations 1974 1974/1681 1975/303

Reporting of Injuries, Diseases and 1985/2023 Dangerous Occurrences Regulations 1985 1985/2023

Safety Representatives and Safety Committees Regulations 1977 1977/500

Safety Signs Regulations 1980 1980/1471

Woodworking Machines Regulations 1974 1974/903 1978/1126

Glossary of Terms

Approved Code of Practice a code of practice approved by the Health and Safety Commission providing practical guidance regarding compliance with statutory provisions. Failure to meet the ACoP is indicative of a contravention of the Associated Statute or Regulation.

Improvement Notice a notice which may be issued by an Inspector in accordance with Section 21 of the HSW Act if the Inspector is of the opinion that there has been a contravention of statutory provisions. The notice would indicate a time scale within which improvements in accordance with a specified schedule issued by the Inspector must be completed. Failure to comply is an offence. Recipients of notices may appeal within a specified period, during which the notice will be temporarily suspended.

Prohibition Notice a notice issued by an Inspector in accordance with Section 22 of the HSW Act if the Inspector is of the opinion that work activities involve risk of serious personal injury, including injury to health. The notice prohibits activities either immediately or over a deferred period and failure to comply is an offence. Recipients may appeal against the notice to an independent tribunal, and the notice remains valid pending the tribunal's decision.

Enforcing Authority the enforcement of health and safety legislation is essentially via the Health and Safety Executive but in certain premises local authorities are designated as the enforcement agents via the Health & Safety (Enforcing Authority) Regulations. Activities scheduled within these regulations are generally premises of a lower risk nature associated with commercial activities warehousing, distribution, catering and servicing.

Recognised Trade Union independent trade union, as defined in Section 30(1) of the Trade Union and Labour Relations Act 1974.

Absolute duty duties are absolute with no regard to cost and inconvenience even though it may render a machine commercially or mechanically inoperable. (*John Summers & Sons v Frost* (1955) AC 740.)

Practicable means something other than physically possible lower standard than 'absolute' but stricter than 'reasonably practicable' precautionary measures must be possible in the light of current knowledge and invention (*Adsett v K. & L. Steel Founders & Engineers* (1953) 1 WOR 733).

Reasonably practicable narrower term than 'physically possible' not as strict as 'practicable'. Implies computation of risk to be balanced against sacrifices (time, effort, financial, etc.). If it is shown that there is a gross disproportion between these, e.g. risk insignificant compared with the cost, the defendant's duty is discharged. It is the defendant's responsibility to prove that precautions are not reasonably practicable. (*Edwards v National Coal Board* (1949) ALL ER 743).

Safe System of Working the term is not defined in the HSW Act but the consensus of case law is that employers are required to assess the risk, taking into account all factors and work out a safe method of doing the job by adopting a safe sequence of operations integrating the use of safety equipment. Employers are required to monitor activities to ensure that systems are maintained. (*General Cleaning Contracts Limited v Christmas* (1952) 2 ALL ER 1110. and *Speed v Thomas Swift & Co* (1943) 1 ALL ER 539).

> **Contractors and safe systems of working:** Employers must assess systems of work of contractors working on his behalf, as well as those adopted by his own workforce where there is interface between his undertaking and contractor' operations. The principal requirements are the joint assessment of risk, exchange of information, planning the sequence of work and monitoring activities. (*Regina v Swan Hunter (Shipbuilders) Ltd and Telemeter Installations Ltd (1981) IRLR 403*).
>
> **Responsibilities of contractors** *J Armour v J Skeen (Procurator Fiscal, Glasgow)* (1977) IRLR 310
>
> **Statute:** Health and Safety at Work etc. Act 1974, S.37(1)
>
> **Duties of Senior Managers**
>
> **Facts:** A workman fell to his death while repairing a road bridge. Mr Armour was the Director of Roads for Strathclyde, whose duty was to supervise safety of council workmen on roads. He had not formulated a written safety policy for road work and was prosecuted under Section 37(1) which imposed a personal duty on executives for breach of statutory duty by a corporate body.
>
> **Decision:** Mr Armour's defence was that he was under no personal duty to carry out the council's statutory duties, one of which was the formulation of a safety policy for the Highways Department. This was rejected as Section 37(1) imposed the personal duty to carry out the council's statutory duty to prepare a written policy, he failed to do this and was guilty of an offence.
>
> Thus, the implication of Section 37 are that health and safety must be effectively managed from the top of an organisation via a policy outlining individual duties, an effective organisation and establishing written safety procedures and systems. Executives and senior managers have a personal duty to ensure that such arrangements are established, maintained and effectively monitored.Article for use at work plant designed for use or operation (whether exclusively or not) by persons at work including components of such plant.

Substance for use at work any natural or artificial substance whether in solid, liquid, gaseous or vapour form intended for use (whether exclusively or not) by persons at work.

Competent person a person with sufficient technical knowledge and experience to achieve the objectives set by the regulation or statute.

BIBLIOGRAPHY

HSE 'Essentials of Health and Safety at Work' HMSO

HSE 'Monitoring Safety' HMSO

HSE 'Effective Policies in Health and Safety' HMSO

HSE 'Managing Safety' HMSO

HSE 'Occupational Exposure Limits 1990', Guidance Note EH 40/90

HSE 'Monitoring Strategies for Toxic Substances' Guidance Note EH 42 HSE

Intellectual Property

Neil Maybury, Michael Servian and Michael Croft

Name: Copyright Designs and Patents Act 1988

Identity/SI No: Copyright Designs and Patents Act 1988

Date effective: 1.8.89

Interpretation:

Preliminary

The Copyright Designs and Patents Act 1988 ("the Act") received its Royal assent in November 1988 and the majority of the provisions came into force on 1st August 1989 ("commencement"). All of the Acts provisions are now in force. Whilst no new categories of copyright are created by the Act considerable changes have been made in an attempt to strike a commercially acceptable balance between the rights of users of material in which copyright subsists and the rights of the copyright holders. The Act attempts to take account of present and anticipated technological advances and contains a new right, design right, which provides protection for certain non-artistic articles. The Act replaces the old law of copyright as provided by the Copyright Act 1956 supplemented and amended by the Design Copyright Act 1968, the Copyright (Amendment) Act 1971, the Copyright (Amendment) Act 1983, parts of the Cable and Broadcasting Act 1984, and the Copyright (Computer Software) Amendment Act 1985. The 1956 Act will however remain important for some time to come in view of the transitional provisions which the Act contains dealing with circumstances where the old law will continue to apply.

The Right

Copyright

Copyright is the exclusive right given to the owner of a copyright work to copy the work, to issue copies of the work to the public, to perform, show or play the work in public, to broadcast the work or include it in a cable programme service and to make an adaptation of the work. Copyright will be infringed by any person who without the authority of the copyright owner does or authorises someone else to do any of these restricted acts.

Copyright will also be infringed by any person who without the consent of the copyright owner imports into the UK otherwise than for his private and domestic use an article which is and which he knows or has reason to believe is an infringing copy. Copyright is similarly infringed by a person who without the consent of the copyright owner possesses in the course of business, sells or lets for hire, exhibits or distributes an article which is and which he knows or has reason to believe is an infringing copy of the work. In essence copyright is the right of the owner of a copyright work to prevent others from copying that work and exploiting it for gain without the permission of the owner.

Types of Work Protected by Copyright

The Act essentially provides for nine categories of copyright work which are capable of protection. These are grouped as follows:

(i) original literary, dramatic, musical or artistic works;

(ii) sound recordings, films, broadcasts or cable programmes;

(iii) the typographical arrangements of published editions.

A literary work is defined in the Act as any work other than a dramatic or musical work which is written, spoken or sung and includes a table or compilation and a computer program. "Writing" includes any form of notation or code, whether by hand or otherwise and regardless of the method by which, or medium in or on which it is recorded. A speech therefore will be treated as a literary work and the lyrics of a song will similarly be protected.

A dramatic work includes a work of dance or mime but under the Act copyright will not subsist in a literary, dramatic or musical work unless and until it is recorded in writing or some permanent form.

In the case of an artistic work the Act states that this means "a graphic work, photograph, sculpture or collage irrespective of artistic quality". Provided the artistic work is original it need not therefore have any particular artistic quality to qualify for copyright protection. A graphic work in accordance with this definition includes any painting, drawing, diagram, map, chart or plan and any engraving, etching, lithograph, wood cut or similar work. The definition of artistic work also includes a work of architecture which will include a building or model for a building and works of artistic craftsmanship.

Sound recordings are now given a new definition by the Act. They are either a recording of sounds from which the sounds may be reproduced, or a recording of the whole or any part of a literary, dramatic or musical work from which sounds reproducing the work may themselves be produced. The definition of a film is a recording on any medium from which a moving image may be reproduced. This is extremely wide and will cover videos and all forms of electronic recording and storage.

Period of Copyright Protection

In the case of literary, dramatic, musical and artistic works the term of copyright protection is the lifetime of the author plus 50 years after the year of the author's death. However, in the case of unknown authors who remain unknown for the full period, copyright will expire 50 years from the end of the calendar year in which the work was first made available to the public. Copyright in a film or sound recording will expire 50 years from the end of the calendar year in which the film or sound recording is made or if it is released before the end of that period, then 50 years from the end of the calendar year in which the film or sound recording is released. Copyright in, for instance, a dramatic work may outlive copyright in a film of that work. Copyright in a broadcast or cable programme will expire 50 years from the end of the year when the broadcast was first made or the programme was included in a cable programme service. Copyright in a computer generated work expires at the end of 50 years from the end of the calendar year in which the work was made.

Ownership of Copyright

The general rule is that the copyright owner is the person who creates the work. That is in most cases the author, but for sound recordings, films and computer generated works it is the person by whom the arrangements are undertaken for making the sound recording or film or computer generated work. For broadcasts the first owner of the copyright will be the person making the broadcast.

There are further exceptions to the general rule, for example in the case of a literary, dramatic, musical or artistic work made by an employee in the course of his employment, the first owner of the copyright, subject to any contractual arrangements to the contrary, will be the employer.

The Act also provides that a photographer will own the copyright in his or her work but in order to protect individuals, a new right of privacy has been introduced for the first time into English Law. A person who for private and domestic purposes commissions the taking of a photograph or the making of a film, has the right not to have copies of the work issued to the public, the work exhibited or shown in public or the work broadcast or included in a cable programme service. Anyone who does or authorises any of these acts will infringe this right. Generally in the case of copyright works the author of a commissioned work owns the copyright, and the old provisions under the Copyright Act 1956 concerning the commissioning of photographs and portraits are not retained.

An agreement can, however, be made whereby a commissioner will become the first owner of copyright in a work of his or her agent, even if that work has not yet been created.

In the case of computer programs, the first owner of the copyright will normally be the author but in the case of computer generated works the Act provides that the author shall be the person by whom the arrangements necessary for the creation of the work are undertaken.

Protection of Copyright

Copyright arises automatically upon the creation of a relevant work. There is no provision for formal registration with any administrative body of copyright or design right in the UK nor are there any depositing requirements, unlike in many other countries. Hence there is no registration fee payable in the case of copyright, although there is in the case of a registered design. There is also no registration or deposit procedure to protect moral rights, performance rights or rental rights.

It is the work itself which is protected, not the idea or principle involved. There is no literary merit, artistic merit or other aesthetic merit test for copyright protection. In the case of drawings, there can be copyright in the drawings of such simple things as nuts and bolts. The test is whether or not sufficient skill, labour and judgment has gone into the creation of an original copyright work. The literary, dramatic, musical or artistic work does not have to be new, but of course it does have to be original and does not qualify as a copyright work if it was copied from a previous known work.

As noted, there is no need to apply for registration of copyright for it to come into effect, nor is it necessary to put any special markings on the work, although it is advisable to indicate that the work is a copyright work owned by the author as a warning to would-be infringers, and also to aid in a claim for damages later (and see below on "qualification for copyright protection and international protection").

Qualification for Copyright Protection and International Protection

A business will often be concerned not only to protect copyright within the UK but to protect it worldwide. Britain is a member of the two central International Conventions, namely the Berne Convention and the Universal Copyright Convention. These Conventions ensure that there is "national treatment" of copyright works within the countries who are signatories to the Conventions. In other words, a foreign copyright work is protected under the domestic legal system with the full force as if that work were a domestic copyright work. The Conventions also guarantee certain minimal levels of protection for works within Convention countries.

It should be noted that in order to secure protection in some countries which are not Berne Convention countries and which have registration requirements, to avoid registration in such countries it is necessary to mark all published copies of a literary work or of drawings and all products or their packaging with the © symbol, together with the name of the copyright owner and the year of first publication or the year of first sale.

UK Copyright Law, then, will apply to a work which qualifies as a copyright work under the laws of another Convention country. The following is an explanation of other circumstances in which the UK law will apply.

A work originating in another country can qualify for UK copyright protection with reference either to the author, to the country in which the work was first published, or, in the case of a broadcast or cable programme, to the country from which the broadcast was made or the cable programme was sent. Most, but by no means all countries are members of one of the International Conventions. The provisions in the UK Act which extend UK copyright protection to what might loosely be called overseas works are therefore important not only in terms of these works gaining UK copyright protection, but also in terms of these works consequently gaining protection in other countries which are members of the Universal Copyright Convention or the Berne Convention.

In what follows, the term "relevant country" will be used to denote one of two things. First, a relevant country is one where there is power in the Act to extend the operation of the Act to that country. By an Order in Council, the Act (subject to modification by the legislature of the host country) may be made to apply to any of the Channel Islands, the Isle of Man or any colony. The Act extends automatically to England and Wales, Scotland and Northern Ireland. Where the Act extends to another country, the Act is effectively part of the internal law of that country. Consequently, where work qualifies for copyright protection under the law of that country, it will also enjoy UK copyright protection. Second, a relevant country is one to which, by Order in Council, the UK Act applies. In this case, the UK Act does not form part of the domestic legal system of the relevant country. However, as with countries to which the Act extends, works first published in countries to which the Act applies also qualify for copyright protection in the UK.

The UK Act, then, applies to a work with reference to author or country. Looking at each of these in turn:

(a) a work qualifies for copyright protection in the UK if the author was at the "material time" (see below) a qualifying person. The author must be either a British National (which is defined quite widely) or must be domiciled or resident in the UK or another relevant country or must be a body incorporated under the law of part of the UK or another relevant country. In the case of a work of joint authorship, the work will qualify for UK copyright protection if at the material time any of the authors satisfies the nationality, domicile or residence requirements. However, where only one of several authors satisfy the author's qualification, then only that author shall be taken into account for the purposes of important aspects of the Act. Most importantly, the duration of the copyright will only be based upon the life of that author.

The meaning of "material time" for these purposes is different for a published and an unpublished work in relation to literary, dramatic, musical and artistic works. If the work is not published, then the material time is the time at which the work was made. If the work is published, then the material time is when the work is first published. In the case of sound recordings, films and broadcasts the material time is when the work is made. In the case of cable programmes, the material time is when the programme is included in a cable programme service. The material time for a typographical arrangement of a published edition is when the edition is first published.

(b) Where a work does not qualify for UK copyright protection with reference to its author, it may still qualify for UK copyright protection with reference to the country in which it is first published. Other than broadcasts and cable programmes, a copyright work enjoys UK copyright protection if it is first published in the UK or in another relevant country. The work will still enjoy UK protection if it is published in the UK or in another relevant country (or, of course, in a Berne or UCC Convention country) within 30 days of its being published elsewhere in the world. For these purposes, publication means the issue of copies to the public.

In the case of broadcasts and cable programmes there is qualification by reference to place of transmission. The broadcast must be made from, or the cable programme sent from a place in the UK or another relevant country. A satellite broadcast is made where the original transmission is uplinked to the satellite. If there is a broadcast from a country which is neither the UK, a relevant country nor a Convention country, and if this broadcast is picked up in the UK and then relayed by means of a cable service, then there will, nevertheless, be no copyright protection for the programme.

Permitted Acts

Fair dealing with a literary, dramatic, musical or artistic work for the purposes of research or private study does not infringe any copyright in the work. Fair dealing with a work for the purpose of criticism or review will not infringe the copyright in the work provided that it is accompanied by a sufficient acknowledgement. Fair dealing for the purpose of reporting current events, other than by means of a photograph, will not infringe any copyright provided again that a sufficient acknowledgement accompanies any publication. So for example, in a recent leading case, it was fair dealing for BSB to broadcast in its sports reporting programmes accredited short excerpts of the "best bits" of the BBC's World Cup coverage. Copyright in a literary, dramatic, musical or artistic work will not be infringed by copying in the course of instruction or preparation for instruction in the world of education. There are sections in the Act which permit general copying by certain librarians and archivists for the purposes of supplying copies to people for research or private study or for preserving or replacing a particular item in a permanent collection.

Moral Rights

Moral rights are prescribed by the Berne Convention. For some time in Europe creative works have been regarded as the expression of the personality of the author. The Act now introduces these rights into the UK and gives (a) the right to the author or director of the work to be identified, otherwise known as the right of paternity; (b) the right for the author or director not to have his or her work subjected to derogatory treatment, called the right of integrity; and (c) the right not to have work falsely attributed to one as author or director.

The right of paternity will apply whenever a work is published commercially, performed, exhibited or shown in public, broadcast or issued to the public. The main proviso is that the right has to be asserted which can be done simply by means of a written statement signed by the author or director. The right of paternity will not however apply in relation to computer programs, computer generated works, works of employees, design of typefaces and works made for the purpose of reporting current events. As in the case of copyright the right will not be infringed where there is fair dealing for the purposes of criticism or review.

The right to object to derogatory treatment means that the author can object to additions, deletions, alterations or adaptations of the work except in the case of translations. Treatment of a work would be derogatory if it amounts to distortion or mutilation, or is in any other way prejudicial to the honour or reputation of the author or director.

A person also has the right not to have a work falsely attributed to him as author or director. There should be no statement, whether express or implied, which falsely indicates that any particular individual is author or director. A person infringes another's moral right not to have the work falsely attributed to him if that person issues copies of the work to the public, exhibits a work, performs, broadcasts or shows a work which he knows or has reason to believe includes a false attribution as to the author or director. The right is also infringed by a person who knowingly in the course of a business possesses or deals with such works containing a false attribution.

The usual civil remedies of injunctions, delivery up and damages will be available to the owners of moral rights. In the case of the right to object to derogatory treatment of a work, the Court may grant an injunction to prohibit the doing of any act unless a disclaimer is made which indicates that the new version of the work is not that of the particular author or director. In the case of the right of paternity, in an action for infringement of the right, the Court can take into account any delay in asserting the right by the author or director. The period of moral right will last for the same amount of time as the period of copyright in the underlying work so that the two rights will for the most part exist in parallel. There is one exception, however, in that the right not to have a work falsely attributed will last for 20 years after the death of the author and not the full 50 year period.

The Rental Right

The rental right, which is limited to sound recordings, films and computer programs, arises from the restricted act under copyright of issuing copies of protected works to the public. "Rental" includes arrangements whereby a copy is made available for payment on terms that it will be returned. The rental right subsists for the length of the copyright term and is protected by the same remedies as protect copyright. The Act provides that the Secretary of State may make an order specifying that the rental of certain sound recordings, films or computer programs shall be treated as licensed by the copyright owner subject to payment of such reasonable royalties as may be agreed or settled by the Copyright Tribunal.

The Performing Right

It is an infringement of the copyright in a literary, dramatic or musical work for that work to be performed in public without authorization. In this context, performance includes delivery of lectures and, generally, includes any form of visual or acoustic presentation. Similarly, it infringes copyright where there is unauthorised public playing or showing of sound recordings, films, broadcasts or cable programmes. The Act however, goes further than this and introduces a right for the performers themselves in their performances. This right is particularly important where the performance is recorded without the performer's permission. Where such a recording occurs, it is quite possible that there will be an infringement of the copyright in a previous recording as well as an infringement of the performer's right in his or her performance. In this context, "recording" means a film or sound recording whether made directly from a live performance, or made from a broadcast of, or cable programme including, the performance. The performer's right is also infringed where a recording is made directly or indirectly from another recording of the performance.

The performer's rights are also infringed where, without the performer's consent, a person knowingly shows or plays in public at least a substantial part of the qualifying performance or broadcasts it or includes it in a cable programme service. It is a defence to an action by the performer to show that the performer's consent was obtained either when the recording was first made, or when the infringing act was done.

The performer's rights are also infringed by a person, without the performer's permission, importing into the United Kingdom (other than for domestic use) or selling, hiring offering or exposing for sale or hire, or distributing in the course of a business a recording of a qualifying performance. The alleged infringer has a defence if he can show that he did not know or have a reason to believe that the recording was illicit. If the recording was "innocently acquired" either by the infringer or by somebody from whom he brought the recording, then the only remedy available to the performer is damages not exceeding a reasonable payment in respect of the act complained of. Notwithstanding this provision, it is still possible that the performer may apply for a Court Order that the infringer hands over or destroys the illicit recording.

Where a recording company has an exclusive recording contract with a performer to make recordings of the performer's performances with a view to their commercial exploitation, the recording company itself enjoys protection of its "recording right". The recording company's rights are infringed if, first, a person records a relevant performance without the consent of the performer. If such consent is given by the performer, this will probably be in breach of his contract with the recording company and the recording company will probably be able to proceed against the performer for this breach of contract. Second, the recording company's rights are infringed if a person, without the consent of the performer or the recording company, shows or plays in public at least a substantial part of the performance or broadcasts it or includes it in a cable programme service where that person knows or has reason to believe that the recording itself was illicit. Third, the recording company has rights against a person who, without the consent of the recording company or the performer, imports into the United Kingdom (other than for domestic use) or in the course of a business possesses, sells or lets for hire, offers or exposes for sale or hire, or distributes a recording of the performance which that person knows or has reason to believe to be an illicit recording. The performer's right and the recording company's right in the performance covers not only performances of literary, dramatic and musical works, but also dance, mime and "variety" acts. The rights expire at the end of 50 years from the end of the calendar year of the performance.

Remedies for infringement of the performer's right or the right of the recording company include damages, an injunction, an order that illicit recordings be handed over and a right to seize illicit recordings found exposed or otherwise immediately available for sale or hire other than at a person's regular place of business. Such seizure requires liaison with the local police. The rights are also protected by certain criminal offenses.

The Copyright Tribunal

It has long been normal practice in the music industry for copyright holders to assign their rights in sound recordings, and in music and lyrics, to collecting societies which then license individual applicants to play the recordings. A Performing Rights Tribunal, was established under the 1956 Act to ensure that these collecting societies did not abuse their strong bargaining position. The Performing Rights Tribunal could settle disputes between the collecting societies and licensees whether concerned with individual licences (or their refusal) or the collecting societies' general terms and conditions for licences. As a consequence of the emergence of other collecting societies, the Copyright Tribunal was established under the 1988 Act to replace the Performing Rights Tribunal. The Copyright Tribunal has wider powers in that it is given jurisdiction and authority over licensing schemes, and licences given by licensing bodies generally.

A licensing scheme is a scheme which sets out the classes of cases in which the collecting societies are prepared to grant licences, and the terms upon which licences would be granted in those classes of case. A licensing body is a society or other organisation which is primarily established for the negotiation or granting of copyright licences in respect of the works of more than one author.

The Copyright Tribunal has jurisdiction over licensing schemes involving most forms of copyright work and their exploitation. As noted, this is a departure from the Performing Rights Tribunal which was concerned only with performing rights. In particular, it is worth noting that the Copyright Tribunal is given specific jurisdiction over the rental of sound recordings, films and computer programs to the public. In the case of sound recordings, broadcasts, cable programmes, published editions and the rental of sound recordings, films and computer programs, the Copyright Tribunal also has jurisdiction over schemes where the scheme is operated by an individual author.

The Copyright Tribunal has a wide discretion to confirm or to vary any particular schemes as is reasonable in the circumstances. The Copyright Tribunal may also take applications from, for example, a person who claims to be unreasonably refused a licence falling under a scheme.

The Copyright Tribunal is also given jurisdiction to settle terms of copyright licences which are available as of right if these cannot be agreed or negotiated between the parties. However, the Copyright Tribunal will have no jurisdiction to hear and to determine disputes relating to the issue of copyright infringement.

The Position in Relation to Industrial Designs

A.   Copyright

Under the Copyright Act 1956, as amended by the Design Copyright Act 1968, designs applied industrially were protected by copyright which usually arose from the copyright in the drawing of an article. Copyright in industrial designs subsisted for the life of the author plus 50 years, unless the design was registrable under the Registered Design Act 1949, in which case there was only 15 years protection. Thus, designs applied industrially with, basically, eye appeal enjoyed a far shorter period of protection than purely industrial designs.

This anomaly was removed by the 1988 Act by its effectively removing copyright protection (subject to a limited exception) for designs of non-artistic, that is industrial , articles:

(i) The Act amends the Registered Designs Act 1949 to allow for a maximum of 25 years protection for registered industrial designs which have "eye appeal" (see below on registrability under the Registered Designs Act 1949.

(ii) There is still copyright in a drawing of a design of an artistic article (and in works of artistic craftsmanship) and it will be an infringement of that copyright to copy the work by reproducing it in any material form. Copying will include the making of a copy in three dimensions of a two-dimensional work and the making of a copy in two dimensions of a three-dimensional work. The copyright subsists for the author's life plus 50 years.

(iii) If an artistic work has been exploited, by or with the licence of the copyright owner, by making artistic articles by an industrial process and marketing them in the United Kingdom or elsewhere, then the period of copyright in so far as it is effective to prevent copying of the design of the article is reduced to 25 years from the end of the calendar year in which the article was first marketed. In respect of copyright drawings of such articles made before the commencement of the Act the old period of 15 years' protection continues to apply.

(iv) The Act provides that the making of an article which is a copy of a copyright work (that is, normally, a drawing) will not be an infringement of the copyright if the design of the article depicted in the copyright work is not artistic. In other words, for industrial designs, there is no copyright protection for the making of articles to the design of a drawing. It is, however, an infringement of the copyright in the drawing for another drawing to be copied from that drawing. This form of copyright protection subsists for the normal period of 50 years after the author's death. However, and subject to the provisos discussed below, it would infringe the new design right (introduced by the 1988 Act) for an article to be made to the design of a non-artistic (that is, industrial) article, for a drawing to be made of the industrial article or for an industrial article to be made to the design of the drawing. Design right subsists for a maximum period of 15 years from the end of the calendar year in which the design is recorded or in which an article was first made to the design. The period of protection is discussed further below.

B. The Design Right

The unregistered Design Right is a property right which subsists in an original design. A design is defined in the Act as any aspect of the shape or configuration (whether internal or external) of the whole or part of an article subject to the following exclusions

(a) a method or principle of construction

(b) features of shape or configuration of an article which:

(i) enable the article to be connected to, or placed in, around or against, another article so that either article may perform its function (the so-called "must fit" exclusion); or

(ii) are dependent upon the appearance of another article of which the article is intended by the designer to form an integral part (the so called "must match" exclusion)

(c) surface decoration.

In order to enjoy design right protection a design must be original. This means that the design must have originated from the author and it must not have been copied from a previous known work. A design will not be original if it is commonplace in the design field in question at the time of its creation. Design right does not subsist unless and until the design has been recorded in a design document or an article has been made to the design.

Design right expires 15 years from the end of the calendar year in which the design was first recorded in a design document or an article was first made to the design, whichever first occurred; or if articles made to the design are made available for sale or hire within 5 years from the end of the calendar year in which the design was first so recorded then design right will expire 10 years form the end of the calendar year in which this first occurred. Thus, if commercial exploitation commences after 5 years but before the end of the 15 years, the period of protection will expire at the end of the 15 years. If commercial exploitation starts within 5 years, the period of protection will expire before the end of the 15 years, specifically 10 years after the start of the commercial exploitation.

Design right is owned by the designer except when either the design is created in pursuance of a commission, in which case the commissioner owns it (the opposite is the case in the context of copyright), or where the design is created by an employee in the course of his employment, in which case the employer owns it.

It is an infringement of design right to reproduce the design for commercial purposes by making articles to that design or by making a design document recording the design for the purpose of enabling such articles to be made. Copying the design substantially is just as much an infringement as copying the design exactly. Copying may be direct or indirect. It will also be an infringement to import into the UK for commercial purposes, or to possess for commercial purposes or to sell in the course of a business an infringing article, but only if the alleged infringer knows or has reason to believe that it is an infringing article.

Any person is entitled as of right to a licence in the last 5 years of the design right term to do anything which would otherwise infringe the design right. If anyone requiring such a licence is unable to reach agreement as to the terms, the matter may be referred to the Comptroller of the Patent Office who will settle the terms. Note that the unregistered Design Right only comes into existence in respect of those designs coming into existence after commencement.

C. Registered Design

A design which is capable of registration must be new and must contain features of configuration or pattern which in the finished article appeal to or are judged by the eye. In addition, the appearance of the article must normally be a material consideration for the acquirers or users of the article, and features dictated by function or dependent upon the appearance of another article of which the article concerned is intended to form an integral part are excluded from registrability.

A registered design has an initial period of protection of 5 years, but this is now renewable on a 5 yearly basis to the maximum of 25 years. Prior to the amendment of the Registered Design Act 1949 by the 1988 Act, the period was a maximum of 15 years.

The author and original proprietor of a registered design is its creator, or the arranger of a computer generated design. An employer of an employee who creates the design is regarded as being the original proprietor of the design, so too is a commissioner who gives money or money's worth for the commissioning of a registered design by another.

Once a design is registered under the Act, the registered proprietor has the exclusive right to make or import for sale or hire, or for use for the purposes of a trade or business, or to sell, hire, or offer or expose for sale or hire an article in respect of which the design is registered and to which that design or a design not substantially different from it has been applied. It is also infringement for an unauthorised person to make something for enabling such an article to be made. Kits for making up an assembled article are also protected.

The registered design right can be lost if the registered design owner fails to work the registered design in the UK.

Remedies include an injunction, damages, or an account of profits. There are also certain criminal offenses.

The registered design right may be assigned, mortgaged or licensed if such arrangements are recorded with the Registrar of Designs.

For further detail, see the section on the Registered Design Act 1949 below.

Practical Considerations in Protecting Designs

All original sketches, designs, drawings and plans should be preserved and kept in a safe place. In the case of important designs, the original drawings should, if necessary, be kept in a Bank and an appropriate dated and signed receipt obtained. The draughtsman should sign and date all the drawings and sketches. All design changes on drawings should be recorded, and employers should ensure that their employees have a contract of service which indicates that the making of drawings comes within the particular employee's normal duties. Drawings should be produced before producing any models or prototypes, and where outside agencies have been responsible for the designs then an assignment of the copyright should be taken from that outside agency since the first owner of a commissioned copyright work will be the designer in the absence of contrary agreement.

Implications for Industry

A major feature of the Act is the concern with design. The Government is committed to encouraging industry to place more emphasis on the design element to British manufactured products. It believes that this will increase the competitiveness of British manufacturing industry in the context of Europe and beyond. However, running contrary to this commitment is a concern that free competition within the UK is not hampered by the creation of long-term monopolies in designs. Moreover, the Government has had to take account of its international commitments in the area of intellectual property.

Consequently, the Government has sought to create a system which offers an incentive for design by offering only a limited monopoly for industrial designs. The monopoly is limited in a variety of senses:

i)   as to duration;

ii) so that it is only available for new/original designs;

iii) so that it does not apply to methods or principles of construction; and

iv) so as not to discourage others from creating alternative designs which do the same job (either with reference to form or function the so-called must-match and must-fit exemptions to design right and registered design right).

With respect to functional articles, the design itself will be protected by design right for usually 10 years from exploitation, with licences of right in the last 5 years. However, industry is encouraged to give even its functional articles eye appeal by the longer protection of 25 years available for registered designs. Moreover, if industry places a surface decoration on the article, the decoration is protected by copyright for the life of its author plus 50 years.

In brief, the message to industry is to take design seriously and the Act offers commercial benefits for so doing.

Provisions of the Act Affecting Computer Software

Copyright subsists in original literary works which specifically include computer programs. However, there is no definition of a "computer program" included in the Act. A computer program like any other copyright work must be recorded in writing or otherwise such as electronically. The program is thus protected whether written in source code or machine-readable object code. The Act indicates that it is an infringement of copyright in a computer program to reproduce the program in any material form, including storage by electronic means, the making of copies which are transient or incidental, or adaptations. This protects computer programs or data from being stored in a computer or on an independent storage media. The problem, as yet unresolved, is whether or not the courts will insist on infringement of copyright in a computer program involving identical reproduction, or whether they will adopt a broader approach as in the United States where the 'look and feel' concept is used to determine infringement. There are indications that the UK Courts are favouring this latter approach.

In addition to computer programs, the Act protects data bases from copying. Where a computer itself is programmed to generate computer programs the Act specifically recognises that the person responsible for making the arrangements for the creating of the computer program is regarded as the author of the new copyright work.

Whilst the Act allows the copyright owner of a computer program to prevent its rental, there are provisions in the Act which allow the Secretary of State to order that the rental to the public of specified computer programs should be treated as licensed by the copyright owner subject to the payment of a reasonable fee. In certain circumstances applications can also be made to the Secretary of State for certification of licensing schemes for computer programs. This can be particularly important in the case of certain computer programs bearing in mind that as literary works computer programs qualify for the full copyright period of the lifetime of the author and 50 years thereafter.

It infringes the copyright in a computer program to broadcast it. For this purpose broadcasting means transmission by wireless telegraphy of the information whether it is in encrypted form or not. Converting a computer program from, for example, source code into object code, or from one type of program language into another is also an act of infringement.

The Act also introduces the right of the copyright owner to prevent any person who makes or sells or advertises for sale or hire a device or means specifically designed or adapted to circumvent any copy protection incorporated in a computer program.

Authors of computer programs apparently do not qualify for the moral rights under the Act, although a program may not apparently be falsely attributed to another author.

Provisions of the Act Affecting Broadcasts, Satellites and Cable

As already noted, copyright subsists in broadcasts and in cable programmes. A broadcast is a transmission by wireless telegraphy (loosely, sent over the air waves and received by an aerial or dish) of pictures, sounds or other information. Other "information" includes computer programs and these are caught even if encrypted and the decoding devices are lawfully available to the public. The broadcast still receives copyright protection if it is ultimately received by means of its being relayed via a telecommunication system, eg a cable system. The broadcast must be intended to be or capable of being lawfully received by the public. The public can mean a section of the public (eg receivers of a specialised service for a particular profession). The maker of the broadcast is the person arranging transmission of or himself transmitting the programme for which he or she has at least part responsibility for its contents.

Broadcasts by means of satellite transmissions are protected by copyright. Such a broadcast is "made" where signals carrying the broadcast are transmitted to the satellite.

The first broadcast determines the copyright term of the 50 years from the end of the calendar year in which the broadcast was made. While repeat broadcasts do not extend the term, they do enjoy copyright protection.

A cable programme is any item included in a cable programme service. A cable programme service means a service involved in sending pictures, sounds or other information by means of a telecommunication system other than wireless telegraphy. The service has to be intended to be received at more than one place or for presentation to members of the public. This means that there will be copyright protection as a cable programme for coverage of, say, a boxing match which is relayed live via a cable to a leisure centre screen. There are certain exceptions to the definition of a cable programme service. Most importantly, there is no copyright protection for a service run for the purposes of business where the apparatus comprised in the system is under the control of the business and the information relayed is solely for purposes internal to the running of the business. Nor is there any copyright protection for a part of a cable programme service which is interactive. In other words, when the programme provider receives messages back from the programme receivers, this part of the cable programme service cannot enjoy copyright protection. Examples are interactive "TV shopping"), and interactive banking services.

As mentioned above, where a broadcast is received at a central point and then relayed by means of a cable service, the broadcast enjoys copyright protection. There is, however, no separate copyright protection for the cable programme as such.

Copyright in a cable programme expires at the end of 50 years from the end of the calendar year in which the programme was included in a cable programme service. As with broadcasts, a repeat cable programme is protected by copyright but only for so long as the copyright in the original cable programme subsists.

In the case of both broadcasts and cable programmes, an infringing broadcast or cable programme does not enjoy fresh copyright. Nor does copyright subsist in a broadcast which infringes the copyright in a cable programme or vice versa.

Remedies Available for Copyright Infringement

The Act makes provision for the owner of a copyright in an action for infringement to have all the remedies and relief which are available in respect of the infringement of any other property right. This means that the remedies available to a copyright owner include the usual claims for damages, account of profits, and injunctions.

The claim of a copyright owner to damages is preserved and the innocent defendant has a good defence to such a claim. Whilst a claim for damages in conversion is abolished save in respect of any proceedings begun before commencement of the Act, the Court may award additional damages where it considers that the infringement has been flagrant, and the defendant has obtained a particular benefit by reason of the infringement. The Courts also have the power to require the infringer to destroy infringing copies or to hand them over to the copyright owner.

The injunctions which are available include orders obtained by the copyright owner on his own without notice to the defendant, to search the defendant's premises and seize any infringing copies (an Anton Piller order), an injunction to restrain the defendant from dissipating his assets whether here or abroad (a Mareva order) and an order requiring the defendant where he is a secondary infringer, for example by importation, to disclose the name and address of his supplier (a Norwich Pharmacal order).

The Act introduces a new right to seize infringing copies which are found exposed for sale or hire but the right is subject to some important limitations. Firstly, before anything is seized notice of the time and place of the proposed seizure must be given to the local police station. No force may be used during the seizure, and no seizure may take place at the permanent or regular place of business of the defendant. Following seizure a notice must be left at the place of seizure indicating by whom the seizure has been made and the grounds on which it has been made.

An exclusive licensee has the same remedies as the licensor against all but the copyright owner himself. However, a non-exclusive licensee must rely upon the licensor taking action and the licence agreement with the licensor should cover this point.

Criminal offenses appear in the Act, however civil remedies such as damages or an injunction will more normally be sought by a copyright owner. The Act also provides a means whereby the assistance of the Commissioners of Customs and Excise might be sought in preventing the importation of infringing copies.

Assignment and Licensing

It is possible to assign copyright, but this must be signed in writing. It is possible to have a partial assignment, that is to say of part of the copyright owner's rights or for part of the copyright period.

A licence granted under the copyright is binding on any successors in title of the copyright, except against a person who in good faith purchases for value without notice of the copyright owner's rights. An exclusive licence is now specifically defined as meaning excluding all parties including the licensor.

Some Transitional Provisions

It is worth noting some important transitional provisions, that is the changeover from the old Copyright Act 1956 to the 1988 Act. These provisions are complex, but some of the main points to remember are as follows:

(i)   A work is 'made' when it is completed, and therefore some works will be made after the 1st August 1989 and the commencement of the Act even though they were begun before.

(ii) The provisions of the Act apply in relation to things existing at the commencement of the Act as they apply in relation to things coming into existence after the Act, subject to some notable exceptions referred to above and below.

(iii) Authorship of an existing work generally depends on the law in force when the work was made.

(iv) In the case of some literary, dramatic, musical works, engravings, and anonymous works in existence prior to 1st August 1989, the period of copyright continues after commencement of the Act until the date of expiry of the copyright period as determined under the Copyright Act 1956. In the case of some other works, for example artistic works, the period of copyright continues until the date on which it expires under the provisions of the Act.

(v)   Acts of infringement prior to commencement of the Act are governed by the Copyright Act 1956, and acts of infringement after commencement are dealt with under the Act. Remedies for infringement under the Act only apply in respect of infringements committed after commencement of the Act. The right to claim conversion damages does not apply after commencement of the Act except in the case of proceedings claiming damages for conversion begun before the date of commencement of the Act.

(vi) The Act excludes copyright protection in relation to works recorded or embodied within a design document which is a copyright work where the work is an article which is non-artistic. However this provision does not apply for ten years after commencement of the Act in respect of works recorded in a design document before commencement.

(vii) Under the Copyright Act 1956 non-functional designs which were applied industrially were protected for a period of fifteen years from the date of first marketing. The period of protection for such designs remain the same.

Major Impact

All areas of Manufacturing, Service and Design Industry, in particular the Entertainment Industry and Consumer Goods Manufacturing.

Name: Berne Copyright Convention (Paris revision 1971)/Universal Copyright Convention (Paris revision 1971)

Identity/SI number: Berne Copyright Convention/Universal Copyright Convention

Date effective: 1971

Interpretation:

The Berne Convention guarantees certain minimum rights throughout the Member States, known as the "Berne Union". The first Berne Convention dates back to 1886 and the most recent revision is that of 1971. There are presently 80 countries in the Berne Union. The United Kingdom is a member and on March 1st

1989 the United States acceded to the Berne Convention. Prior to this the United States was, significantly, a member of the Universal Copyright Convention. With the accession of the United States to the Berne Union, the Berne Convention has now become of primary importance on the international stage of copyright protection. The United Kingdom is also a member of the Universal Copyright Convention, it should be noted that this Convention contains many but not all of the same countries as the Berne Convention. However, the Berne Convention generally has precedence over the Universal Copyright Convention.

Name: (EEC) Council Directive on the legal protection of computer programs

Identity: 91/250/EEC

Date effective: 4.5.91

Interpretation:

Preliminary

UK domestic law will have to be brought in line with the requirements of the Directive by 1st January 1993. The Directive will create a uniform minimum level of protection throughout the EEC, however member states may offer additional protection if they wish. As will be seen below the main alteration to existing UK law will be the inclusion of the "decompilation" right whereby the code of a computer program may be reproduced and translated with a view to designing a method of interfacing the program with another program for interoperability.

Copyright Works

As is already the case in the UK, original computer programs will be protected throughout the EEC as literary copyright works. Originality in this context means little more than "not copied". The term "computer programs" includes programs written in object code, application programs and their preparatory design material.

As with other copyright works, the expression of the program rather than the idea or principle behind it is protected. Ideas and principles involved in the logic, algorithms and programming languages of a computer program are not protected under the Directive. An opportunity for harmonisation has been lost in that the Directive gives no guidance as to how literal any copying must be to infringe.

Ownership

The creator of a program is its author and will be its owner, unless the program was created in the course of his employment in which case the employer will be the first owner.

Infringement

Infringement includes even temporary unauthorised reproduction of a computer program and will thus include loading, displaying, running, transmitting or storing the program. Unauthorised translation of a program, for example in and out of particular languages and codes, will also infringe.

Only the copyright owner (or someone he authorises) may distribute the computer program or copies of it to the public. This includes rental. Whenever the copyright owner sells or authorises the sale of a computer program, his rights in that program are "exhausted" and others may deal with it as they wish (save that the copyright owner may reserve the right to prevent further rental of the program).

Position of Licensees and the "Decompilation" Right

Under the Directive, a person who acquires a program will automatically also gain the right to use it for its intended purpose including "error correction" and the production of a back-up copy. The copyright owner can contract that the acquirer may not correct errors, but he cannot avoid the acquirer's right to produce a necessary back-up copy.

An authorised user, then, has the right to use the program for its intended purposes whether this involves loading, displaying, running, transmitting or storing the program. In exercising these rights, the user may "observe, study or test" the program to ascertain the underlying ideas or principles behind the program. This provision is unremarkable in that it merely restates conventional copyright rights. As under existing UK Law, a copyright work may be investigated to determine its underlying ideas and (subject to any obligations of confidence) these ideas, but not the expression of them, may be copied. The preamble to the Directive is clear that the right to test does not confer the right to infringe copyright in the program, for example by making alterations to the program.

Probably the most significant provision in the Directive is the right conferred upon an authorised user to reproduce the code of the program and to translate it in order to investigate means of interfacing the program with another program to create interoperability. The investigation must only be for the purposes of obtaining the necessary information for interoperability. No right is conferred whereby the authorised user may alter the program, but it must be implied that he can tag on the necessary instructions to create interoperability with the other program (if necessary, through the medium of a third program). The Directive states that the investigation must be confined to parts of the original program which are necessary to achieve interoperability. However, again the right is meaningless unless it also implied that the investigation may be of the whole code in the first instance so that the relevant part of the code may be identified and be investigated in further detail. The reproduction and translation may only be carried out by or on behalf of a legitimate user of the program, and where the information necessary to achieve interoperability has not previously been readily available to that user or to the person whom he authorises to carry out the investigation on his behalf. Once obtained, the information may only be used to seek to achieve interoperability of the program with another, and the information may only be given to others if this is essential for interoperability of the programs. The information must not be used to make or to market an infringing program or otherwise to infringe copyright in the program. Moreover, this "decompilation" right is subject to not unreasonably prejudicing the copyright owner's legitimate interests or conflicting with his normal exploitation of the program. What this means remains to be seen. This "decompilation" right will have specifically to be written into English law by legislation. It will not be possible to contract out of these provisions.

Remedies

UK law need not change as a result of the Directive's requirement that member states provide remedies against a person knowingly possessing for commercial purposes or putting into circulation, infringing copies of computer programs. UK law includes a provision whereby a copyright owner has rights against a person who puts into circulation a device designed to circumvent copy protection of a computer program. The Directive may require a slight alteration to UK law in that it also requires that there be remedies for the copyright owner as against a person who merely possess for commercial purposes such a device. UK law already provides, as required under the Directive, for the seizure of infringing copies of computer programs and devices designed to circumvent copy protection.

Direction

The Directive requires protection for the copyright in the program to be for the life of the author and for 50 years after the end of the calendar year of his death. This is in accordance with present UK law.

Transitional Provision

The Directive's effect is retrospective, but is without prejudice to any rights which may have accrued up until 1st January 1993.

Other Forms of Protection of Computer Programs

The terms of the Directive are without prejudice to other forms of protection of computer programs (for example, contractual obligations or obligations of confidentiality). The Directive's provisions are, of course, subject to the application of EEC competition laws and, in particular, it should be noted that if a dominant supplier refuses to make information available which is necessary for interoperability, this may infringe article 86 of the Treaty of Rome.

Name: The Design Right (Semiconductor Topographies) Regulations 1989

Identity/SI No: SI 1989/1100

Date effective: 1.8.89

Interpretation:

Preliminary

These Regulations give exclusive rights in the topographies of semiconductor products. A semiconductor product is an article which performs an electronic function and which consists of layers, where at least one of these layers is composed of semi conducting material. On at least one of the layers there must be a pattern appertaining to an electronic function. The semiconductor topography refers to the design placed on that layer. The design or pattern need not actually be fixed so long as it is intended to be fixed upon the semiconductor product.

Ownership of Design Right in Semiconductor Topography

The first owner will be the designer, the person who commissioned the design, or the employer of a person who made the topographic design in the course of his employment. There can be agreement in writing to prevent the commissioner or employer becoming the first owner.

Duration of Right

The design right in a semiconductor topography expires 10 years from the end of the calendar year in which the topography or articles made to the topography were first made available for sale or hire anywhere in the world by or with the licence of the design right owner. However, the design right expires if either the topography or articles made to the topography are not made available within a 15 year period starting with the earlier of the time when the topography was first recorded in a design document or when an article was first made to that design. Generally, confidential disclosure of the design does not start time running.

Infringement

Only the owner of the design right in the topography may reproduce the design by making articles to that design or by making a design document recording the design for the purpose of enabling such articles to be made. However, the design may be reproduced by another without infringing if that other reproduces the design privately for non commercial aims or does so to analyze or evaluate the design or the ideas behind it. In the latter case, it also does not infringe the design right to create another original semiconductor topography as a result of this analysis.

No Licences of Right

It should be noted that, unlike provisions relating to design right generally, there can be no licences of right for semiconductor topography.

Name: Public Lending Right Act 1979

Identity/SI number: Public Lending Right Act 1979

Date effective: In force

Interpretation:

Preliminary

This Act provides a public lending right for authors. When a book is sold to a library, the author will clearly only receive one royalty payment notwithstanding that the book might be widely borrowed. This Act ensures that authors whose works are lent to the public by local library authorities receive at least some income from this. The Right only applies to books.

Administration

The Scheme under the Act is prepared by the Secretary of State and there is a Registrar of public lending right who administers the Scheme. The Registrar keeps a register of books in which the Public Lending Right subsists and a register of the persons entitled to the Right with respect to each book. The Registrar pays a fee, under the terms of the Scheme, to the appropriate people according to number of borrowings of the books.

Duration

The Right lasts from the date of first publication (or, if later, the beginning of the year in which application is made for it to be registered) until 50 years after the end of the calendar year in which the author dies.

Assignment

The author can freely assign this right to his publisher or to others. The right can be left in his or her will.

Name: Trade Marks Act 1938

Identity/SI number: Trade Marks Act 1938

Date Effective: In force

Interpretation:

Preliminary

A trade mark may be a business's most valuable asset. It identifies the goods or services of the business and serves to distinguish them from those of its competitors. To customers and clients the mark usually represents a particular type or quality of product or nature or standard of service, and therefore it is often by reference to the Mark that they place further orders for the product or use the services again and also recommend them to others. A trade mark may therefore play a valuable role in the promotion and advertising of a business.

What is a Trade Mark?

A trade mark may be:

(1) a word or words which in some cases may be represented in a special style of lettering,

(2) a name,

(3) a signature,

(4) a logo, for example a picture or a geometrical device,

(5) a complete label,

(6) a combination of letters or a monogram,

(7) a combination of numerals,

(8) a combination of colours applied to a product,

(9) a particular shape of a product or its container,

(10) any combination of these.

Goods and Services

Trade marks generally fall into two categories, first those used upon and in relation to goods and second those used in relation to services, and there are of course some marks which apply to both. In fact, the Act specifies that marks used in respect of goods are referred to as "Trade Marks" and marks used for services are called "Service Marks", and these terms will therefore be used hereafter.

Common Law Rights and Registration

Trade marks and service marks are protected in two ways:-

(1) by registration of the mark which provides statutory protection under the Act enforceable by proceedings for infringement,

(2) by use which, through acquiring a reputation, establishes rights in the mark at common law enforceable by proceedings for passing off.

For the purposes of registration a mark is essentially a distinctive mark used or proposed to be used in relation to specific goods or services. A mark can only be registered if it complies with certain requirements set out in what are effectively different versions of the Act as applied to trade marks (for goods) and to service marks. A registered trade or service mark is infringed only by visual misuse of the mark in relation to the goods or services for which it is registered. Common law rights can provide broader protection. In some circumstances marks which are incapable of registration, may nevertheless be protected against passing-off and the protection may extend beyond the scope of the actual goods or services in respect of which the mark is used. Passing-off applies to oral as well as visual misuse.

Trading Names

Trade and service marks, and trading names are frequently confused. Strictly speaking they are distinct but there is frequently a degree of overlap. For example, common law protects the trading name of a business as such against passing off but it becomes a trade mark or service mark insofar as it is used upon and in relation to goods sold by the business or in relation to services provided by the business. Also, if a registered company name is used without "Limited" or "Plc" in respect of goods or services it may become a trade mark or service mark as the case may be.

A business may have a corporate or house mark which is used in respect of all the goods or services provided by the business and/or a number of marks for individual goods or services.

Registration of a Trade Mark or Service Mark

General Procedure

Registration for either a trade mark or a service mark involves filing an application at the Trade Marks Registry with a filing fee. The Registry examines the application for registrability and possible conflict with existing registrations, and if any objections are raised the applicant is given the opportunity to deal with them by argument and/or amendment of the application and/or by filing evidence of past use of the mark. When the application has been accepted it is advertised in the weekly Trade Marks Journal to enable any interested third party to oppose registration. If no opposition is lodged, or there is an opposition which is successfully defeated, the mark then proceeds to registration. It can take up to two years or even longer from filing an application to obtain registration although the registration is effective from the filing date.

In more detail the application procedure is as follows:-

(a) Filing

The application for registration should be by the proprietor of the mark. Usually this is the company, partnership or individual using or proposing to use the mark. If the application is filed in another name, it must be accompanied by an application to register as a registered user the actual user or proposed user of the mark.

It is necessary to specify the goods or services for which registration is sought. All marks are classified according to the goods or services for which they are registered, and there are 34 classes of goods and 8 service classes in the classification. An application can only cover goods or services in a single class and if protection is required for a range of goods or services falling into more than one class it is necessary to file a corresponding number of separate applications.

(b) Examination

The registrability of a mark depends mainly on its distinctiveness, that is to say its ability to distinguish the applicant's goods or services from those of its competitors.

Generally speaking marks which are descriptive of the goods or services for which registration is sought, common surnames and geographical names are considered not to be distinctive, although in some cases registration is possible on the basis of evidence of a number of years' use of the mark which shows that the mark has nevertheless become distinctive through use. The Trade Marks Register is divided into two parts—Part A and Part B—which are for marks of differing degrees of distinctiveness. Generally a mark will qualify for registration in Part A if it is inherently distinctive, for example if it is an invented word or, in the event that it is a dictionary word, it nevertheless has no direct reference to the character or quality of the goods or services concerned, or if the mark has already gained a sufficient degree of distinctiveness by use. If a mark is not inherently distinctive and there has been no (or insufficient) past use, but it is nevertheless capable of becoming distinctive after a (longer) period of use, registration can usually be obtained in Part B. The difference is perhaps best illustrated by the attitude of the Registry to "Master" marks. "Lawnmaster" for lawn mowers has been refused registration in either Part A or Part B as it was deemed to have a direct and relatively close reference to the character or quality of the goods concerned. "Swingmaster" for golf clubs has been refused in Part A but accepted in Part B as it was deemed to have a less pointed reference to the character or quality of the goods, but "Globemaster" for cycles has been allowed in Part A.

Applicants always apply initially for registration in Part A because such a registration gives broader protection than a Part B registration and has partial immunity from attack after being registered for seven years, and the Registry then decides whether the application should proceed in Part A or Part B.

The Registry also refuses to register deceptive marks. A mark is considered to be deceptive if its use in relation to the goods or services concerned is likely to deceive or cause confusion, for example because such use would lead to confusion with another mark already in use for the same or similar goods or services. The Registry will also reject marks which are deceptive as to the quality or composition of the goods or services concerned. For example, "Orlwoola" has been refused for textile goods because it would be deceptive if used on goods not made of wool.

Another ground of refusal is that the mark conflicts with an existing registration, i.e. the mark itself is identical or confusingly similar to the registered mark and the goods or services for which registration is sought are identical or similar to, or are associated with the goods or services in respect of which the existing mark is registered.

(c) Registration

Registration is initially for a period of seven years from the filing date and the mark can then be renewed on payment of renewal fees for further periods of fourteen years.

Infringement Of A Registered Trade Mark Or Service Mark

A registered trade mark or service mark is infringed by the unauthorised use upon or in relation to any goods or services covered by the registration of the identical mark or a mark nearly resembling it.

The use of a particular mark constitutes an infringement of a registered mark only if the following requirements are fulfilled:

1. The mark must be used within the territory covered by the registration. Whilst most marks are registered for the whole of the United Kingdom, there are registrations whose scope is confined to only part of the UK (usually when registration has only been possible on the basis of evidence of use which was restricted to the area concerned).

2. The goods or services for which the offending mark is used, must fall within the scope of the goods or services for which the mark is registered and within the same class of the classification.

3. The mark must be identical with or confusingly similar to the registered mark. The question of whether a mark is confusingly similar may involve a number of factors, and each case has to be considered on its merits.

Passing Off

Passing off is a tort which has its basis in common law. It does not derive from the Act.

In the case of a trade mark or service mark common law rights are established by use of the mark. If as a result the mark becomes well-known to customers and to clients, goodwill is thereby created in the business providing the goods or services concerned. It is this goodwill that is protected by common law rights. The first requirement for a plaintiff in an action for passing off, therefore, is to establish that there is an existing goodwill arising from use of the mark.

Having established that there is goodwill, in order to succeed the plaintiff then has to show that there is a misrepresentation made by the defendant in the course of trade which causes or is likely to cause damage to goodwill. In the case of a trade mark or service mark, such misrepresentation usually arises from the defendant's use of the identical or a confusingly similar mark which results in customers or clients being confused into thinking that the defendant's goods or services are those of the trade mark owner or associated with the owner in some way. In other words the defendant is passing off his goods or services as and for those of the trade mark owner.

One defence frequently advanced by the defendant in a passing off action is that the mark involved is descriptive. If a mark is descriptive, the plaintiff needs to show by evidence of use that the mark has acquired a secondary meaning as denoting the goods or services of the plaintiff. Generally speaking, the more descriptive a mark is, the more use there has to be in order to found a passing off action.

It is no defence to show that in fact the defendant's goods or services are not inferior to the trade mark owner's goods or services. Also, the goods or services need not necessarily be the same as those in respect of which the trade mark owner is using his mark, although there does usually have to be what is commonly referred to as a common field of activity. Generally this means that the nature of the goods or services of the unauthorised user is such that the public are likely to think that they originated from or are connected in some way with the trade mark owner. In the case of goods, for example, this may be because they are sold through the same trade channels or they may be thought to be a natural diversification of the trade mark owner's product range. Although common law protection is automatic, that does not mean that the user of the mark should do nothing. It is advisable to keep evidence of the past use of the mark, including turnover figures, advertising material, copies of advertisements in trade magazines and other publications for use in any litigation. Such material will also be useful if the user decides at some time to apply for registration of the mark and it is necessary to file evidence of use to support the application.

Advantages of Registration of Marks Already Protected Against Passing Off

There are disadvantages in relying on protection against passing off, one of which is the trouble and expense involved in compiling the necessary evidence of past use of the mark to support legal proceedings (in some cases it may be necessary to produce evidence to obtain registration but at least this only has to be done once).

It is preferable to register a mark for a number of reasons:

(a) Registration gives protection even before use of the mark has commenced.

(b) Generally proceedings for infringement of a registered trade mark are less complicated than proceedings for passing-off.

(c) In the absence of a registration of the mark the Trade Marks Registry would allow someone else to register the same mark or a confusingly similar mark for the same or similar mark for the same or similar goods or services even if the unregistered mark is in use and as a result protected be common law rights, because the Registry would not know of such use. The owner of the unregistered mark, even if he gets to know of the application for registration which is unlikely, would have to go to the trouble and expense of opposing it on the basis of his prior common law rights which would have to be proved by evidence of use.

(d) Any third party proposing to adopt the same or a similar trade mark but not knowing of the use of the existing mark would, if the mark is registered, find the registration in a search in the register of trade marks and thus be deterred from proceeding to use the proposed mark.

(e) A registered trade mark is usually effective throughout the whole of the United Kingdom whereas if a mark has only a local reputation as a result of its use being confined to a particular part of the UK, the trade mark owner relying on his common law rights may not be able to prevent others using the mark in other parts of the UK.

(f) Use of the mark can be licensed on a proper legal basis without prejudicing the mark, which may not be possible if the mark is not registered.

(g) A registration in Part A (but not in Part B) is effective to prevent others "importing a reference" to the trade mark owner of his goods or services, the most common example of which is comparative advertising where a competitor compares his goods or services with those of the trade mark owner. There is no passing-off in this case because the mark is being used in relation to the genuine goods or services of the owner, not the competitor's goods or services. However, there is infringement if the mark is registered in Part A because the infringer is importing a reference to the mark and thereby appropriating some of the goodwill associated with the mark.

Remedies for Infringement and Passing-off

The remedies available in proceedings for both causes of action are generally the same. The trade mark owner or plaintiff is entitled to (a) an injunction to restrain further infringement or passing off, (b) delivery up or destruction of any goods, advertising literature, labels and other matter carrying the offending mark, or obliteration of the mark, and (c) an enquiry as to damages or an account of profits. Further remedies are also available in certain circumstances. If the plaintiff is likely to suffer irreparable damage should the defendant continue to use the offending mark until the trial of the action, which could be a year or more after the commencement of proceedings, the plaintiff may apply to the Court for an interlocutory injunction to restrain the defendant until the trial. Such an application must be made without delay and if it is granted the plaintiff must give an undertaking to pay damages to the defendant for preventing him using the mark in the event that the plaintiff loses at the trial.

If the defendant is likely to dispose of products, packaging, advertising literature and other material carrying the offending mark, the plaintiff may apply to the Court for a so-called Anton Piller Order which enables the plaintiff, without prior warning, to enter the defendant's premises and search for, and seize such material.

If the defendant is likely to dispose of assets before the trial with the result that the plaintiff will not be able to recover any damages awarded by the Court, the plaintiff may apply for a Mareva Injunction which is an order freezing the defendant's assets.

These further remedies are commonly used in counterfeiting cases.

Assignment And Licensing

Registered marks and marks which are protected at common law against passing off, can be assigned to others but whilst a registered mark may be assigned with or without the goodwill of the business in the goods or the business of providing the services for which the mark is registered, a common law mark can only be assigned with goodwill, which is of course logical because without goodwill an unregistered mark has no protection.

In the case of an assignment of a registered mark without goodwill it is necessary to advertise the assignment in an appropriate publication as a warning to customers that the goods or services concerned have not been provided by the same business as previously and therefore the nature or quality of the goods or services may not be the same.

It is also possible to license others to use both registered and common law marks but it is important that the owner of the mark is in a position to exercise control over the manner in which the mark is used by the user since any use without proper control can affect the validity of the mark and the owner can lose his rights.

Name: Patents Act 1977

Identity/SI Number: Patents Act 1977

Date Effective: 1.6.78

Interpretation:

Preliminary

Patentability

To be patentable an invention must exhibit three features. It must be new, involve an inventive step and be capable of industrial application. Looking at each of these in turn:

(a) Novelty

The invention must not be known to the public anywhere in the world at the date of the filing of the patent application either because:

(i)   others have previously thought of and publicly disclosed the same idea; or

(ii)   because the inventor has publicly disclosed his own idea himself (see below); or

(iii)   because another patent application has been filed even if that patent application has not yet been published (this is a strong argument for early application for a patent)

(b) Inventive Step

The invention must not merely be an obvious development in the light of existing knowledge. The question is whether or not a person skilled in the specific field of the invention would have regarded the step as obvious at the time of the filing of the application.

(c) Capable of Industrial Application

"Industry" is construed widely and includes almost any commercial enterprise and agriculture. The invention may be relate to a product or to a process.

Exclusion from patentability

It is not possible to obtain a patent for a discovery, scientific theory or a mathematical method. Nor are patents obtainable for aesthetic creations, ways of thinking or ways of presenting information. Specifically, patents are not obtainable for computer programs as such, or for animal or plant varieties. However, the way in which computer programs control manufacturing processes and equipment can be patented, and computer programs *per se* are protected by copyright. New plant varieties can be protected under the *Plant Varieties and Seeds Act 1964*. The patentability of inventions relating to medical treatment is also severly curtailed.

Disclosure of invention prior to patent application

Since the invention must be "new" at the time of filing, the strict rule is that there should be absolutely no prior disclosure to the public. This includes disclosure in the course of conversation. However, there are two limited exceptions where any prior disclosure to the public occurring within 6 months prior to filing is not detrimental. First, if someone makes public disclosure in breach of an obligation of confidence to the inventor, the invention will still be regarded as "new". Second, the novelty of an invention will not be affected by its display at an officially recognised trade exhibition provided written evidence of the display is provided at the time of filing. In both cases, however, there must not be any other public disclosure before the filing date.

Prior disclosure to one or more individuals under obligations of confidence (which should preferably be expressed in writing) will not undermine the "novelty" of the invention.

Entitlement to a patent

Primarily the inventor, or where more than one person has devised the invention, the joint inventors. However, commonly the inventor is an employee of a company and in this case the question arises of whether the company or the employee is entitled to the patent.

Employee inventions

The 1977 Act set down for the first time in statute law the circumstances in which an invention made by an employee belongs to his employer. Prior to the Act the issue was determined on the basis of the "master and servant" principles of common law.

An employee is defined in the Act as a person who works (or where the employment has ceased) worked under a contract of employment. The relevant provisions do not therefore apply to consultants engaged by companies and an invention made by a consultant will only belong to the company if there is an agreement to this effect which should preferably be entered into when the consultant is engaged.

The Act provides that an invention made by an employee belongs to his employer only if:

(i) The invention was made in the course of the employee's normal duties or specifically assigned duties, which in either case were such that an invention might reasonably be expected to result from the carrying out of those duties. Clearly, therefore, inventions made by employees working on research and development and in design departments belong to their employers. Inventions made by employees not normally involved in such work will only belong to the employer if the employee has been specifically asked to undertake a job which is likely to result in the making of an invention.

(ii) The invention was made in the course of the duties of the employee and at the time because of the nature of those duties and the responsibilities arising from them the inventor was under a special obligation to further the interests of the employer's business. This covers inventions made by directors and persons in senior management irrespective of whether or not their duties involve or are likely to lead to the making of inventions.

The Act states categorically that in any other circumstances an invention made by an employee belongs to the employee himself.

Compensation for Employees

A further new feature of the 1977 Act was the introduction of a provision that an employee is entitled to compensation from his employer but only in certain circumstances:

(i)   The invention must have been patented. An employer owning an employee's invention can therefore avoid paying compensation simply by not patenting the invention but of course this has the potentially much more serious drawback that the invention will not then be protected.

(ii) If the invention was initially owned by the employer under the circumstances outlined above, the inventor can claim compensation if the patent is of outstanding benefit to the employer.

(iii) The compensation provisions are not however limited to inventions initially owned by employers. If the invention was initially owned by the employee and he has either granted an exclusive licence or assigned the patent to his employer he can claim compensation if the benefit derived by the employee is inadequate relative to the benefit which the employer derives from the patent.

Note that it is the value of the patent rather than the value of the invention which has to be considered.

An application for compensation may be made to the Patent Office or the Court.

The inventor's rights may not be diminished in any way by his terms of employment or by any other agreement.

The provisions regarding compensation for employee-inventors can be overruled only when the employee is a member of a Union at the time the invention is made and that Union has a collective agreement with the employer (or an employers' Association to which the employer belongs) and such collective agreement has other provisions for the payment of compensation in respect of employee-inventions.

Application for a patent

A patent for the United Kingdom can be obtained either:

(a)   by application to the British Patent Office for a national UK patent

(b)   by a single application under the European Patent Convention for a European Patent covering a number of European countries (including the UK)

(c)   by a single application under the Patent Cooperation Treaty for separate patents in a variety of countries throughout the world (including the UK)

At some time in the future, a Common Market Patent will be obtainable under a proposed Community Patent Convention.

In the case of an application to the British Patent Office for a national UK patent it is necessary to file:

(a)   a form requesting the grant of a patent

(b)   a statement of inventorship

(c)   a description of the invention including if appropriate drawings illustrating a preferred form of the invention

(d)   claims defining the scope of the invention for which protection is sought

(e)   an abstract briefly outlining the main features of the invention

(f)   a filing fee.

The applicant must also request a "preliminary examination and search" and pay a search fee. The Patent Office then conducts a search usually in earlier patent specifications and sometimes in other literature for any documents which are likely to be relevant to the patentability of the invention claimed.

The application is published 18 months after the filing date or if the application claims the priority date of an earlier UK or foreign application, 18 months after the priority date, and with it the results of the search. Not until then are the contents of the application available to the public.

Within 6 months of publication of the application the applicant (who has by now had the opportunity to study the search results and decide whether or not it is worth proceeding with the application) may apply for "substantive examination" which involves paying a further fee. A Patent Office examiner then considers the patentability of the invention in the light of the documents revealed in the search, and issues a report.

If the examiner raises any objections to the application the applicant can argue against the objections or amend the application to overcome them. In the event of an objection that the invention as defined in the claims is not new or it is obvious in view of the search results, it may be necessary to amend the claims to distinguish the invention claimed from the disclosures in the documents revealed in the search.

During the course of the application, third parties can make observations to the Patent Office on the novelty or inventiveness of the invention claimed which the examiner will take into account.

Duration

The patent may subsist for a maximum of 20 years from the filing date subject to the payment of annual renewal fees for the fifth and subsequent years.

Dealings with patent rights

Patent applications and patents may be sold (by means of an assignment) or mortgaged and others may be licensed to exploit the patented invention. Such transactions must be registered at the Patent Office to protect the position of the person acquiring the rights concerned. Assignments and mortgages of patents or patent applications must be in writing signed by both parties. Licences may arise out of oral agreements, but clearly written agreements are to be recommended.

Contracts concerning patent rights

Contracts relating to the exploitation of patent rights must not infringe UK or EEC Competition Law. The 1977 Act also contains certain restrictions applicable to licences and contracts for the supply of patented products.

Licences

The patentee may be happy to grant licences at commercial rates to all-comers. If so, he can apply to the Patent Office to endorse his patent "licences of right" which means that anyone is entitled to a licence under the patent as of right. An advantage of such endorsement is that the annual renewal fees are reduced by half. If the patentee and an applicant for a licence cannot agree the terms including the royalty payable, the Comptroller of Patents can be asked to settle the terms.

There are certain limited situations where the patentee has no choice but to grant licences. The Patents Act provides for the grant of compulsory licences at any time after three years have elapsed from the grant of the patent if the applicant for a licence can show that the patentee has harmed the public interest by failing adequately or reasonably to exploit the patented invention or to meet public demand. Such applications are rare.

Publication

The publication of patent applications 18 months after filing means that details of new developments often available before they reach the market. There are facilities for watching for the publication applications in any particular field and searches can also be made for all patents and applications relating to a particular subject.

Attacks on validity

After the patent has been granted, any person can apply to the Patent Office or to a Court for revocation of the patent. Most attacks on the validity of a patent arise as a defence in proceedings initiated by the patentee for infringement of the patent.

The grounds upon which the patent can be revoked are:

(i) the invention was not patentable at the date of filing of the application (that is, it lacked novelty or did not involve an inventive step or it was not capable of industrial application)

(ii) the patent was granted to someone not entitled to the patent

(iii) the patent specification contains insufficient disclosure of the invention

(iv) the granted patent extends beyond the disclosures in the patent application as filed

(v) an amendment to the patent has extended the protection conferred by the patent beyond what should have been allowed.

Infringement

It is a common misconception that a patent gives to the patentee the right to exploit the invention. It is possible to obtain a patent for an invention, the exploitation of which infringes someone else's patent. All a patent does is to give to the patentee the right to prevent others exploiting the invention. The extent of this right is determined by the claims the patentee has made. What amounts to an infringement differs with respect to patented products, patented processes and to products made by patented processes.

A person infringes a patent, if, without the patentee's consent, he does any of the following:

(a) Patented Product

Makes, sells, offers to sell, uses, imports or merely possesses the product.

(b) Patented Process

Uses the process or offers it for use in the UK when he knows (or should have realised) that its use without the patentee's consent would infringe the patent.

(c) Product made by Patented Process

Sells, offers to sell, uses, imports or merely possesses the product.

It should be noted that if a product or process does not fall within the scope of the claims on a literal interpretation of their wording, it may nevertheless still be an infringement because the Courts can apply a broader interpretation to the claims.

A person also infringes a patent if without the consent of the patentee be supplies or offers to supply in the UK to a person not entitled to work the patented invention any of the means, relating to an essential element of the invention, for putting the invention into effect when he knows, or it is obvious to a reasonable person in the circumstances, that those means are suitable for putting and are intended to put,

in the UK. Thus, for example, in the case of a patent for a piece of apparatus
mponent parts, it can be just as much an infringement of the patent to supply one
the whole apparatus. If the supply is of a staple commercial product, however,
.gement if the supplier is actually inducing infringement.

..C law, where the patentee or his licensee has sold a patented product in one part of the
.cnt rights in the EEC are said to be "exhausted" and it will not be infringement for this product
oe imported into the UK.

As well as the patentee of course, the holder of an exclusive licence under the patent may bring
proceedings in respect of infringements committed after the date of his licence.

Defences

The two most common defences to an action for infringement are:

(a) the patent is not in fact being infringed on a proper interpretation of the claims, and

(b) the patent is invalid as the invention was not patentable as at the date of filing the patent application,
perhaps in view of some prior art not known to the Patent Office.

Additionally, the patent is not infringed by otherwise infringing acts which are done, for example, for
private and non-commercial purposes, for experimental purposes, or simply by virtue of a ship or
aeroplane with the invention on board temporarily or accidentally coming within UK jurisdiction.

Other defences are that the patent is not infringed by acts which are done, for example, for private and
non-commercial purposes, for experimental purposes, or simply by virtue of a ship or aeroplane with the
invention on board temporarily or accidentally coming within UK jurisdiction.

Threats

An unjustified threat of proceedings for infringement of a patent (except in relation to the making or
importing of a patented product for sale, or the use of a patented process) is actionable and the person
threatened is entitled to apply to the Court for an injunction against continuance of the threat. He may also
seek damages in respect of any loss he has sustained by reason of the threat. A threat is unjustified if the
patent is invalid or is not in fact being infringed.

Remedies

In proceedings for infringement of a patent the plaintiff is entitled to an injunction restraining further acts
of infringement and to damages in respect of the past acts of infringement, usually past sales in the case of
a product, or (at the plaintiff's option) to an account of the profits the defendant has made as a result of the
infringement. The damages or account of profits can in certain circumstances date back to the date of
publication of the patent application. The plaintiff may also apply for an order requiring the defendant to
deliver up to him or to destroy any infringing products and for a declaration that the patent is valid. Neither
damages nor an account of profits are available where the defendant proves that at the date of the
infringement he was not aware and had no reasonable grounds for supposing that a patent existed. It is
therefore sensible to place on products, the subject of a patent, the word "patent" along with the number of
the patent. "Patented" alone is not sufficient.

In certain circumstances if urgent action is needed the Plaintiff can immediately apply for:

(a) an interlocutory injunction to restrain the infringer until the trial of the action,

(b) an Anton Piller Order enabling the Plaintiff, without the infringer being forewarned, to enter the
infringer's premises and search for and seize infringing products and other relevant materials thereby
preventing the infringer from destroying or disposing of incriminating evidence,

(c) a Mareva injunction freezing the infringer's assets thereby preventing the infringer from d. of the means to pay damages.

A foreign Plaintiff may be required to provide security for costs so that the Defendant will be sur recover his costs if the Plaintiff loses; and similarly in an application for an interlocutory or Mare injunction or an Anton Piller Order the Plaintiff has to give a cross-undertaking as to damages to satisfy th Court that he can pay damages to the Defendant if he loses at the trial and therefore the grant of the injunction turns out to be unjustified.

Patents County Court

In the past, proceedings for patent infringement have always had to be taken in the High Court where the procedure is complicated and cases can take years to come to trial. Under the 1988 Copyright Designs & Patent Act, Patents County Courts were introduced. The Act provides that the Lord Chancellor may designate any County Court as a Patents County Court and for the reasons explained below this will provide a simpler, more informal, speedier and cheaper forum for patent disputes. So far only one Patents County Court has been established at Wood Green in London, but others are expected to follow in due course.

The Patents County Court can deal not only with patent infringement but also with other proceedings relating to patents. Its jurisdiction, in fact, also includes matters relating to registered designs and design rights. The rules governing the Patent County Court empower the Court to do anything that the High Court can do. Therefore the Patents County Court can grant interlocutory injunctions, Anton Piller Orders and Mareva injunctions.

The procedure in the Patents County Court should ensure a speedier trial not least because before a case reaches trial, unsustainable and unsupported points will have been eliminated so that only the essential points need be argued and decided at the trial. The same Judge will follow the case from its early stages through to the trial. Importantly, the parties at a Patents County Court will be able to be represented by either patent agents or solicitors: there is no need to involve both nor is there any need to involve barristers.

Name: Registered Designs Act 1949 (as amended by the Copyright Designs and Patents Act 1988)

Identity/SI No: Registered Designs Act 1949

Date Effective: In force - amendments from 1.8.89

Interpretation:

Preliminary

It is difficult to discuss registered designs outside of the context of the protection afforded by the law to industrial designs generally. Reference should therefore be made to the text following the heading "the position in relation to industrial designs" in the discussion of the Copyright, Designs and Patents Act 1988 above.

pe, configuration, pattern or ornament. These features must be applied to an ... by any industrial process. The features, in the finished article, must appeal to ...ye. There is therefore an aesthetic criterion for registrability.

...n registrability are features of shape or configuration of an article which:

...e necessary simply so that the article can fulfil its function and

(b)   are necessary only because the article must match with another article where the author intends the design to form an integral part of that other article. This replicates the "must-match" exception to design right (see above).

The design can also only be registered if people acquiring or using articles of this sort are concerned how this sort of article looks or how the particular article looks.

The design of a particularly attractive cog in a piece of clockwork would be unlikely to be registrable. People do not normally take into account the attractiveness of the cogs of a clock in purchasing a clock. If the workings of the clock were in a transparent casing, it might be argued that a purchaser would take the attractiveness of the cog into account in purchasing the clock. However, the design of the cog would still not be registrable if its features of shape or configuration were dictated by its function within the clock or if it was of that design simply so that it would match the design of other parts inside the clock.

Novelty

A design may only be registered if it is "new". It is not new if it is substantially the same as a design which is already registered or already published in the United Kingdom. Where there has already been registration or publication of a design, there can be no fresh registration of a design which merely replicates features which are common trade variants to the design. It is possible to register the same design in respect of other articles.

Registration can still occur where prior disclosure of the design has taken place, but only where this prior disclosure was in confidence. In other words, if a person tells his friend about a design and makes it clear that his friend is not to tell anybody else about the design or use it himself, then it may still be possible to register the design. It is also still possible to register even if the friend has breached his duty of good faith by disclosing the design to another person. If the design is shown at certain exhibitions, then it may nevertheless be registered within six months of the opening of the exhibition.

Where one person owns the copyright in an artistic work, another person may (with the permission of the copyright owner) apply for registration of a corresponding design notwithstanding any use to which the copyright work has been put. The design will still be "new" for the purposes of the Act. However, this does not apply if the previous use of the copyright work, with the copyright owner's permission, consisted of or included the exploitation of the copyright work by means of its having been applied industrially to articles which were then offered for sale or hire. In this case, the design is not "new" and therefore not registrable under the Act..

Proprietorship of Designs

The author, that is the person who creates the design, is normally treated as the original proprietor of the design. However, where a design is created in the course of his employment by an employee, the employer is the proprietor of the design. Where employees may create designs, a clause should be included in the contracts of employment to ensure that there is no doubt that such designs are created in the course of employment. A commissioner is treated as the original proprietor where the design is created in pursuance of a commission for money or money's worth. This is similar to the rule with regard to design rights, but the opposite of the rule as regards artistic copyright. The original proprietor of a computer generated work is the person by whom the arrangements necessary for the creation of the design are made.

Note that where design right subsists in a design, the applicant for registration must be the design right owner.

Right Given by Registration

Once the design is registered under the Act, the registered proprietor has the exclusive right:

(a) to make or import for sale or hire, or for use for the purposes of a trade or business, or

(b) to sell, hire or offer or expose for sale or hire

an article in respect of which the design is registered and to which that design or a design not substantially different from it has been applied. Anyone who, without the registered proprietor's licence, does any of these acts infringes the exclusive right of the proprietor. It would also be infringement for a person without authorization to make something for enabling such an article to be made and this provision applies to the U.K. and abroad. Protection is also afforded to kits for the making of an assembled article over which there is registered design right.

If a feature of the design of an article was left out of account in the determination as to whether the design was registrable, then this feature can be copied with impunity.

Failure To Work

Any person may apply to the Registrar for the grant of a compulsory licence in respect of a registered design if that design has not been worked in the U.K.

Remedies For Infringement

The registered proprietor may seek an injunction. He or she may also seek damages or an account of profits. It is an offence punishable by a fine for a person falsely to represent that a design applied to any article sold by him is registered in respect of that article.

Duration of Protection

The right subsists for five years from the date of registration; however, on the payment of the appropriate renewal fees, the term can be extended by up to four further periods of five years. A maximum term of 25 years is therefore possible. Where the design corresponds to a previously made copyright work, then the registered design expires with the expiration of the copyright term even if this is prior to the end of the full 25 year period from first registration.

Assignments

Transactions such as assignments, mortgages and licenses may be undertaken with registered designs, however, these must be recorded in the Register of Designs. An application must therefore be made to the Registrar. There can be assignment of ownership of a design, or of the permission to apply that design to articles. The proprietor of the design for the purposes of the Act will be either the assignee or the assignee along with the original proprietor.

Overlap Between Registered Design Right and Unregistered Design Right

Only the design right owner may apply for registration of that design. Where the owner of the design right and the registered design right are the same person, an assignment of the registered design is taken also to be an assignment of the design right subject to contrary intention being shown. Given the possibility that the design right and registered design right owners are different people, there would seem to remain the possibility of the singular owner of both the design right and the registered design right taking an infringement action under either or both regimes. This also creates a situation where a licence of right may be available as regards the design right, but such a licence proves virtually valueless given the concurrent rights under the Registered Design Act.

Implications for Industry of the Amendments to The Registered Design Act by The Copyright, Designs And Patents Act 1988

The most significant new use of the Registered Design Act will be in the situation where there is a drawing recording the design of a non-artistic article. It is in this area that the full significance of the new 25 year Registered Design Act term can be seen (previously the maximum term was only 15 years) and it is also in this area that registration of designs may prove to be a more normal part of the protection of the intellectual property rights of industry than was previously the case. There is no significant copyright protection for designs of non-artistic articles. The maximum duration of the design right in the design of a non-artistic article is 15 years, and a maximum of 10 years from the first marketing of articles to the design. Further, during the final 5 years of the term, licenses of right are available. As noted, Registered Design Act protection can subsist for 25 years (without the availability of licences of right). Registered Design Act protection will therefore prove attractive where the design of non-artistic articles can be registered. Moreover, if the registered design does not prove to be profitable, the 5 yearly renewal fees need not be paid.

Name: Commission Regulation (EEC) No 2349/84 of 23rd July 1984 on the Application of Article 85(3) of the Treaty to certain categories of patent licensing agreements

Identity/SI No: Commission Regulation (EEC)No.2349/84 of 23.7.84

Date Effective: from 1.1.85 to 31.12.94

Interpretation:

Preliminary: Block Exemptions

A block exemption Regulation ("block exemption") is a Regulation passed by the European Commission which grants certain categories of agreements an automatic exemption from the EEC Competition Rules. Article 85(1) of the Treaty of Rome prohibits any agreement between undertakings or decisions by an association of undertakings or concerted practices which may affect trade between Member States and which restrict competition within the Common Market.

Article 85(2) specifies that such agreements, decisions or concerted practices are "automatically void" and consequently cannot be enforced in any Court in a Member State. However, Article 85(3) states that the provisions of article 85(1) may be declared inapplicable to an agreement by an individual exemption, or to a category of agreements by a block exemption when the resulting restrictions on competition are outweighed by economic advantages. Economic advantages would be improved production or distribution of goods or promotion of technical or economic progress while allowing consumers a fair share of the resulting benefits.

The parties to an agreement may apply to the Commission for "negative clearance", that is to say a declaration that the agreement falls outside article 85(1). Alternatively, or in addition, the parties may also notify the Commission of the agreement for the purpose of obtaining an individual exemption under article 85(3). One of the consequences of this notification is that the parties to the agreement will not have to pay fines for breaches of the competition rules which occur after the date of notification pending a final decision of the commission.

Apart from agreements covered by negative clearance or an individual exemption, the following will also be exempted from competition rules:

(a) agreements having no appreciable effect on trade between Member States (for guidance, see the Notice on Agreements of Minor Importance (Notice of 3rd September 1986)); and

(b) agreements covered by one of the block exemption regulations. As noted, the block exemption is a Regulation by which the European Commission grants blanket automatic exemption from the Competition Rules for particular categories of agreements. Individual notification is therefore unnecessary where a block exemption applies.

Block exemptions state which clauses may or must not be contained in an agreement if it is to benefit from the exemption, and the conditions which must be satisfied by the agreements.

Preliminary: Patent Licensing Block Exemption

This block exemption applies to patent licensing agreements in respect of national patents granted in EEC countries or European patents granted in respect of EEC countries and licences in respect of inventions a term of which is that a patent application will be made within one year. It will also apply to Community patents when it becomes possible to apply for these. Patent licensing agreements containing additional provisions relating to know-how or trademarks are also included in the scope of this block exemption (however, see below on the relationship between patent and know-how licensing agreements). The Regulation also applies to such licensing agreements as patent licensing agreements where the licensor is not the patentee but is authorised by the patentee to grant a licence or sub-licence.

It should be noted that the Block Exemption does not cover patent pools or licensing agreements entered into in connection with joint ventures.

Restrictions Which Can Be Included in a Patent Licensing Agreement

A patent licensing agreement will benefit from this block exemption if it contains provisions restricting competition which are expressly authorised by the block exemption; for example the following:

(a) a provision obliging the licensor not to exploit the patent himself or license other undertakings to exploit the patent in the territory within the EEC covered by the licence;

(b) a provision obliging the licensee not to exploit the patent in a territory in the EEC reserved for the licensor or to the manufacture the patented product or use the patented process in a territory reserved for other licensees in which there is patent protection;

(c) a provision prohibiting the licensee from pursuing an active sales policy (e.g. advertising or establishing a branch office) in other licensees' territories in which there is patent protection;

(d) a provision prohibiting the licensee from pursuing a passive sales policy (i.e. responding to unsolicited demands from customers established in other licensees' territories in which there is patent protection). However, this prohibition must be limited to a period not exceeding five years from the date when the product is first marketed within the common market;

(e) a provision obliging the licensee to mark the products produced pursuant to the patent licensing agreement with the licensor's trademark. However the licensee may identify himself as the manufacturer of the product;

(f) a provision obliging the parties to exchange any experience obtained in exploiting the licensed patent and to grant each other non-exclusive licences in respect of patents relating to improvements to the licensed patent;

(g) a provision obliging the licensee to pay a minimum royalty to the licensor or to produce a minimum quantity of products pursuant to the licensed patent. The purpose of this type of clause is to avoid the possibility of a licensee bringing the exploitation of the patent to a standstill;

(h) a provision restricting the use of the invention to specific technical fields of application.

Restrictions Which Must Be Excluded from a Patent Licensing Agreement

The block exemption provides a list, commonly called the "black list", of certain provisions which must not be included in patent licensing agreements if these are to benefit from the block exemption. However an individual exemption might be granted under Article 85(3). The following are examples of provisions in the black list:

(a) a provision stating that the licensee may not challenge the validity of the licensed patents, without prejudice to the right of the licensor to terminate the licensing agreement in the event of such challenge.

(b) a provision limiting the maximum quantity of the licensed products that can be manufactured or sold pursuant to the agreement or the maximum number of operations the licensee may carry out using the patent;

(c) a provision preventing the free determination of price or discounts for products made pursuant to the licensing agreement or restricting the customers which the licensee is entitled to supply;

(d) a provision obliging the licensee to enter into further patent licensing agreements with the licensor or to agree to use patents, goods or services provided by the licensor unless they are necessary for a technically satisfactory exploitation of the invention (this is commonly known as a tie-in requirement);

(e) a provision extending the agreement automatically to cover any new patents which the licensor might obtain unless each party is entitled annually to terminate the agreement after the expiry of the patent which was originally licensed;

(f) a provision preventing competition between the parties in the field of research and development;

(g) any provision or arrangement affecting either or both of the parties which has the effect of preventing the goods circulating freely throughout the common market once they have been put on the market.

If restrictive clauses are included which are not expressly permitted but which are not on the black list the "opposition procedure" explained in the Chapter on "Competition Law" may be of assistance.

Relationship Between Patent and Know-how Licensing Agreements

The transfer of complex technology often includes patented and non-patented elements. The block exemption on patent licensing agreements also covers provisions relating to know-how provided that both the licensed patent and the know-how are necessary for the exploitation of the licensed technology and the know-how is secret.

However, there are a large number of agreements concluded solely for the exploitation of non-patented technical information or where the patent component is not essential for the exploitation of the licensed technology. The Commission is interested in encouraging not only the exploitation of patents but also the transfer of know-how which is vital for strengthening the competitiveness of European firms and to establish a technological community in Europe. The increasing importance of know-how has made it desirable to give greater legal certainty to agreements governing the transfer of such technical knowledge and the Commission therefore subsequently adopted a block exemption for know-how licensing agreements (see below).

Patent Licensing Agreement Including Other Categories of Clauses May Still Benefit from the Block Exemption

The Commission may be notified of patent licensing agreements which include clauses which are not specifically mentioned in the Block Exemption. Once notified, the Commission has six months to oppose exemption under the Block Exemption. If the Commission fails to oppose exemption within this period, the licensing agreement will be exempted from the Competition Rules.

The Right of the Commission To Withdraw the Benefit of the Block Exemption on Patent Licensing Agreements

The Commission may withdraw the benefit of the Block Exemption with respect to a particular licensing agreement. It will do so if it finds an agreement otherwise exempted by this Block Exemption nevertheless has certain effects which are incompatible with Article 85(3) of the Treaty. The Commission looks in particular such matters as:

(a) whether there is sufficient competition within a licensed territory from either identical products or services, or products or services which users consider interchangeable with the licensed products or services

(b) whether the licensor or the licensee without good reason are refusing to meet demand from users or resellers in their respective territories who would market the products in other territories within the EEC.

Implications for Industry

The Commission considered that the Block Exemption would contribute to improving the production of goods and to promoting technical progress. The Regulation should make patentees more willing to grant licences and licensees more inclined to undertake the investment required to exploit new products or processes. It is therefore possible, to some extent at least, to carve-up the EEC into specific territories in which licensees might exploit the patent of the licensor.

Name: Commission Regulation (EEC) No.556/89 of 30 Nov.88 on the application of Article 85(3) of the Treaty to certain categories of know-how licensing agreements.

Identity/SI No: Commission Regulation (EEC)No.556/89 of 30.Nov.88

Date effective: from 1.4.89 to 31.12.99

Interpretation

Preliminary

For an explanation of the meaning of a "block exemption" see the preliminary comments under the patent licensing block exemption above.

Meaning of Know-how

The term "know-how" is an abbreviation of the expression "to know how to do it". For the purposes of the Regulation, know-how means a body of technical information that is secret, substantial and identified in any appropriate form. The know-how is secret if it is not generally known or easily accessible. The idea behind this is that part of the value of the know-how consists in the lead-time that the licensee gains when the know-how is communicated to him or to her. Although individual components of the know-how might be known, the package as a whole must not generally be known or easily accessible. "Substantial" means that the know-how includes information which is of importance for the whole or a significant part of a manufacturing process, a product or service, or for the development of either of these. The information must therefore be neither trivial nor obvious. The know-how must also be identified in the sense that it must be described or recorded in such a manner as to make it possible to verify that it fulfils the criteria of secrecy and substantiality and to ensure that the licensee is not unduly restricted in his exploitation of his own technology. If the licensor wishes to avoid spelling out the know-how in the licence agreement itself, then the licensor may incorporate the information in a separate document.

Categories of Know-how Licensing Agreements which are covered by the Block Exemption

The block exemption applies to know-how licensing agreements to which there are only two parties and which include certain restrictions on the use which is made of the know-how. The block exemption also applies to certain mixed know-how and patent licensing agreements (in which, for example, the patent is necessary for the exploitation of the licensed technology but the know-how is the decisive element) such agreements not being covered by the block exemption on patent licensing agreements.

The block exemption will not cover agreements where the know-how relates solely to the sale or marketing of goods or services such as franchising arrangements. Commercial franchising agreements are governed by a separate EEC block exemption discussed below.

What Restrictions May Be Included In Know-how Licensing Agreements?

The block exemption specifies which restrictions can be included in know-how licensing agreements. The following are examples of provisions

(a) a provision preventing the licensor from exploiting or appointing other licensees to exploit the know-how in the licensed territory covering all or any part of the common market;

(b) a provision obliging the licensee not to exploit the licensed know-how in territories within the EEC which are reserved for the licensor and not to manufacture or use the licensed product, or use the licensed process, in the territories reserved for other licensees;

(c) a provision obliging the licensee not to pursue an active sales policy in other licensees' territories within the common market and in particular not to engage in advertising the licensed product or establishing any branch office in those territories;

(d) a provision obliging the licensee not to divulge the know-how even after the agreement has expired;

(e) a provision obliging the licensee not to exploit the licensed know-how after termination of the agreement unless it has ceased to be secret.

Agreements including (a) (b) and (c) are exempted for a period of ten years from the date of signature of the first licence agreement entered into by the licensor in the EEC in respect of the technology.

Restrictions Which Have To Be Excluded from Know-how Licensing Agreements

The block exemption regulation also specifies what restrictive clauses are not to be included in a know-how licensing agreement if it is to the benefit from an automatic exemption from the competition rules. However, even if an agreement does contain one of these restrictions it may still be possible to apply for an individual exemption from the European Commission. Examples of provisions which may not be contained in an agreement if it is to benefit from the block exemption are:

(a) a provision preventing the licensee from using the know-how after the agreement has expired if it has by then become public knowledge otherwise than by default of the licensee;

(b) a provision prohibiting the licensee from contesting the secrecy of the licensed know-how or from challenging the validity of any accompanying patents; however the licensor may be permitted to terminate the licensing agreement in the event of such a challenge;

(c) a provision preventing the free determination of prices or discounts for the products made using the licensed know-how;

(d) a provision obliging the licensee to assign to the licensor rights in, or to grant an exclusive licence to the licensor in respect of, improvements to or new applications of the licensed know-how;

(e) a provision restricting competition between the licensor and the licensee in relation to research and development into or use of competing products;

(f) any provision or arrangement affecting either or both of the parties which has the effect of preventing the goods circulating freely throughout the common market once they have been put on the market.

Know-how Licensing Agreement Including Other Categories of Clauses May Still Benefit from the Block Exemption.

The block exemption establishes a simplified procedure (the so-called "opposition procedure") for notifying to the Commission of know-how licensing agreements which include clauses which are restrictive of competition within the Common Market but which are neither expressly authorised to be, nor are expressly prevented from being, included in the agreement. If the agreement is notified to the Commission under the opposition procedure and the Commission does not oppose the exemption within a period of six months, it will be exempted from the competition rules.

The Right of the Commission to Withdraw the Benefit of the Block Exemption on Know-how Licensing Agreements

The Commission retains the right to withdraw the benefit of the block exemption Regulation from an individual agreement where, in exceptional circumstances, that agreement has effects which are incompatible with the conditions laid down by Article 85(3); for example, if the licensed products are not subject to effective competition in the licensed territory or if the parties without justification withhold supplies from customers who wish to resell the goods in other Member States.

Implications for Industry

Once know-how has been transferred, this will frequently be irreversible. The Block Exemption provides legal certainty with regard to the status of such agreements and encourages the dissemination of technical knowledge within the EEC. The Block Exemption recognises that know-how will often be an extremely valuable resource for a business and facilitates that business in transferring this resource on the basis of a licence agreement.

Name: Commission Regulation (EEC) No. 4087/88 of 30th November 1988 on the application of Article 85 (3) of the Treaty to categories of franchise agreements.

Identity/SI No.: Commission Regulation (EEC) No. 4087/88 of 30th November 1988

Date effective: From 1st February 1989 to 31st December 1999

Interpretation:

Preliminary

For an explanation of the meaning of a "block exemption" see the preliminary comments under the Patent Licensing block exemption.

Meaning of Franchise

For the purposes of this regulation franchise means a package of industrial or intellectual property rights relating to trade marks, trade names, shop signs, utility models, designs, copyrights, know-how or patents, to be exploited for the re-sale of goods or the provision of services to end users. The regulation therefore defines franchise extremely widely and catches both sales of goods and of services to the public.

The franchised information will particularly concern the presentation of goods for sale, the processing of goods in connection with the provision of services, methods of dealing with customers and administration and financial management. The franchised know-how must give the franchisee some competitive edge either by improving its performance or by helping it to enter a new market.

Categories of Franchise Agreements Which Are Covered by the Block Exemption

The block exemption applies to franchise agreements to which two undertakings are party. The block exemption also applies to so-called "master franchise agreements" to which two undertakings are party. For these purposes, a master franchise agreement means an agreement whereby the franchisor for financial consideration (direct or indirect) grants the right to a master franchisee to sub-franchise to third party undertakings.

A franchise agreement will include at least obligations relating to the use of a common name or shop sign and a uniform presentation of contract premises and/or means of transport. The franchisor will also communicate know-how to the franchisee. For the purposes of this block exemption, know-how is defined in a similar fashion to its definition under the know-how block exemption discussed above. Further, in a franchise agreement, the franchisor will continue during the term of the franchise agreement to provide to the franchisee commercial or technical assistance.

The franchisor's goods are goods produced by the franchisor or according to its instructions. These goods may, but need not, bear the franchisor's name or trade mark.

Conditions for the Application of the Block Exemption

The block exemption will only apply if the franchisee is free to obtain the franchised goods from fellow franchisees or from any within a network of authorised distributors. Where the franchisee is obliged by the agreement to honour a guarantee, the franchisee must also honour similar guarantees by its fellow franchisees. The franchisee is also obliged to indicate its status as an independent undertaking. Having done so, there is no objection to the franchised network enjoying a common identity through uniform appearance or other specified means.

What Restrictions May Be Included in Franchise Agreements?

The block exemption specifies the restrictions which may be included in franchise agreements, and the following are important examples of the provisions:

(a) an obligation on the franchisor, in a defined area of the Common Market (known as the "contract territory") first not to grant the right to exploit all or part of the franchise to third parties; second not itself to exploit the franchise, or itself market the goods or services which are the subject matter of the franchise under a similar formula; or third not itself to supply the franchisors goods to third parties;

(b) an obligation on the master franchisee (see above) not to conclude franchise agreements with third parties outside of its contract territory;

(c) an obligation on the franchisee to exploit the franchise only from the contract premises;

(d) an obligation on the franchisee to refrain, outside the contract territory, from seeking customers for the goods or services which are the subject matter of the franchise;

(e) an obligation on the franchisee not to compete with the franchisor's goods which are the subject matter of the franchise. The obligation may not, however, be imposed in respect of certain spare parts or accessories.

The Block Exemption applies even with the presence of certain other obligations on the franchisee, but only if these other obligations are necessary to protect the franchisor's intellectual property rights or to maintain the common identity and reputation of the franchised network; these other obligations can include:

(a) minimum quality specifications

(b) not to compete during, or for up to one year after, the existence of the franchise agreement with the other members of the franchise network

(c) to use its best endeavours to sell the goods or provide the services

(d) to stock and to offer for sale a minimum range of goods and to achieve a minimum turnover

(e) to pay to the franchisor a specified proportion of its, the franchisee's revenue, for advertising and itself carry out advertising for the nature of which it shall obtain the franchisor's approval.

Additionally, the Block Exemption will apply even if the franchisee is bound, for example:

(a) not to disclose the know how provided by the franchisor to third parties (and the franchisee can be held to this even after termination of the agreement)

(b) to communicate to the franchisor any experience gained in exploiting the franchise and grant it, and other franchisees, a non-exclusive licence for the know how resulting from that experience

(c) to inform the franchisor of infringements of the franchisor's intellectual property rights and then either to take legal action against infringers or to join with the franchisor in taking such legal action

(d) only to use the franchisor's know how to exploit the franchise

(e) to attend or have its staff attend training courses arranged by the franchisor

The franchisor may also demand the right to carry out checks on the franchisee's contract premises and even ensure that its means of transport are appropriate.

Finally, the franchisor can make the rights and obligations under the franchise agreement only assignable with its, the franchisor's, consent.

Restrictions Which Have To Be Excluded From Franchise Agreements

The Block Exemption Regulation also contains a "Black List", specifying what restrictive clauses are not to be included in a franchise agreement if it is to benefit from the automatic exemption from article 85(1) of the Treaty. The exemption shall, for example, not apply where:

(a) undertakings producing goods or providing services which are identical or which are considered by users as interchangeable enter into franchise agreements in respect of such goods or services

(b) the franchisee is prevented from continuing to use the licensed know-how after termination of the agreement where the know-how has become generally known or easily accessible other than by breach of an obligation by the franchisee

(c) the franchisor can fix prices (although, the franchisor is permitted to recommend prices)

(d) the franchisor prohibits the franchisee from challenging the validity of the intellectual property rights forming part of the franchise

(e) franchisees are obliged not to supply within the Common Market the goods or services which are the subject matter of the franchise to end users because of their place of residence

The Right of The Commission To Withdraw the Benefit of the Block Exemption

If the Commission finds in a particular case that an agreement otherwise falling within this Block Exemption nevertheless has certain effects which are anti-competitive, then it may withdraw the benefit of the Block Exemption to that agreement. In determining whether to withdraw the benefit of the Block Exemption, the Commission will look in particular at agreements where territorial protection is awarded to the franchisee and this has the effect of, for example, significantly restricting access to the relevant market or diminishing competition within that territory by means of the cumulative effect of parallel networks of similar agreements established by competing manufacturers or distributors. Similarly where territorial protection is awarded to the franchisee, the Block Exemption may be withdrawn where franchisees engage in concerted practices relating to the sale prices of goods or services. These and the other grounds for withdrawing the benefit indicate that there must be some serious effect on competition for the removal of the Block Exemption in particular circumstances.

Franchise Agreements Including Other Categories of Clauses May Still Benefit from The Block Exemption

The Block Exemption establishes a procedure (the opposition procedure) for notifying the Commission of franchise agreements which include clauses which are restrictive of competition within the Common Market but which do not fall squarely within the prohibitions and permissions of the franchise agreement Block Exemption. The Commission has six months from notification to oppose exemption of the agreement. If the Commission fails to act within the six months, then the agreement is effectively deemed within the Block Exemption. Generally, where the Commission does oppose an agreement it can withdraw that opposition at any time. The situation is different where the opposition was raised at the request of a Member State.

Implications for Industry

The Commission, in this Block Exemption, recognises that franchise agreements often improve the distribution of goods and services in that they give franchisors the opportunity to establish a uniform network with limited investment. The Block Exemption is designed to encourage the development of small businesses which can benefit from the franchisor's experience and assistance. These small business should then be able to compete more effectively with large distribution undertakings. The benefit for the consumer is said to be consistency in quality. © **Pinsent & Co 1991**

Business Contracts of Supply, Product Liability, and Negligence

Robert Bradgate and Shane Russell

The Common Law of Contract

Preliminary

Most goods are supplied in the course of business pursuant to contracts of supply. Although special statutory rules apply to contracts involving the supply of goods, the basic common law of contract applies to those contracts as to any other, except as modified by the relevant statutes. The common law therefore underpins the statutory rules which govern supply contracts. It governs the formation and variation of contracts and provides the basic rules concerning the incorporation of terms into contracts.

1. Agreement

A contract is a legally binding agreement between two or more parties. The legal basis of a contract is agreement. Subject to certain restrictions, the parties are free to agree any terms they like and the court will not make a contract for them. No contract is formed until the parties reach agreement on all its essential terms. However, agreement is analyzed artificially in terms of "offer" and "acceptance". The parties are deemed to be in agreement when one party has made an offer which is accepted by the other. Agreement is judged objectively, by examining the outward appearance created by the words and conduct of the parties. Thus the parties will be deemed to be in agreement provided that objectively they appear to be in agreement, even if in fact they intend different things.

1.1. Offer

An offer is a statement by one party which indicates a definite intention to be bound if the other party agrees to its terms. An offer can be made in writing, orally or by conduct. If its terms are accepted it will be converted into a binding contract. It follows therefore that if the person making a statement reserves the right to negotiate further, the statement is not an offer but merely a stage in negotiations.

Since an offer is converted into a contract by acceptance, it must set out the essential terms of the contract with sufficient clarity and certainty to allow a court to enforce them if necessary. If the terms of an agreement are incomplete or unclear a court may conclude that the parties have not yet made a contract.

Certain situations have been analyzed by the courts in decided cases. The decisions of the courts in previous cases do not lay down hard and fast rules, but generally:-

(a) Estimates (e.g: to manufacture goods or machinery) will be regarded as offers.

(b) Tenders will be treated as offers (so that the person who requested the tenders will have the right to choose which to accept).

(c) Price lists are generally not offers but may be so if circulated by a manufacturer of products or to a limited number of customers. A person who sends out a price list may include terms in the list and make it clear that any orders will be made subject to those terms.

(d) Advertisements are generally not offers.

(e) Displays of goods in shop windows are generally not offers.

1.2. Acceptance

An acceptance is an unequivocal agreement to all the terms contained in the offer. If the offeree responds to the offer by attempting to add to or vary its terms his response is not an acceptance of the offer but is regarded as a counter offer which is treated as rejecting the first offer and making a new offer on the terms it contains. Once an offer has been rejected, it cannot be accepted unless a fresh offer is made.

E.g: A offers to sell goods to B for £1000. B replies that the price is too high but that he will pay £850. B has rejected A's offer and made a new offer of his own. A can choose whether to accept or reject it. If A does not accept B's price, B cannot "accept" A's original offer to sell for £1000. If he tries to do so he actually makes a new offer to A to buy for £1000 which A can choose to accept or reject.

1.2.1. Notification of Acceptance.

Acceptance may be by words or by conduct.

Generally acceptance must be notified to the offeror, but the offeror may waive the need for notification. Therefore (e.g.) if A orders goods from B, B may accept A's order by despatching the goods to him.

An acceptance is not valid, and there is therefore no contract, until the offeree notifies the offeror of his acceptance. However, it is generally held that where the parties use the post for their communications, a posted acceptance is effective, and binds both parties, as soon as it is posted. It is possible for the offeror to exclude this rule in the terms of his offer, for instance by stipulating that any acceptance must actually reach him.

1.3. Incomplete Agreements

Agreements which contain vague or ambiguous terms, or where the parties have not agreed all essential terms, or which show that the parties are still negotiating, will not be recognised as contracts and enforced by the courts. However, the courts will normally try to find a binding contract where business people have acted on the basis that they have a contract. The court may be able to imply terms into a contract to fill in any gaps in the agreement: see below. In contracts for the sale and supply of goods there will normally be implied terms dealing with delivery and price of the goods if the parties make no express agreement. It will be implied that the price should be a reasonable price and that delivery will take place within a reasonable time. However, if the parties' agreement shows that they are still negotiating over the price or other terms the court cannot imply any such term. Thus an agreement to sell goods "at a price to be agreed" is incomplete and does not amount to a contract.

1.4. Withdrawal

An offeror may withdraw his offer at any time before it is accepted. He must notify the offeree of the withdrawal. A posted notice of withdrawal will only be effective when it reaches the offeree. If the offeror attempts to withdraw unilaterally after the offeree has accepted, he will be in breach of contract.

1.5. Standard Terms

It is common for businesses to use standard terms to govern their business contracts and to set out those terms on business stationery, order forms etc. Thus a manufacturer of goods might have standard conditions of supply and a potential customer may have standard conditions of purchase. If A places an order with B using his own terms, but B responds with an order acknowledgement including his own terms, there is what has been called a "battle of the forms". The courts have tended to analyze this situation in accordance with the rules of offer - acceptance - counter offer set out above. The effect of this is that there will be no contract until one party accepts the other party's terms. Acceptance may occur if (e.g.) one party returns a signed acknowledgement slip from the other party's terms. Acceptance may also occur by conduct: for instance a supplier may accept his customer's terms if he despatches goods in response to an order on the customer's terms. Alternatively, if the supplier sends out goods together with a delivery note including his own terms, the customer may accept those terms if he retains the goods without objection.

Implications for Industry

These rules are applicable to all business contracts whether for the supply of goods or services. Businesses should take care to include their own standard terms of trading on all company documentation and avoid accepting any offer made by a customer. Tear off slips and other documents originating with the other party should not be returned. No terms should be agreed without reading them.

A party may accept its trading partner's terms inadvertently. Care must be taken to avoid this by ensuring that all staff are aware of the dangers of returning tear off slips etc.

Where neither party is prepared to give way and agree to the terms put forward by the other then there may be no contract at all in law. In that situation it may be desirable for the parties to negotiate a compromise agreement.

2. Consideration

Contract terms are promises which the courts will enforce. The courts will only enforce a promise for which consideration has been given. Essentially this means that gratuitous promises will not be enforced. One promise can be consideration for another: for instance in a contract to supply goods in the future the seller's promise to deliver is consideration for the buyer's promise to pay, and vice versa. Since business contracts normally involve payment, there is generally no problem finding consideration for the creation of a contract. However, the doctrine is important in relation to the variation of existing contracts and in relation to the incorporation of terms into a contract. The law will not recognise "past consideration" as valid consideration for a promise. This means that an act already done, or a promise already made by A, cannot be consideration for a later promise by B. The practical impact of this is that new terms cannot be introduced into a contract after there has been a valid offer and acceptance creating a binding contract. Once a contract has been made, new terms can only be introduced by varying the contract. For a variation to be binding each party must provide consideration, for instance by each promising to do something extra.

Practical Implications

If a contract is made by telephone, or at a meeting, a form sent out afterwards will not alter the terms of the contract unless both parties agree to a variation and provide consideration. A business which wants to rely on its standard terms of trading should take care when taking orders by telephone or in person to make it clear either that all contracts are made subject to those standard terms, or that the telephone conversation (etc.) is not intended to create a contract and that a written document containing the contract terms will be sent out.

An invoice sent out after the goods have been delivered will be ineffective to introduce new terms into the contract.

3. The Terms of the Contract

Contracts may contain express and implied terms. Express terms are those actually agreed by the parties, orally or in writing. Implied terms may be implied by the courts in order to give effect to the intentions of the parties or in order to make their contracts effective. In addition certain terms are automatically implied into contracts for the supply of goods by virtue of the **Sale of Goods Act 1979**, the **Supply of Goods (Implied Terms) Act 1973**, and the **Supply of Goods and Services Act 1982**.

3.1. Express Terms

Express terms are the terms actually agreed by the parties. They may be agreed orally or in writing. Because of the rules of offer and acceptance governing the formation of contracts, express terms will normally be contained in the offer.

3.1.1. Written Contracts

Where the parties enter into a formal written contract it is assumed that agreement is intended to contain all the terms of their contract. A court may refuse to allow a party to use evidence of other documents, letters, conversations, promises etc to add to or vary the terms of the written contract. However, this is not a strong rule and only applies where the written contract was intended to comprise the whole agreement. It does not prevent the parties using external evidence to explain what the terms of the contract mean.

Practical Implications

When entering into a formal written contract make sure that it contains all the terms of the agreement which it is intended to include.

3.1.2. Signed Documents

A person who signs a document will generally be bound by any terms contained in that document, even if he has not read or understood them. The only exception generally available in business transactions is where the signor has been misled by the other party.

Practical Implications

Care should be taken not to sign any document containing contract terms without reading it first. It is unlikely that a business will be able to escape from terms contained in a signed document.

A supplier may use the signature rule in order to incorporate its own terms into its contracts with customers.

A supplier might require all orders to be placed on forms supplied by it and including its own terms of trading. Alternatively it might require customers to sign an initial agreement agreeing that all contracts should be made on the suppliers' terms.

3.1.3. Unsigned Documents

Terms also may be incorporated into contracts from unsigned documents provided reasonable notice of those terms is given to the other contracting party. What is reasonable will vary from case to case but certain general rules are clear:-

1. The document must be of a sort which a reasonable person would expect to contain contract terms. It has been held that this excludes documents such as car park and deck chair tickets, but most business documents such as order forms etc. can be assumed to be contractual documents.

2. The recipient of the unsigned document will not be bound by terms on it if he did not know there was writing on it.

3. The recipient will be bound by terms on the document if he realised that it contained contract terms.

4.   If the recipient knew that the document contained writing but not that it contained contract terms he will be bound by those terms provided the person putting forward the document has taken reasonable steps to bring those terms to his attention.

Reasonable notice requires that the terms should be printed clearly and legibly. They should appear on the face of the document, or, if not, a notice on the face of the document should draw attention to the terms. The document can refer to terms in another document and incorporate those terms by reference, but it will generally be preferable to show that a copy of the document containing the terms has been made available to the other party.

3.1.4. Particular Terms

Where a contract term is unreasonable or unusual, special notice should be drawn to that term. In the absence of special notice, the party seeking to rely on the term will be unable to do so. Terms which are in common use in business contracts, such as retention of title and exclusion clauses, will generally not be regarded as "unusual", but if a term is more stringent or wider in ambit than similar terms used by other businesses in the same field, the term may be regarded as unreasonable and require special notice. Special notice of a term can be given by printing the term in red ink, or by highlighting it; Lord Denning, suggested that such terms could be highlighted by using a red hand to point to them.

Practical Implications

A business wishing to rely on standard or other terms of business should ensure that those terms are printed clearly and legibly on its business documentation. The terms should be included, or mentioned, on the face of documentation: e.g: by including a notice such as "This document includes contract terms which are printed overleaf". Terms should be compared with those used by other similar businesses: any terms which are unusual in nature or in extent should be highlighted in some way.

3.2. Implied Terms

In addition to its express terms a contract may contain implied terms to which the parties are taken to have impliedly agreed. Terms may be implied by the court subject to very strict rules. In general, terms will only be implied if necessary to make the contract work in the way in which the parties as business people must have intended. The court will only imply terms if the parties have reached agreement on sufficient of the important terms to show that they have actually reached the stage of making a contract.

In addition a number of terms are implied automatically by statute into contracts for the supply of goods. There are provisions governing the time when property passes from seller to buyer and the duties of the parties. The most important of the terms relate to the state and quality of the goods delivered under the contract and are examined below (see *Sale of Goods Act,* 1979, *Supply of Goods (Implied Terms) Act,* 1973, *Supply of Goods and Services Act,* 1982.)

In general the parties to a contract can avoid a court implying terms into a contract by agreeing all essential items between themselves: an implied term cannot normally override an express term. However, terms may have to be implied to deal with events not foreseen by the parties. The statutory implied terms may be excluded by an express term, but the right of the seller of goods to exclude the statutory implied terms relating to the quality of goods supplied under the contract is severely restricted by statute. This is examined below.

3.3. Classification of Terms

Traditionally contract terms have been classified into three categories. The classification of a term affects the remedies available if the term is broken.

1. A condition is an important term. If it is broken, the innocent party automatically has the right, if he wishes, to end the contract and refuse to perform it any more. In addition he may claim damages for any loss caused by the breach.

2. A warranty is a less important term. If it is broken, the innocent party may claim damages but may not end the contract.

3. Most terms are now classified as "intermediate terms". If such a term is broken, the innocent party has the right to claim damages for any losses, but may only have the right to terminate the contract if the effects of the breach are serious. It may be difficult to decide if the results of a breach are sufficiently serious to justify termination of the contract.

The parties may classify the terms of their contract by referring to them as "conditions" or "warranties", but classifications are not necessarily binding on a court and in order to avoid uncertainty it may be preferable to classify the term by defining the rights available to the other party if it is broken. A party who regards a term as important and who may want to terminate the contract if that term is broken should seek to have it classified as a condition, or include an express right to terminate the contract if it is broken. A party who wishes to prevent his contract partner from terminating the contract should classify his own contractual obligations as "warranties", or expressly state that breach will only give rise to a claim for damages and not to a right to terminate the contract.

4. Defects in the Formation of Contracts

Statements made or events occurring during the negotiation of a contract may affect its enforceability. Most importantly, a contract may be defective if there is a misrepresentation by one party to another during negotiations.

4.1. Misrepresentation

Statements made during negotiations for a contract may become terms of the contract. If so they bind the parties as indicated above. Even if not terms, statements made during negotiations, either orally or in writing, may be representations. A representation is a statement of fact made before the contract is concluded which induces the other party to enter the contract. Thus a statement about the materials of which goods are made, or their performance capabilities, will normally be a representation. Such a statement may also be a term of the contract.

If a representation is false, it is a misrepresentation and the innocent party will have legal remedies for misrepresentation. The innocent party may rescind the contract and/or claim damages for any losses he has suffered because of the misrepresentation. Rescission involves returning the parties to their position before the contract was made: for instance in a contract for the sale of goods, the buyer would return the goods and recover the price paid for them. Where the misrepresentation was made fraudulently the innocent party may rescind the contract and claim damages for any additional losses. Where the misrepresentation was not fraudulent, damages may be awarded under the **Misrepresentation Act 1967**.

Section 1 allows the victim of the misrepresentation to rescind the contract even though the misrepresentation has become a term of the contract. Thus the victim of a misrepresentation may be able to choose between remedies for misrepresentation and breach of contract in respect of the same statement.

Section 2 allows the court to award damages for misrepresentation even though it was not fraudulent.

Under s.2(1) the court may award damages for additional losses as well as rescinding the contract, unless the person making the misrepresentation shows that he was not negligent; but the court has a general discretion to refuse rescission and under s.2(2) it may award damages instead of rescission in any case where the misrepresentation was not fraudulent; the court might exercise this power where the misrepresentation was relatively trivial.

The combined effect of s.2 is complicated. In essence the court may always give damages instead of rescinding the contract except where the victim of misrepresentation can prove fraud. However, unless the maker of the misrepresentation can show that he took all reasonable care when making the statement in question, the court has power to rescind the contract AND give damages for any losses suffered by the victim.

Section 3 of the Act restricts the right of any contracting party to exclude or restrict his liability for misrepresentation. A contract term which excludes or restricts liability for misrepresentation is ineffective unless it can be shown to be a fair and reasonable term, in accordance with the term laid down by the **Unfair Contract Terms Act 1977**. (See below.)

Practical Implications

Care should be taken during negotiations that any statements made relating to the contract are true. If reasonable care is taken to ensure that statements are accurate, any misrepresentation will be wholly innocent and if a dispute arises, the court will have no power to award damages for additional losses under s. 2(1) of the Misrepresentation Act.

Any exclusion clauses in the contract should cover liability for misrepresentation as well as for breach of contract.

4.2. Other defects

Other defects in formation of the contract may affect the validity of the contract and give one party a right to escape from it. The most important defect which is likely to affect business contracts is duress. In recent years the courts have recognised that the validity of a contract may be affected by "economic duress" where one party uses illegitimate economic pressure to force the other to enter into the contract. The ordinary commercial use of market bargaining power does not amount to duress. If there is duress, the victim of duress may be allowed to have the contract rescinded. The most important application of duress appears to be in relation to variation of contracts (see below).

5. Variation of Contracts

The parties to a contract may vary its terms at any time. A variation will only be effective if both parties agree to it. A variation cannot be unilaterally imposed by one party on the other, and an attempt to vary a contract without the agreement of the other party may amount to a breach of contract.

A variation will generally only be binding if each party gives consideration for it. There will be consideration if the variation can benefit both parties, or if it may work for the benefit of either, but if the variation can only benefit one of the parties, the other will not be bound unless some other consideration is provided. For instance, if A has agreed to build a machine for B for £5000 and then finds that the price is uneconomic, he may seek an increase in the price. Unless the contract terms already include provision for a price increase, a variation will be necessary. If B merely agrees to pay £6000, his promise to pay the extra is not binding because there is no consideration for it. The promise will only be binding if A promises something extra over and above his existing duties, of benefit to B: for instance delivery earlier than the originally agreed delivery date.

Even if there is consideration for a variation, it will not be binding unless both parties freely agree to it. If one party is forced to agree by duress, the variation will not be binding on him. Duress in this context can include unfair economic pressure.

Practical Implications

Because of the difficulties of varying a contract once made, care should be taken to ensure that all required terms are included in the initial agreement. If a variation becomes necessary, if possible, the variation should be so arranged that there is consideration. Alternatively, the variation will be binding without consideration if it is recorded in a deed under seal (when no consideration is necessary.)

6. Privity of Contract

The doctrine of privity of contract states that a contract can only be enforced by or against a person who is a party to that contract. Although there are some exceptions to the general rule, for instance where a contract is made by an agent on behalf of someone else (his principal) the general rule applies to most contracts.

The rule means that a third party affected by a contract made between other people cannot sue on the contract. For instance a manufacturer who sells goods to a retailer for resale cannot be sued *in contract* by a member of the public injured by a defective product. Instead the injured consumer can sue the retailer on his contract and the retailer can sue the manufacturer on the contract between them. However, the rule of privity may be evaded by suing in the tort of **Negligence**; or, in the context of defective products, by the injured consumer suing the manufacturer under the **Consumer Protection Act 1987**. In such a case the rule of privity of contract remains important because the manufacturer will not be able to rely on any clauses in either his contract with the retailer or in the retailer's contract with the consumer to exclude or restrict his liability in tort to the consumer: there is no privity of contract between manufacturer and consumer.

7. Remedies for Breach of Contract

The principle remedy for a breach of contract is a claim for damages. In some cases a court may order that a contract should be specifically performed, but such orders are rare and are mainly used in relation to contracts for the sale of land or other unique items.

7.1. Types of Damages

A person injured by a breach of contract may claim damages to cover losses incurred by relying on the contract, such as wasted expenditure incurred in order to perform the contract, and also for disappointed expectations. For instance, the buyer of defective goods can claim damages being the difference between the value of the goods as they should have been and the value of the defective goods actually delivered. Damages may also be claimed to cover other losses provided that it can be shown that they were caused by the breach of contract. Such damages could include compensation for:-

1. personal injuries suffered by the Plaintiff;

2. damage to the Plaintiff's other property;

3. economic losses suffered due to the breach of contract: for instance a person who bought a machine to use in his business would be able to claim damages to cover the profits he would have made by using the machine if the machine proves defective;

4. an indemnity to cover damages etc. paid to other people as a result of the breach of contract: for instance if a retailer buys goods from a manufacturer and resells them to a consumer the retailer will have to pay damages to the consumer if the goods are defective; the retailer can claim an indemnity from the manufacturer to cover the damages paid to the injured consumer;

5. in some cases, especially of consumer contracts, disappointment and mental distress.

Such damages are recoverable provided it can be shown that the loss in question was caused by the breach of contract, subject to the rules on remoteness of damage and mitigation which are intended to limit the extent of the contract-breaker's liability.

7.2. Remoteness of damage

No damages will be awarded in respect of any loss which was "too remote". To be compensatable, the loss or damage in question must either have resulted directly from the breach as a normal and natural consequence of it, or have been in the reasonable contemplation of both parties at the time the contract was made as likely to result from a breach. For instance, a person buying a machine for use in his business can claim the costs of repair if the machine is defective. He can also claim damages for lost profits, provided the supplier of the machine knew that the machine was to be used in the business to make profits. If the buyer expected to make specially high profits because of special circumstances, he will not be able to claim for those special profits unless the special circumstances were known to the other party.

Practical Implications

A person entering a contract who because of special circumstances affecting him is likely to suffer special losses if the contract is broken should make sure that those special circumstances are made known to the other party. The other party who is notified of such special circumstances should try to take steps to protect himself against becoming liable for damages due to those special circumstances: for instance, he may insert a clause in the contract excluding or limiting his liability (subject to the **Unfair Contract Terms Act 1977**), or arrange insurance to cover any special risk, and increase the contract price to reflect the cost of the insurance.

7.3. Mitigation of Damage

The victim of a breach of contract must take reasonable steps to mitigate his loss arising from any breach: this means that he must try to reduce his damages so far as he can and so far as is reasonable. Mitigation may involve buying replacement goods, accepting an offer to have them repaired, or hiring a replacement while the goods are unavailable. Damages will be assessed on the basis that the victim of the breach did take reasonable steps available to him. A person who fails to take proper steps by way of mitigation may find that he is unable to recover all of his actual losses.

Statutes and other instruments

Name: Sale of Goods Act 1979.

Identity/SI Number: Sale of Goods Act 1979.

Date Effective: 1/1/80.

Interpretation:

Preliminary

The Act applies to all contracts for the sale of goods: that is where ownership of goods is transferred in exchange for a money consideration. It does not apply to other contracts of supply including hire purchase (regulated by the Supply of Goods (Implied Terms) Act 1973), hire, work and materials, barter or exchange (regulated by the Supply of Goods and Services Act, 1982). The Act applies to contracts between businesses and consumer and to contracts between businesses, and lays down a detailed code for contracts for the sale of goods which modify the common law rules applicable to contracts generally. However, where there is no special statutory rule the ordinary common law rules apply. In particular, common law rules govern the formation of the contract.

The Act covers most aspects of the contract of sale, including the price, delivery, the passing of ownership from seller to buyer and the rights of the parties. Most of the provisions of the Act can be excluded or modified by the terms of the contract, although in the important area of the implied terms relating to the quality etc. of the goods delivered under the contract, the seller's right to exclude or modify the terms or his liability for breach of them is restricted by the **Unfair Contract Terms Act 1977**.

There are three main areas of the Act which are particularly important in the context of business contacts and product liability: the implied terms relating to the quality etc. of the goods; the rules governing delivery etc; and the rules governing remedies.

1. Implied Terms Relating to Quality etc

The Act lays down a series of implied terms relating to the quality and condition of the goods to be delivered under the contract. The implied terms are all classified by the Act as either "conditions" or "warranties". The Act makes it clear that where a condition is broken, the buyer has the right to reject the goods and terminate the contract, in addition to claiming damages for any loss suffered due to the breach.

1.1. Title

s.12(1) provides that in a contract of sale there is an implied condition that the seller has the right to sell the goods, or, where the contract requires property to pass from seller to buyer in the future (for instance under a conditional sale where property does not pass until payment), that the seller will have such a right at the time when property is to pass. There can be a breach of this term where the seller sells goods which he does not own, or where the goods breach some right of a third party which allows the third party to restrict their sale or use: for instance where the goods breach a patent or copyright.

This is probably the most fundamental requirement in a contract of sale. Where the seller delivers goods he does not own, case law suggests the buyer will be able to claim a full refund of any money paid under the contract even where he has used the goods for a considerable time.

s.12(2) implies two additional warranties: that the goods are free from encumbrances other than those disclosed to the buyer; and that the buyer will enjoy quiet possession of the goods.

Practical Implications

The implied terms in s.12 should not normally cause difficulties for businesses. However, it should be noted that there will be a breach of the implied condition in s.12(1) if the seller sells goods in breach of copyright etc. This could mean that there will be a breach if the goods are marketed in a way which infringes a trade mark owned by a third party. It also has serious implications for the computer software industry: sale of a program which breaches copyright will not only give rise to copyright liability vis a vis the copyright owner but also be a breach of s.12 vis a vis the buyer of the program. Neither the implied terms in s.12 nor liability for their breach can be excluded by an express contract term, by virtue of s.6 of the **Unfair Contract Terms Act**.

1.2. Description and Quality

Sections 13–15 imply a series of conditions concerned with the quality and physical condition of the goods delivered. Breach of these implied terms will give rise to contractual product liability, and liability for breach is strict. The terms apply equally to sales to consumers or to businesses, although where the buyer is a business it may be possible to exclude them or limit liability for breach.

1.2.1. Goods must comply with their description.

S.13 implies a condition into all sale contracts that where goods are sold by description they should conform to that description. Older cases have held that the following are all part of the description of the goods: the thickness of pieces of timber; the date of shipment of goods bought from overseas; details of the packaging of tins of fruit (tinned fruit to be packed in 24 tins per case: there was a breach when goods were delivered packed 30 tins to the case). The trend of modern case law has been to narrow the ambit of the words "sold by description" and it now seems that goods are sold by description where descriptive words define some essential commercial characteristic of the goods. There can be a sale by description even though the buyer chooses the goods in person: for instance, a person who buys a television set described on its box as having a 24" screen buys the goods by description and there is a breach of this condition if the television does not in fact have a 24" screen.

The section has been strictly applied: a slight variation from the contract description has been held to be a breach entitling the buyer to reject the goods. It is irrelevant that the seller was not at fault.

Practical Implications

Parties should take great care when making contracts for the sale of goods to define what constitutes the contractual description of the goods. Sellers will wish to define the goods in the broadest terms possible; buyers will seek to define the goods precisely in order to maximise the chances of taking advantage of s.13.

1.2.2. Quality and Fitness for Purpose

S.14 modifies the basic rule of *caveat emptor* by implying two conditions into contracts for the sale of goods concerned with the quality and condition of goods delivered under the contract. These two conditions only apply where the seller sells the goods in the course of a business. Recent case law concerned with a similar expression in the **Unfair Contract Terms Act 1977** suggests that a sale may only be in the course of business where the seller sells an item which is part of his stock in trade or where the item sold was bought with a view to resale. However, these implied terms will still apply to most business transactions.

S.14(2) implies a condition that the goods delivered under the contract should be of merchantable quality. "Merchantable quality" is defined by **s.14(6)** which requires them to be "as fit for the purpose or purposes for which goods of that kind are commonly bought as it is reasonable to expect having regard to any description applied to them, the price (if relevant) and all the other relevant circumstances." It is clear that the section creates a flexible standard and there is a great deal of case law on "merchantable quality". The following points can be made:-

1. Where goods can be bought under one description for a range of purposes, the goods will be merchantable provided they are fit for at least one of that range of purposes.

2. Defective or misleading packaging, warnings and instructions may all make goods unmerchantable.

3. Goods are required to be merchantable only at the time of sale, but that involves that at that time they should be reasonably durable. Goods which break down or wear out prematurely may well be regarded as unmerchantable, provided the failure is not due to misuse.

4. Minor or cosmetic defects may make goods unmerchantable, depending on the description used and the price paid.

5. Sale goods and second hand goods are still required to be merchantable, but the standard required may be lower where the goods are described as "second-hand", "used" etc.

Liability under s.14(2) is strict. If the goods are unmerchantable, the seller is liable regardless of the fact that he was not at fault, or that he did not create or even know of the defect; for instance, a dairy was held liable under this section for supplying milk infected with typhoid.

The section also recognises two exceptional situations where there is no implied condition of merchantability. Those are:-

(a) where defects are drawn to the buyer's attention, there is no implied condition as regards those defects and

(b) where the buyer examines the goods before buying them, there is no implied condition as regards defects which that examination ought to reveal (but there is no requirement that the buyer should examine them at all).

s.14(3) implies an additional condition that where the buyer indicates the purpose for which he requires the goods, the goods must be reasonably fit for that purpose. The buyer may make his purpose known expressly or impliedly; where he buys goods for their normal purpose he will impliedly make his purpose known to the seller. The implied condition of fitness for purpose does not apply where the seller can show that:-

(a) the buyer did not rely on the seller's skill or judgement (e.g. where the buyer asks for goods by a trade name) or

(b) it was unreasonable for him to rely on the seller's skill or judgement (e.g. where the seller makes clear that he has no expertise in the particular field).

The terms implied by s.14 can be excluded, or liability for their breach be limited or excluded, by an appropriate term in the contract but only subject to the terms of the **Unfair Contract Terms Act 1977**

Practical Implications

The implied terms in s.14 are very important. They apply to all business sales in all sectors and form the basis for most contractual product liability claims. Sellers should seek to minimise liability by drawing known defects to the attention of the buyer and by encouraging the buyer to inspect goods where possible. Where the buyer states a specific purpose the seller should make it clear if he has no expertise in that area, in order to exclude the operation of s.14(3).

Buyers should maximise their chances of relying on the implied conditions. In particular, a buyer who wishes to use goods for a particular purpose should expressly make that purpose known to the seller, in order to allow himself to rely on s.14(3).

1.2.3. Sales by sample

When goods are sold by sample, **s.15** implies three further terms:-

1. that the bulk will correspond to the sample in quality.

2. that the buyer will have a reasonable opportunity to compare the bulk with the sample; and

3. that the bulk will be free from any defect rendering the goods unmerchantable but not apparent on reasonable examination of the sample.

1.3. Remedies for breach of the implied terms

All of the implied terms apart from those in s.12(2) are expressly classified as conditions. Where a condition is broken, the Act allows the buyer to reject the goods and, if he wishes, treat the contract as repudiated, so that he may terminate the contract, refuse to perform his obligations and recover any money he has paid. In addition the buyer can claim damages for any further losses he suffers due to the breach. Where the seller has delivered defective goods such damages may include damages for personal injuries, property damage, economic losses or indemnities against claims by third parties. Breach of a warranty entitles the buyer to claim damages but not to reject the goods.

However, **s.11(4)** restricts the buyer's right to reject the goods for breach of condition: he loses the right to reject if he has accepted the goods or any part of them. The buyer may not normally accept part of the goods and reject the rest, unless the contract is a severable one (under which the goods are delivered and paid for by instalments). (If the contract is severable, the buyer is generally only entitled to reject the defective instalment, unless the breach is so serious as to undermine the whole contract). This position may be modified by terms in the contract, subject to the terms of the **Unfair Contract Terms Act 1977.** The result is that if any of the goods are defective the buyer is entitled to reject all of them.

Acceptance is defined by s.35 as qualified by s.34.

s.35 indicates that the buyer may be taken to have accepted goods so as to lose the right to reject them in the following three situations.

1. He expressly indicates that he accepts the goods.

2. He does any act "inconsistent with the seller's ownership". This seems to mean an act inconsistent with rejection of the goods, such as reselling the goods or giving them away as a gift; consuming the goods; or making attempts to have them repaired without consulting the seller. **s.34** provides that, unless the contract provides otherwise, when the goods are delivered to the buyer the seller must allow him a reasonable opportunity to examine the goods. An inconsistent act will not amount to acceptance until the buyer has had a reasonable opportunity to examine the goods.

3. He retains the goods beyond any time limit for rejecting them stipulated in the contract, or, in the absence of a time limit, beyond a reasonable time. It seems that what is a reasonable time will depend on the facts of the case and in particular on the nature and complexity of the goods. Recent cases suggest that the right to reject may be lost very quickly, even before a defect has manifested itself.

Practical Implications

These provisions are of great importance to both buyers and sellers.

Buyers should take care not to lose the right to reject. They should examine the goods at the earliest opportunity after delivery and notify the seller of any defects as soon as possible. In the event that any of the goods are defective they should notify the seller of their intention to reject all of the goods. (In practice the parties may then negotiate some settlement in which the seller may agree to replace or repair the defective goods.) In order to protect the right to reject, buyers should not attempt to repair defective goods independently of the seller.

Sellers should seek to minimise the risk of the buyer rejecting the goods. The contract may restrict the right of rejection, allowing the buyer to reject only those of the goods which are defective, although such a term will be subject to the provisions of the **Unfair Contract Terms Act 1977.** The contract should also fix a time limit for rejection. Alternatively the seller may require the buyer to sign an acceptance note indicating that the goods have been accepted.

If the buyer rejects where he is not entitled to do so, either because there is no breach of condition or because he has already accepted the goods, he will be in breach of contract and the seller may be able to claim damages for non-acceptance.

2. Delivery and related matters

The terms of the contract of supply will normally fix matters such as the time, place and means of delivery. In the absence of such agreement, **s.29** provides that delivery should take place at the seller's place of business. within a reasonable time after the making of the contract and at a reasonable time of day.

The provisions of **s.30** are of much greater practical significance. They give the buyer extensive rights to reject the goods if the wrong quantity is delivered.

s.30(1) provides that if the seller delivers a smaller quantity than required by the contract the buyer may either (a) keep the goods delivered and pay the relevant proportion of the contract price or (b) reject the goods delivered.

ss.30(2) and 30(3) together provide that if the seller delivers a larger quantity than required by the contract, the buyer (a) may keep the contract quantity and reject the rest or (b) reject all of the goods or (c) keep all the goods and pay for the extra at the contract rate.

s.30(4) applies where the seller delivers the goods he contracted to sell together with other goods not of the contract description. The buyer may accept the goods which conform to the contract and reject the rest, or reject all of the goods delivered.

Practical Implications

These sections give the buyer wide powers to reject goods which conform to the contract where the wrong quantity is delivered. The buyer may seek to rely on these rights to escape from the contract if it proves to be uneconomical. To avoid this the seller should take care to deliver the correct quantity and should protect himself by including in the contract appropriate provisions allowing him to deviate by small amounts from the contract quantity: e.g: "plus or minus 5%".

Buyers should examine all deliveries carefully as soon as possible after delivery to ensure that the correct quantity of goods has been delivered.

3. Remedies

The right of the buyer to reject goods which do not conform to the contract or for breach of the implied terms has already been noted. If the buyer rejects, the seller is treated as if he has not delivered and the buyer may claim damages for non-delivery.

The rules governing damages for breach of sale contracts are basically similar to those applying in the general law of contract but are modified slightly by the provisions of the Act.

s.51 applies where the seller fails to deliver, including where the buyer has rejected the goods for breach of condition. The buyer's damages will ordinarily be assessed by reference to the difference between the contract price and the market price for similar goods at the date when the goods should have been delivered. This rule only applies if there is an "available market" for goods of the contract description, which for this purpose means that demand does not exceed supply, so that the buyer can buy an alternative. The section will not apply if the goods are unique so that there cannot be said to be an "available market": e.g. for second hand goods or for goods manufactured to the buyer's order.

The practical effect of s.51 is to modify the rule on mitigation of damages in sale of goods cases. The buyer's damages will normally be fixed by reference to the market price and so the buyer should seek an alternative supply as soon as possible after the seller fails to deliver or after rejecting the goods. However, the buyer may be allowed a reasonable time to decide what to do: for instance to try to persuade the seller to deliver, or to replace the goods. In a rising market a buyer should take steps to obtain alternative goods as quickly as possible once it is clear that the seller will not deliver.

If the buyer chooses to keep defective or substandard goods, **s.53** applies. Damages are basically calculated in accordance with the general rules applying in contract, and in general where the buyer complains of defective quality the damages are the difference between the value of the defective goods actually delivered and the value the goods would have had they conformed to the contract; where the goods can be repaired, this will often be the cost of repair. The buyer may make his claim by withholding part or all of the price.

s.54 allows the buyer to claim additional damages for any special losses where the ordinary rules of contract law would allow him to do so. This means that the buyer may claim additional damages, e.g:

for lost profits he would have made by reselling the goods or by using them;

for injuries he suffers or for damage to other property;

for an indemnity against damages paid to other persons injured by the goods; or

(in consumer cases) for distress or disappointment,

subject to the general contract rules on mitigation of damages and remoteness of damage.

The seller may seek to limit his liability in damages for breach of contract by including appropriate terms in the contract of supply. Such a term may be effective but will be subject to the terms of the **Unfair Contract Terms Act 1977**.

Name: Supply of Goods (Implied Terms) Act, 1973

Identity: Supply of Goods (Implied Terms) Act, 1973

Date effective: 18.5.1973 (original); 19.5.1985 (as amended)

Interpretation

Preliminary

Much of this Act has now been superseded by provisions in the **Unfair Contract Terms Act 1977** and the **Sale of Goods Act 1979** but parts of the Act remain in force and govern contracts of hire purchase. Broadly the Act implies into hire purchase contracts similar terms as to quality etc. of the goods supplied as those implied into sale contracts by the **Sale of Goods Act 1979**, but with some important modifications.

"Hire purchase agreement" is defined in s. 15(1) as an agreement under which (i) goods are bailed to the customer in return for periodical payments and (ii) property in the goods will pass to the customer if the terms of the agreement are complied with and the customer exercises an option to buy or some condition specified in the agreement is fulfilled.

1.1. Title

s.8. is the equivalent of **s.12** of the **Sale of Goods Act 1979**. It implies into hire purchase contracts a condition that the supplier will have a right to sell the goods at the time when property is to pass under the contract, and warranties that the goods are free from undisclosed charges and encumbrances and that the hirer/purchaser will enjoy quiet possession of the goods.

These implied terms cannot be excluded.

1.2. Quality and Description

s.9 is the equivalent of s.13 of the **Sale of Goods Act 1979**. It implies into hire purchase contracts a condition that if the goods are hired by description they should correspond to that description.

The condition can be excluded, subject to the **Unfair Contract Terms Act 1977**

---

s.10 is the equivalent of s.14 of the **Sale of Goods Act 1979**. It implies into hire purchase contracts a condition that the goods should be of merchantable quality and fit for the hirer/purchaser's purpose where that is made known to the seller.

"Merchantable quality" is defined in s. 15(2) of the Act. It has the same meaning as in s. 14(6) of the **Sale of Goods Act 1979**.

Both implied conditions are subject to the same exceptions as apply to the equivalent conditions in the **Sale of Goods Act 1979**.

The conditions can be excluded, subject to the **Unfair Contract Terms Act 1977**.

s.11 is the equivalent of s.15 of the **Sale of Goods Act 1979**. It implies into hire purchase contracts a condition that where the goods are hired by reference to a sample

(a) the goods should correspond to the sample

(b) the hirer/purchaser will have a reasonable opportunity to compare bulk and sample and

(c) the bulk will be free of defects making the goods unmerchantable not apparent on a reasonable examination of the sample.

The conditions can be excluded, subject to the **Unfair Contract Terms Act 1977**.

2. Remedies for the customer under a hire purchase contract

The remedies available to the customer under a hire purchase contract are broadly similar to those available to a buyer under a sale contract. However there is one notable difference. There is no equivalent in the 1973 Act to the rules on acceptance in the **Sale of Goods Act 1979**. A hirer/purchaser only loses the right to terminate the contract for breach of implied condition if he has affirmed the contract. Affirmation cannot take place unless the hirer/purchaser is aware of the breach. Thus under a hire purchase contract the hirer/purchaser cannot lose the right to reject defective goods before he is aware of the defect, in contrast to the position of a buyer under a sale contract.

In practice it may be difficult to distinguish between hire purchase and conditional sale agreements. **Ss.14–15** therefore apply to conditional sale agreements where the buyer deals as a consumer as defined in the **Unfair Contract Terms Act 1977** and provides that in such conditional sale agreements the buyer will not lose the right to reject the goods by acceptance under s.11(4) of the **Sale of Goods Act 1979**. This only applies to a "conditional sale agreement" where the seller retains title to the goods until he is paid or some other condition is satisfied AND the price is payable by instalments. The result is that in such a case, the buyer's right to reject goods is substantially extended.

Where the goods supplied under a hire purchase contract are defective and the hirer/purchaser rejects them, he may not be able to recover the whole of instalments already paid under the contract as he will have had the benefit of using the goods. Subject to that, if the goods are defective the hirer/purchaser has the same rights to damages for injuries, damage to property, loss of profits and other losses as the buyer under a sale contract.

Name: Supply of Goods and Services Act 1982

Identity: Supply of Goods and Services Act 1982

Date effective: 4.1.1983

Interpretation

Preliminary

This Act applies to a wide range of contracts not covered by the **Sale of Goods Act 1979** or the **Supply of Goods (Implied Terms) Act 1982.** Part I of the Act is concerned with contracts for the supply of goods. Broadly the purpose of the Act is to imply into all contracts of supply terms relating to the quality etc. of the goods supplied similar to those implied into sale contracts by the **Sale of Goods Act 1979**. Part II of the Act is concerned with contracts for the supply of services.

Sections 1–5 govern contracts for the transfer of property in goods and sections 6–10 govern contracts for the hire of goods.

1. Supply Contracts

1.1. The contracts covered

s.1 identifies the contracts covered by ss1-5. Any contract under which one person transfers or agrees to transfer the property in goods to another person is covered except:

1) a contract of sale of goods;

2) a hire purchase agreement;

3) a contract for the supply of goods in exchange for trading stamps.

4) a transfer made in a deed for no consideration.

5) a contract for the transfer of goods intended to operate as a mortgage, pledge or security.

The Act therefore applies to contracts of barter, exchange, part-exchange and work and materials (where goods are supplied and work is done for the customer, as where a car is serviced or a domestic appliance repaired with new parts). The result is that all contracts involving the transfer of property in goods are regulated by either the **Sale of Goods Act 1979**, the **Supply of Goods (Implied Terms) Act 1982** or by this Act.

1.2.1. Title

s.2 is the equivalent of s.12 of the **Sale of Goods Act 1979**. It implies into contracts for the supply of goods a condition that the supplier will have a right to sell the goods at the time when property is to pass under the contract and warranties that the goods are free from undisclosed charges and encumbrances and that the customer will enjoy quiet possession of the goods.

These implied terms cannot be excluded.

1.2.2. Description and Quality

s.3 is the equivalent of s.13 of the **Sale of Goods Act 1979**. It implies into contracts for the supply of goods a condition that if the goods are supplied by description they should correspond to that description.

The condition can be excluded, subject to the **Unfair Contract Terms Act 1977**

s.4 is the equivalent of s.14 of the **Sale of Goods Act 1979**. It implies into contracts for the supply of goods conditions that the goods should be of merchantable quality and fit for the customer's purpose where that is made known to the supplier.

"Merchantable quality" is defined in s. 4(9) of the Act. It has the same meaning as in s. 14(6) of the **Sale of Goods Act 1979**.

Both implied conditions are subject to the same exceptions as apply to the equivalent conditions in the **Sale of Goods Act 1979**.

The conditions can be excluded, subject to the **Unfair Contract Terms Act 1977**.

s.5 is the equivalent of s.15 of the **Sale of Goods Act 1979**. It implies into contracts for the supply of goods a condition that where the goods are supplied by reference to a sample

(a) the goods should correspond to the sample

(b) the customer will have a reasonable opportunity to compare bulk and sample and

(c) the bulk will be free of defects making the goods unmerchantable not apparent on a reasonable examination of the sample.

The conditions can be excluded, subject to the **Unfair Contract Terms Act 1977**.

1.3. Remedies for the customer under a supply contract

The remedies available to the customer under a supply contract are broadly similar to those available to a buyer under a sale contract. However there is no equivalent in the 1982 Act to the rules on acceptance in the **Sale of Goods Act 1979**. A customer only loses the right to terminate the contract of supply for breach of implied condition if he has affirmed the contract. Affirmation cannot take place unless the customer is aware of the breach. The position is the same as under a hire purchase or conditional sale contract and the customer cannot lose the right to reject defective goods before he is aware of the defect, in contrast to the position of a buyer under a sale contract.

If the customer does terminate a supply contract for breach of implied term, he may not be able to recover payments already made if he has received a benefit under the contract, for instance under a contract for work and materials where the work is satisfactory. However, the customer's right to claim damages for any losses caused by defective goods are exactly the same as under a contract of sale and damages may include compensation for personal injuries, damage to property, the cost of repairing or replacing the defective goods themselves, loss of profits, indemnities against compensation paid to third parties and (in a consumer case) possibly disappointment or distress.

2. Hire Contracts

Ss.6–10 apply to any contract by which one person agrees to hire goods to another is covered, except a contract of hire purchase or a contract of hire in exchange for trading stamps.

2.1. Title

s.7 is the equivalent of s.12 of the **Sale of Goods Act 1979**. It implies into contracts of hire a condition that the supplier has right to transfer possession of the goods by way of hire for the duration of the hiring and a warranty that the hirer will enjoy quiet possession of the goods for the period of the hiring.

These implied terms can be excluded subject to the terms of the **Unfair Contract Terms Act 1977**.

2.2. Quality and Description

s.8 is the equivalent of s.13 of the **Sale of Goods Act 1979**. It implies into contracts of hire a condition that if the goods are hired by description they should correspond to that description.

The condition can be excluded, subject to the **Unfair Contract Terms Act 1977**

s.9 is the equivalent of s.14 of the **Sale of Goods Act 1979**. It implies into contracts of hire conditions that the goods should be of merchantable quality and fit for the customer's purpose where that is made known to the supplier.

"Merchantable quality" is defined in s. 9(9) of the Act. It has the same meaning as in s. 14(6) of the **Sale of Goods Act 1979**.

Both implied conditions are subject to the same exceptions as apply to the equivalent conditions in the **Sale of Goods Act 1979**.

The conditions can be excluded, subject to the **Unfair Contract Terms Act 1977**.

s.10 is the equivalent of s.15 of the **Sale of Goods Act 1979**. It implies into contracts of hire a condition that where the goods are hired by reference to a sample:

(a) the goods should correspond to the sample

(b) the customer will have a reasonable opportunity to compare bulk and sample and

(c) the bulk will be free of defects making the goods unmerchantable not apparent on a reasonable examination of the sample.

The conditions can be excluded, subject to the **Unfair Contract Terms Act 1977**.

Remedies for the hirer under a hire contract.

Where an implied condition is broken, the hirer has the right to terminate the contract. There is no equivalent to the rules on acceptance in the **Sale of Goods Act 1979** so that the hirer only loses the right to terminate the contract if he affirms it. A contract can only be affirmed if the hirer knows of the breach so that the hirer cannot lose the right to terminate the contract until the defect has become apparent.

If the hirer does terminate the contract for breach of condition, hire charges already paid may not be recoverable since the hirer has had the use of the goods. However, if the goods are defective the hirer will be entitled to damages which may include compensation for personal injuries, damage to property, the cost of repairing or replacing the defective goods themselves, loss of profits, indemnities against compensation paid to third parties and (in a consumer case) possibly disappointment or distress.

3. Contracts for the supply of services

Part II of the Act regulates contracts for the supply of services. By **s. 12** this part of the Act applies to all contracts for the supply of services including contracts for the supply of services and goods, such as a contract to service a car or repair machinery. The Act implies terms into such contracts including a term governing the degree of skill required of the supplier of the service.

s.13 implies into contracts for the supply of services a term that the service should be carried out with reasonable skill and care. Unlike the implied terms relating to goods, the term is not classified as a condition or warranty. Therefore if the work is not carried out with proper skill and care, the customer will only have the right to terminate the contract if the breach is serious.

The term requires the supplier of the service to exercise reasonable skill and care. The standard is the same as that in the tort of **Negligence**. Liability is not strict, in contrast to liability for goods.

In some cases, particularly where the contract is for work and materials (e.g: servicing a car) it may be difficult to say whether damage was caused by defective goods or poor workmanship. Because liability for goods is strict whereas liability for work is only imposed where there is a lack of proper care it is important for a customer who wishes to complain to obtain evidence as to whether the defect was caused by poor work or by defective parts.

If work is not carried out with reasonable skill and care, the customer may claim damages for any losses suffered, which may include compensation for personal injuries, damage to property, the cost of repairing or replacing the defective goods themselves, loss of profits, indemnities against compensation paid to third parties and (in a consumer case) possibly disappointment or distress.

Liability under s.13 can be excluded or restricted by terms in the contract, subject to the **Unfair Contract Terms Act 1977.**

Name: Unfair Contract Terms Act 1977.

Identity: Unfair Contract Terms Act 1977.

Date effective: 1.2.1978

Interpretation

Preliminary

This is a very important piece of legislation. It affects all businesses and restricts the extent to which a business may use notices or contract terms to exclude, limit or restrict liability for breach of contract or for the tort of negligence. The Act applies to a wide range of contract terms and notices and contains a number of provisions designed to prevent its rules being evaded. However, despite its title, the Act does not give a general power to the court to intervene in contracts which are thought to be unfair, but only prevents reliance on certain contract terms which restrict or exclude legal liability.

The effectiveness of a notice or contract term may depend on:-

1. the nature of the loss suffered: the Act distinguishes in some cases between personal injuries (including death) and other types of loss;

2. the legal basis of liability: contract or tort; strict liability or negligence; liability under statutory implied terms or otherwise;

3. the capacity of the Plaintiff; where the Plaintiff is "dealing as consumer" it is generally more difficult to exclude liability;

4. the extent to which liability is modified: in general restrictions on liability are more likely to be effective than blanket exclusions of liability.

Care must be taken when drafting contracts or using notices or contract terms. Some clauses may be made wholly ineffective by this Act and in some cases the use of an ineffective term or notice may constitute a criminal offence.

1. The types of clause covered by the Act.

s. 13. This section lists the types of clause/notice regulated by the Act. Any clause which excludes or restricts liability (e.g: "our liability shall not exceed £500", "our liability is restricted to the refund of the price"), or which imposes restrictions on the enforcement of liability (e.g. "claims must be notified within 3 days"), or which excludes or restricts remedies (e.g. "no refunds"), or which excludes or restricts rules of evidence (e.g. "no refunds without production of receipt", "the decision of our engineer shall be final") is regulated by the Act. In addition it has been held that a clause which purports to prevent liability arising (e.g. "the implied terms in the Sale of Goods Act do not apply to this contract", "we accept no duty of care in negligence") is also regulated by the Act.

2. Negligence Liability

s.2. restricts the extent to which a business may exclude or restrict its liability for loss caused by its negligence. This includes the liability in **negligence** of a manufacturer of a defective product to a person injured by that product but also includes any other liability for failing to take reasonable care, including the liability of occupiers of business premises to visitors to their premises under the Occupiers' Liability Act 1957 and breach of a contract term requiring reasonable skill and care, such as that in s.13 of the **Supply of Goods and Services Act 1982.**

The section provides that liability for personal injury or death caused by negligence can never be excluded or restricted. Liability for other kinds of loss can be excluded or restricted if such exclusion/restriction is reasonable.

This section does not affect a term in a contract between A and B whereby A agrees to indemnify B against any liability B may incur to a third party. This section therefore does not prevent a manufacturer requiring his customers to indemnify him against any liability he may incur in **negligence**, or under the **Consumer Protection Act 1987** to consumers of his products. However, such an indemnity will generously be coupled with a term excluding B's liability to A under the contract, and that exclusion will be regulated by the the Unfair Contract Terms Act.

Practical implications

This section severely restricts the ability of a negligent person or body to exclude or restrict liability for that negligence. Contracts and notices should not purport to exclude or restrict liability for personal injury caused by negligence. In other cases careful consideration should be given to what is likely to be regarded as reasonable.

Because liability for personal injury and/or death cannot be excluded, businesses should ensure that they have adequate insurance cover to protect them in case of such liability being imposed.

3. Supply of Goods

Ss.6-7 severely restrict the ability of a supplier of goods to exclude or restrict liability for breach of the implied terms in contracts for the sale and supply of goods implied by s.12-15 of the **Sale of Goods Act 1979** and the similar provisions in the **Supply of Goods (Implied Terms) Act 1973** and the **Supply of Goods and Services Act 1982.**

Liability for breach of the terms concerned with title in sale, hire purchase, or other supply contracts (s.12 Sale of Goods Act, s 8 Supply of Goods (Implied Terms) Act 1973 and s.2 Supply of Goods and Services Act 1982) can never be excluded or restricted. Liability for a breach of the implied term in hire contracts that the hirer has a right to transfer possession of the goods (s7 Supply of Goods and Services Act 1982) can be excluded/restricted if the excluding/restricting term satisfies the test of reasonableness. Liability for breach of the terms concerned with correspondence with description, quality, fitness for purpose and correspondence with sample (ss. 13–15 Sale of Goods Act, ss. 9–11 Supply of Goods (Implied Terms) Act

1973, ss. 3-5 Supply of Goods and Services Act 1982) can never be excluded or restricted where the buyer deals as a consumer. In other cases exclusion/restriction of liability is permitted if the clause is reasonable.

"Consumer" has an extended meaning. It is defined in s.12 of the Act. A person deals as a consumer if he does not buy the goods in the course of a business, the supplier supplies the goods in the course of a business and the goods are of a type ordinarily supplied for private use or consumption. A wide range of goods, including motor cars, furniture, electrical equipment etc., other than for resale, may fall into this description. It has been held that a business may be dealing as consumer if it buys goods of a type it does not ordinarily deal in.

Practical Implications

A business which supplies goods to the public is unlikely to be able to restrict its liability for breach of the statutory implied terms in the supply contract. Because of the strict standard of liability created by the implied terms, many product liability claims will be brought against the retailer/supplier.

Businesses which supply goods to other businesses may be able to restrict liability for breach of the implied terms, provided any exclusion clause is considered reasonable by the court. The combined effect of these rules may be that contractual product liability claims have to be borne by retailers.

All businesses should consider their terms of business carefully and take legal advice. If dealing with the public, no attempt should be made to exclude the statutory implied terms. Appropriate insurance should be taken out to cover potential product liability claims. Businesses should also check the terms of business used by their suppliers to ensure that product liability claims can be passed back to the manufacturer if necessary.

S.3. This section regulates any attempt to exclude liability for any other breach of contract. Such a clause will be ineffective unless reasonable if either (a) the other party to the contract deals as a consumer or (b) the clause appears in the written standard terms of business of the party seeking to rely on it.

Indemnities

The Act imposes some restrictions on indemnity clauses which might otherwise be used to evade the restrictions on exclusion clauses. However, as between businesses, indemnities against liabilities to third parties may be perfectly valid.

S.4 provides that a contract term may not be used to make a consumer indemnify the other party of a contract against liability to the consumer himself or to anyone else, for breach of contract or for negligence, unless the term is reasonable.

In contracts between businesses, an indemnity against a third-party liability (e.g., in a contract between A and B, a clause whereby B indemnifies A against liability to C) is unaffected by the Act and perfectly valid. However, an indemnity against liability to the indemnifier is treated as as exclusion of liability and subject to the Act.

Practical implications

This section covers a wide range of clauses, including, e.g., clauses allowing late delivery or giving a right to replace the goods ordered with other similar goods etc. Since most businesses use standard terms of trading, most exclusion clauses are likely to be subject to the reasonableness test under s.3. Consideration should be given to linking limitations of liability to the amount of insurance cover available to the business, as this is likely to be factor affecting reasonableness.

4. Guarantees

s.5. applies to exclusion and similar clauses in guarantees. No clause in a guarantee may exclude or limit (etc.) liability for any loss or damage caused by a product which proves defective while in consumer use due to negligence in manufacture. Goods are in consumer use provided they are not used exclusively for business purposes.

Practical implications

This is a very wide provision. A manufacturer generally has no contract with the ultimate user of his product but if the product causes loss to the user the manufacturer may be held liable in the tort of **negligence**. This section means that the manufacturer cannot use a clause in a guarantee to exclude or limit that liability. Any attempt to do so is likely to be a criminal offence under the **Consumer Transactions (Restrictions on Statements) Order 1976.** This section is wider than s.2 (above) because it prevents exclusion of liability for any type of loss caused by negligence. The manufacturer is therefore unable to limit or exclude liability to the ultimate consumer. Manufacturers of products intended for consumer use should therefore:-

1. take appropriate steps to ensure that liability in negligence will not arise (see: **"Negligence"**);

2. take out appropriate insurance to cover potential liability;

3. consider requiring their customers to indemnify them against such liability; whilst such a clause is not prohibited by the Act, it must be used together with an exclusion of contractual liability to the customer, and that exclusion will be regulated by ss.6–7.

5. Reasonableness

Many exclusion and limitation clauses are subjected to a reasonableness test which gives the court a discretion to prevent reliance on the clause unless it is found to be reasonable. S.11 defines the test and Schedule 2 of the Act lists a number of factors which the court will take into account in deciding if a clause is reasonable. Factors include the relative bargaining power of the parties to the contract, the degree of notice given to the clause, and the availability to the customer of any choice.

Practical implications

Businesses should take legal advice on the effectiveness of any exclusion clauses they wish to rely on. In the light of decided cases the following matters should be borne in mind, as likely to influence a court's decision on reasonableness:-

(a) clauses should be printed clearly, legibly and in intelligible language;

(b) the customer should be offered a choice: e.g: to pay a higher price for a contract without the exclusion clause (a "two-tier service");

(c) a limitation of liability is more likely to be reasonable than a total exclusion;

(d) any limitation should be linked to the level of insurance cover available to the business;

(e) consideration should be given to the practice of other similar businesses: a clause which is much more stringent than those used by similar businesses may be regarded as unreasonable;

(f) if a business adopts a policy of settling claims without reference to its exclusion clause, a court may refuse to allow it to rely on the clause should it wish to do so; a business which has such a clause in its terms of trading should therefore rely strictly on it if disputes arise.

General overview

The Unfair Contract Terms Act affects all businesses by restricting their ability to restrict or exclude liability for supplying defective products or other legal liabilities. Businesses dealing with the public and those manufacturing consumer items are most seriously affected since the Act prevents any exclusion of liability for breach of the implied terms relating to quality etc. in a consumer contract or any exclusion of liability for manufacturer's negligence in a consumer guarantee.

Name: Consumer Transactions (Restriction on Statements) Order 1973

Identity: SI 1976 no 1813.

Date effective: 1.12.1976

Interpretation

This order supplements the **Unfair Contract Terms Act 1977** and makes it a criminal offence to display certain types of notice or contract term made ineffective by the 1977 Act. The Order is made under the Fair Trading Act 1973.

Art 3 makes it a criminal offence to display a notice or advertisement or include in a contract any term which purports to exclude or restrict liability, as against a person dealing as a consumer, for breach of the implied terms in ss. 12–15 of the Sale of Goods Act 1979 or ss.8–11 of the Supply of Goods (Implied Terms) Act 1973.

In view of the wide definition given to "deals as consumer" by case law, businesses should take care not to display notices such as "No refunds" etc. or to include invalid exclusions in terms of business. A business which occasionally deals with "consumers" as defined in the Unfair Contract Terms Act may consider it appropriate to have a separate set of contract terms for use when dealing with "consumers". Legal advice should be taken.

Art 4. makes it a criminal offence for the supplier of goods to supply goods to a consumer with any statement about the liability accepted by the supplier (e.g: a statement of willingness to exchange goods) unless that statement also contains a clear statement that the consumer's statutory rights are not affected.

Art 5. applies where any person supplies goods to another in the reasonable expectation that those goods will in the future be supplied to a consumer. If the original supplier makes any statement on the packaging or in any document with the goods about the liability accepted by him in relation to the goods, such as a guarantee, he must also state that the consumer's statutory rights are not affected. Failure to do so is a criminal offence.

This is important to all manufacturers of consumer goods. If the manufacturer offers any guarantee, or makes any statement about his liability on the packaging of the goods, he must include a further statement that the consumer's statutory rights are not affected.

Name: Consumer Protection Act 1987.

Identity: Consumer Protection Act 1987.

Date Effective: 1.3.1988 (Part I); 1.10. 1987 (Part II)

Interpretation

Preliminary.

The Consumer Protection Act contains two groups of provisions relevant to this chapter. Part I was passed to implement **EEC Directive 85/374/EEC on Liability for Defective Products**. It creates an important new system of civil liability for defective products. Part II replaces provisions in earlier legislation and is concerned with criminal liability for unsafe products and with administrative measures to ensure that only safe products are placed on the market.

Part I is the most significant part of the Act for industry. Its importance lies in the fact that it makes a manufacturer (and certain other parties) **strictly liable** for damage caused by defects in his products. Prior to the Act the manufacturer was strictly liable in contract to his immediate customer; and each person in the distribution chain was similarly liable to his customer. The manufacturer could also be liable in the tort of **negligence** to a person injured by the product, but the victim of the defective product was required to prove that the manufacturer had been negligent in order to recover damages. The Act now allows the injured party to sue the manufacturer direct without the need to prove negligence; he need only prove that the product was defective and that the defect caused his injury or loss. The Act therefore extends the manufacturer's strict liability for his products beyond the limits of privity of contract. It is still necessary for the injured victim of the product to prove that the defect caused his injuries. The rules of causation applying in the tort of **Negligence** are likely to be used for this purpose. However, the Act does not prevent a claim being made on the grounds of negligence or breach of contract and in many cases the victim may prefer to bring a contractual action against the supplier; in that case the retailer will bring a similar action against his supplier claiming an indemnity and liability will be passed back up the chain of supply by a series of contract actions (subject to any exclusion clauses in the relevant contracts).

Part I of the Consumer Protection Act does not protect only consumers. Any person can make a claim under the Act provided he/she has suffered damage of a kind covered by the Act.

s.1. declares that the Act was passed to give effect to the European Directive and that it should be construed accordingly. This is important. In several places the Act appears not fully to implement the Directive. It is open to the courts to give an extended meaning to such provisions to make them accord with the Directive.

1. Who is Liable?

s.2 identifies the persons who may be held liable in respect of damage caused by a defective product. It must be read together with the definitions of "producer" and "product" in s.1 of the Act. The following persons may be held liable:-

1. the manufacturer of a finished product; liability may be imposed both in respect of defects in the finished product and in respect of defects in components;

2. the manufacturer of a defective component in a product;

3. in the case of non-manufactured products, such as oil, coal or gas, the person who won or abstracted it;

4. an own-brander who by putting his name, mark etc. on the product holds himself out as the manufacturer;

5. in the case of a product manufactured outside the EEC, the person who imported it into the EEC.

In addition a supplier may be held liable. A supplier will be held liable where the injured person asks him to identify either the manufacturer or his own supplier and he fails to identify either within a reasonable time.

More than one person may be held liable under the section for the same damage.

Practical implications

This section considerably extends the liability of several possible defendants. Effectively, all businesses involved in the manufacture or supply of products of all descriptions are affected by the Act and may be held liable for damage caused by defective products. In particular, own branders, suppliers and importers may find themselves liable to persons with whom they have no contract. All businesses involved in the supply chain should seek to protect themselves from supplier liability by keeping such records as will enable them to identify their own suppliers in order to respond to any request for identification, and, if necessary, to make a claim for an indemnity against liability on the basis of the implied terms in the contract of supply (see **Sale of Goods Act 1979**). This may pose particular problems for businesses which obtain supplies of similar products from a number of different suppliers, such as pharmaceutical product manufacturers and suppliers. The records must be sufficient to identify the supplier of individual items. It must be possible to identify which consignment of raw materials was used to manufacture each consignment of manufactured products.

All potential defendants should seek to minimise their exposure by taking the following steps:-

(a) ensuring that their suppliers are competent and reputable;

(b) negotiating to obtain appropriate indemnities against liability from their suppliers;

(c) ensuring that their suppliers have adequate insurance cover to satisfy any claim;

(d) ensuring that they themselves are insured against possible liability.

2. What Products are Covered?

The act applies to "any goods or electricity", including components and raw materials. It is not clear if computer software can be regarded as "goods" so as to impose liability on the supplier of software containing "bugs".

Special rules apply to agricultural produce. No person is liable as "producer" or as supplier of game or agricultural produce if, at the time he supplied it to another person, the produce had not undergone any "industrial process". Once agricultural produce or game has undergone such a process, the person responsible for the process is treated as the "producer" of the product and is liable for any defects, including defects not attributable to his process. Once food has undergone "industrial processing", subsequent suppliers may also incur liability. "Industrial process" is not defined. It probably includes canning, packing, freezing, drying, grading and washing as well as preparation of meals etc.

It is arguable that the **EEC Directive 85/374/EEC on Liability for Defective Products** imposes wider liability.

Practical implications

Businesses which process or package food are at particular risk. They may be held liable as producers for defects in the food even though such defects are not attributable to their process: e.g: a business which cans fruit treated with a harmful insecticide may be held liable for any harm caused by the insecticide. To minimise exposure such businesses should take the steps indicated above and also obtain supplies, wherever possible, from reputable suppliers and test all food supplied to them before processing.

3. When is a Product Defective?

s.3. defines "defect". There is a defect in a product if the safety of the product is not such as persons generally are entitled to expect. A defect may arise from the design of the product, or from an error in manufacture. Design defects are potentially more serious than manufacturing defects because design defects are likely to affect a larger group of victims.

A court considering whether a product is defective will consider a wide range of factors including:-

(i)   the purpose of marketing the product;

(ii) the way the product was marketed;

(iii) any instructions, packaging, warnings supplied with it and the use of any mark on it;

(iv) what might be expected to be done with the product; and

(v)   the time when the product was supplied by the defendant; the Act recognises that safety standards may improve as technology develops and a product will not be regarded as defective merely because later products are safer.

Practical Implications

Courts will take into account all aspects of the marketing of a product in assessing whether it meets the required standard of safety. Manufacturers should ensure that all products are supplied with accurate, legible and comprehensible instructions for use and, where appropriate, warnings of steps to be taken by the user or of safety hazards etc. Importers, who may be held liable as producers under s.2, should ensure that imported goods are accompanied by adequate instructions, accurately translated into English or the language of the EEC country into which they are imported. Inaccurate or insufficient instructions may also render a product unmerchantable under the **Sale of Goods Act 1979**.

Advertising should be accurate. It will be taken into account along with other aspects of marketing in assessing product safety. It will shape public perception of the intended use of the product.

Manufacturers should monitor safety developments in their field. Safety will be judged by reference to current standards prevailing at the time of supply. Products may therefore have to be improved or redesigned as safety standards improve.

5. What Kinds of Damage are Covered?

s.5. defines the categories of damage in respect of which a claim may be made under the Act. Any person injured by a defective product may claim damages for those injuries. Damages will also be awarded if a defect in a product causes death. In addition, damages will be awarded for loss of or damage to private property other than the defective product itself. No damages are available for damage to business property, so that businesses will not be Plaintiffs under the Act. No damages are available in respect of damage to the product itself or of any item in which the defective item is supplied: for instance if a new car is damaged due to a defective tyre, the Act does not provide compensation for the damage to the car or the tyre. Such claims must be brought under the contract of sale relying on the implied terms in the **Sale of Goods Act 1979**.

The Act seeks to prevent small claims for property damage being brought. No claim for property damage may be made unless the total damages which would be awarded to the victim exceed £275. The wording of the **EEC Directive 85/374/EEC on Liability for Defective Products** on this point is different from that of the Act.

Claims for purely financial or economic loss may not be brought under the Act.

5. What Defences Are Available?

Manufacturers and other persons liable under the Act may be able to raise a number of defences to a claim. Some of the possible defences are expressly set out in **ss.4 and 6** of the Act. The following is a list of possible defences.

(1) The product is not defective; it is as safe as persons are entitled to expect in view of its purpose and the way it is marketed.

(2) The damage was not caused by any defect but was caused by an unexpected use or by the Plaintiff ignoring instructions or warnings.

(3) The defect in the product is attributable to compliance with a requirement imposed by or under statute or any EEC obligation; this will only apply where the defect is unavoidably due to compliance with a mandatory legal requirement.

(4) The defendant did not supply the product; this will apply where damage is caused by: a prototype or test product; a stolen product; a product intended only for the manufacturer's use (although in some cases liability may be imposed under other legislation or in tort).

(5) That the only supply was not in the course of business; this will have no application to businesses.

(6) That the defect did not exist in the product at the "relevant time"; "relevant time" means different things for different defendants; for manufacturers, producers and importers, it is a defence to show that the defect did not exist at the time they supplied the product; for suppliers held liable on the basis of failure to identify the manufacturer or supplier, the relevant time is the last time the product was supplied by a manufacturer, producer or importer; therefore if it can be shown that the product has been damaged or has deteriorated since it left the manufacturer, the manufacturer may be able to raise this defence, but the defence will not be available where any deterioration is due to the condition of the product at the time of its supply.

(7) The "development risks defence". The inclusion of this defence has been criticised by consumer groups; it was included because it was feared that imposition of strict product liability might obstruct the development of new products, especially in areas of developing scientific or technological knowledge. The defence is optional under the **EEC Directive 85/374/EEC on Liability for Defective Products** and it seems that the provision in the Act does not accurately implement the Directive. The defence is likely to be strictly applied. It is available if the defendant can show "that the state of scientific and technical knowledge at the relevant time (see above) was not such that a producer of similar products might be expected to have discovered the defect if it had existed in his products while under his control". It will be of most relevance to manufacturers in high technology or similar industries such as pharmaceuticals. In order to rely on the defence they must show that manufacturers of similar products could not have discovered the defect; compliance with accepted industry standards will not guarantee that the defence can be raised, but failure to comply with such standards will always mean that the defence cannot be raised. Manufacturers in high technology industries should establish strict research procedures to ensure that they are fully up to date with technological and scientific developments in their field and that they are aware of developments n relation to similar products. Under the Directive, the availability of the defence is to be reviewed in 1995.

(8) There is a special component manufacturers' defence. It is a defence for a component manufacturer to show that any defect constitutes a defect in the finished product in which his component is incorporated and that the defect is due entirely to the design of the finished product or to compliance with instructions given by the manufacturer of the finished product. In order to rely on this defence, component manufacturers should keep records of communications with their customers, including details of any requirements imposed by customers in relation to their products.

(9) Contributory Negligence. It is a partial defence to show that the Plaintiff suffered harm partly due to the defect in the product and partly due to his/her own negligence. The Law Reform (Contributory Negligence) Act 1945 applies to claims under the Act. Failure by the victim to follow instructions or warnings may well make this defence available.

(10) Consent. In extreme cases a court may be prepared to hold that a victim has agreed to run the risk of injury. In such a case the manufacturer or other defendant has a complete defence. The defence is likely only to apply where full and accurate instructions and warnings are offered to the user of the product. In general such cases will be seen as cases of "no defect" or of contributory negligence. Consent may be especially important in relation to products such as pharmaceuticals, especially where a new drug is undergoing trials or tests. Testers should sign consent forms indicating that they have been made aware of and agree to accept possible risks of side effects etc. More generally, new products should be accompanied by full and complete warnings and instructions.

(11) Limitation and time limits: The Act lays down a limitation period for claims under the Act. In general claims must be brought within three years of the Plaintiff suffering damage or injury, or of knowing of the injury and the possibility of bringing a claim under the Act against the particular defendant. However, two overriding rules further restrict claims. No claim may be brought in respect of damage caused by a product supplied by its producer before the Act came into force and in any case, no claim may be brought against a manufacturer/producer/importer or own brander after ten years from the date when that defendant supplied the product, or against a supplier after ten years from the date of the last supply by a manufacturer/producer/importer or own brander.

Practical Implications

The long stop limitation period of ten years means that any person potentially liable under the Act should keep records relating to products for a period of at least ten years from the date of supplying that product. Records relating to product development and testing procedures should be kept for ten years from the date of last supply of that line of products.

s.7. provides that liability under the Act cannot be excluded by any contract term, notice or other provision. Businesses must therefore seek to avoid liability by ensuring that they can establish that their products are safe, or that they can take advantage of the statutory defences listed above. In addition, businesses should ensure that they have adequate insurance to cover potential liability under the Act.

Part II: Product Safety

Part II of the Act deals with product safety. It replaces legislation contained in earlier Acts. It creates a criminal offence of supplying consumer goods which do not conform to a minimum safety standard prescribed by the Act and contains detailed provisions for the enforcement of the standard.

s.10. creates a general safety requirement with which goods must comply. This requires goods to be reasonably safe having regard to all the circumstances including the purpose for which they are marketed, the way they are marketed, instructions, warnings, published safety standards for similar goods and the existence of any means by which the goods could have been made safer; the cost and extent of any improvement in safety from such measures will be taken into account. "Safe" is defined in s.19 as meaning that there is no, or only a minimal, risk that the goods or their keeping, use or consumption, assembly, leakage from them or reliance on them will cause death or personal injury. The standard of safety is intended to be linked to the standard required by the product liability provisions of Part I of the Act. The general safety requirement applies to all goods. It is a criminal offence to supply, or, in general, to possess for supply any consumer goods which do not comply with the requirement, although there are important exceptions for growing crops, water food and feedstuffs, fertilisers, gas, aircraft, motor vehicles, controlled drugs or licensed medicinal products and tobacco. Products in these categories are covered by specific legislation governing safety standards. In addition second hand goods are largely excluded.

A number of defences are provided.

1. It is a defence to show that the goods complied with mandatory statutory requirements or with published safety standards for such goods.

2. It is a defence to show that the Defendant did not reasonably expect the goods to be used or consumed in the U.K. so that exporters should be protected from the requirement.

3. It is a defence for retailers to show that they did not know and had no reasonable grounds to believe that the goods failed to satisfy the safety requirement.

4. S. 39 provides a defence where the defendant can show that he took all reasonable steps and exercised all due diligence to avoid committing an offence.

Practical Implications

All businesses concerned in the manufacture, supply or distribution of any goods normally supplied for private use or consumption are potentially caught by this section, unless the goods fall into the exempted categories. In particular, domestic appliances and toys are likely to be caught by the general safety requirement. Businesses should ensure that where there are particular safety standards published for the goods in question, those standards are complied with. Where no such standards are published, businesses should take all possible steps to ensure that the goods are reasonably safe. This will involve undertaking appropriate and careful research and testing before marketing a new product, establishing appropriate procedures to minimise the risks of defects in manufacture and batch testing procedures to try to detect rogue products. Such steps will parallel those required to minimise the risk of civil liability under Part I of the Act.

ss.11–12. These sections allow the Secretary of State for Trade and Industry to make regulations to ensure that products are reasonably safe, and make it a criminal offence to contravene any such regulations. In addition any person injured as a result of any contravention of safety regulations made under this section may bring a claim for damages against the person who contravened the regulations. Regulations may be made to ensure that goods are safe, to restrict the availability of goods to persons generally or to particular classes of persons, or to require information to be provided with goods. Regulations may relate to a wide range of matters including:- design, composition, construction, contents, packaging of goods; testing, inspection and approval of goods; requiring warnings, instructions or information to be provided with the goods or otherwise.

Similar power was contained in earlier legislation and the following regulations have been made:-

Stands for Carry Cots (Safety) Regulations 1966, SI 1966 No 1610;

Electrical Appliances (Colour Code) Regulations 1969, SI 1969 No 310; 1970, SI 1970 No. 811; 1977, SI 1977 No 931;

Electric Blankets (Safety) Regulations 1961, SI 1971 No. 1961;

Cooking Utensils (Safety) Regulations 1972, SI 1972 No. 1957;

Heating Appliances (Fireguards) Regulations 1973, SI 1973 No. 2106; 1977, SI 1977 No. 167

Pencils and Graphic Instruments (Safety) Regulations 1974, SI 1974 No. 226;

Toy (Safety) Regulations 1974, SI 1974 NO. 1367;

Glazed Ceramic Ware (Safety) Regulations 1975, SI 1975 No. 1241;

Electrical Equipment (Safety) Regulations 1975, SI 1975 No. 1366; 1976 SI 1976 No. 1208; 1987 SI 1987 No. 603;

Children's Clothing (Hood Cord) Regulations 1976, SI 1976 No. 2;

Vitreous Enamel Ware (Safety) Regulations 1976, SI 1976 No. 454;

Oil Heaters (Safety) Regulations 1977, SI 1977 No. 167;

Babies' Dummies (Safety) Regulations 1978, SI 1978 No. 836;

Cosmetic Products Regulations 1978, SI 1978 1354; 1978 SI 1978 No. 1477; 1984, SI 1984 No. 1260; 1985 SI 1985 No. 1279;

Perambulator and Pushchairs (Safety) Regulations 1978, SI 1978 No. 1372;

Oil Lamps (Safety) Regulations 1979, SI 1979 No. 1125

The Dangerous Substances and Preparations (Safety) Regulations 1980 SI 1980 No. 136; 1985, SI 1985 No.127;

Upholstered Furniture (Safety) Regulations 1980, SI 1980 No. 725;

Novelties (Safety) Regulations 1980, SI 1980 No. 958;

The Filament Lamps for Vehicles (Safety) Regulations 1982, SI 1982 No. 444;

The Pedal Bicycles (Safety) Regulations 1984, SI 1984 No. 145;

The Motor Vehicles Tyres (Safety) Regulations 1984, SI 1984 1233;

Cosmetic Products (Safety) Regulations 1984, SI 1984 No. 1260; 1985, SI 1985 No. 2045; 1988, SI 1988 No. 802;

Gas Catalytic Heaters (Safety) Regulations 1984, SI 1984 No. 1802;

Food Imitations (Safety) Regulations 1985, SI 1985 No. 99;

The Asbestos Products (Safety) Regulations 1985, SI 1985 No. 2042; 1987, SI 1987 No.1979;

Nightwear (Safety) Regulations 1985, SI 1985 No. 2043; 1987, SI 1987 No. 286;

Pushchair (Safety) Regulations 1985, SI 1985 No. 2047;

Child Resistant Packaging (Safety) Regulations 1986, SI 1986 No. 758;

Fireworks (Safety) Regulations 1986, SI 1986 No. 1323;

Plugs and Sockets etc. (Safety) Regulations 1987, SI 1987, No. 603;

Benzene in Toys (Safety) Regulations, 1979, SI 1987 No. 2116;

Cosmetic Products (Safety) (Amendment) Regulations 1988, SI 1988 No. 802;

Furniture and Furnishings (Fire) (Safety) Regulations 1988, SI 1988 No.1324;

Ceramic Ware (Safety) Regulations 1988, SI 1988 No 1647;

Cosmetic Products (Safety) (Amendment No.2) Regulations, 1988, SI 1988 No. 2121;

Three Wheeled All-Terrain Motor Vehicles (Safety) Regulations 1988, SI 1988 No. 2122;

Gas Cooking Appliances (Safety) Regulations 1989 SI No. 149

ss.13–18. contain extensive powers to assist the Secretary of State and enforcement authorities in the enforcement of the product safety provisions. The Secretary of State may issue prohibition notices, forbidding the supply of goods specified in the notice, and notices to warn, requiring the person to whom the notices are addressed to publish warnings about the safety of any goods specified in the notice. It is a criminal offence to contravene such notices. A person to whom such a notice is directed may make representations to the Secretary of State with a view to persuading him to revoke the notice.

Enforcement authorities, which are weights and measures departments in England and Wales, may issue suspension notices where there has been a breach of the general safety requirement, specific safety regulations or any prohibition notice or notice to warn. A suspension notice may prohibit the person to whom it is addressed supplying products specified in the notice for a period of up to six months. A person on whom such a notice is served may appeal to a magistrates court against the notice.

The Secretary of State may serve notice on any person requiring him to supply any information which the Secretary of State considers he needs in order to decide whether to exercise his powers under the Act. It is an offence to fail to comply with such a notice.

Enforcement authorities may apply to the court for forfeiture of any goods which contravene any safety provision. They also have extensive powers to make test purchases, test goods, enter premises, inspect goods or premises and search for and seize goods and records.

Name: Directive on the approximation of the laws, regulations and administrative provisions of Member States concerning liability for defective products.

Identity/No: Product Liability Directive; (85/374/EEC)

Date Effective: 25. 7. 1985

Interpretation.

The Directive is intended to harmonise the law of EEC member states in relation to liability for defective products and requires all member states to introduce a regime of strict liability. because of the difficulty in obtaining agreement between all members to all provisions of the Directive, the Directive permits derogations from its provisions in three areas. Members are allowed the option of including a development risks defence, fixing a maximum limit to the compensation payable in respect of identical items (i.e: a particular product type) and of exempting primary agricultural produce from the strict liability scheme. The Directive was to be implemented throughout the EEC by July 1988. It has been implemented in the U.K. by part I of the Consumer Protection Act 1987. Implementation in member states is patchy so far, and some members have still not implemented it. Others have implemented the Directive but have not done so completely. The U.K. legislation falls into this category. The U.K. has chosen to include a development risks defence and an exclusion for primary agricultural produce, but has not included a financial ceiling for identical items. The three optional derogations are to be reviewed by the Commission in 1995.

Because the Directive has been implemented by the **Consumer Protection Act 1987** its detailed provisions are not set out here. However businesses should note that similar provisions will apply throughout the Community so that exporters to other EEC countries may find themselves held liable in the courts of other member states (and that the injured victim of a defective product may be able to choose between different jurisdictions in deciding where to bring his action, so as to take advantage of favourable differences between domestic legislation: for instance, in Germany the development risks defence only applies to pharmaceuticals, so that a German citizen injured by a non-pharmaceutical product imported from the U.K. could sue under German law, depriving the manufacturer of the development risks defence) and that in the following areas the 1987 Act does not fully correspond with the Directive.

Art 2. allows primary agricultural produce to be excluded from the strict liability scheme where it has not undergone "initial processing". The U.K. legislation refers instead to "an industrial process". It is possible that the Directive offers a narrower defence than that included in the U.K. legislation.

Art 7. describes the defences to be available to producers. Art 7(e) contains the development risks defence. The defence in the Directive is narrower than that included in the U.K. legislation. The defence in the Directive is only available if the state of scientific and technical knowledge when the product was put into circulation was not such as the defect could have been discovered at all. This would require producers to monitor all research relevant to their field of manufacture, regardless of the practice of other manufacturers in the same field. The EC Commission is commencing legal action against the U.K. Government to test the U.K. provisions.

Art 9. defines the types of damage in respect of which a claim can be brought. It provides that in a claim for compensation for damage to property the first 500 ecu (equivalent to £275) are to be paid by the Plaintiff and not be recoverable from the Defendant. In contrast the U.K. legislation provides that no claim can be brought for damages under £275 but that in the case of larger claims the defendant is liable for the whole of the claim.

Summary of Practical Implications of Product Liability.

Product liability may affect all businesses involved in the manufacture, supply or distribution of any type of product. All businesses in all product sectors are potentially at risk, although there may be a particular risk for manufacturers of pharmaceutical, chemical and medicinal products, where a defect may affect a large number of victims, giving rise to a large number of claims, and to manufacturers of high technology products, especially where individual claims may be for very large amounts.

Liability may arise in contract, tort or under the product liability provisions of the Consumer Protection Act 1987. In addition there may be a risk of criminal liability for failure to comply with the provisions of Part II of the Consumer Protection Act 1987 or related regulations. The standard required of a manufacturer or supplier may vary according to the legal basis of liability, but the following practical steps are of general application. All potential defendants should assess their product liability risk and take steps to minimise the risk of liability and to enable any liability which is imposed to be transferred.

1. Steps to Minimise the Risk of Liability

(a) Establish adequate research and development systems to assess safety of designs and prototypes before marketing. BS5750 lays down a national standard for manufacturing quality procedures.

(b) Output testing: inspect and test actual finished products: this may involve testing individual products or testing batch samples according to the nature of the product.

(c) Input testing: inspect and test all goods purchased for use in manufacture, components for incorporation in finished products and food for packaging or processing. Input testing is relevant to:-

    (i) avoiding product liability for components;

    (ii) avoiding product liability for foods which are packaged/processed;

    (iii) making a contract claim against the supplier and avoiding the risk of acceptance of goods.

(d) Choose suppliers carefully. Suppliers should:

    (i) be reputable;

    (ii) have adequate quality control and testing procedures;

    (iii) be solvent and likely to remain so;

    (iv) have adequate insurance cover, so that they are able to meet any product liability claims made against them and to provide indemnities against liability.

(e) Care should be taken in advertising and marketing. No excessive claims should be made, especially in relation to product safety. Marketing etc. will affect the standard of safety expected by the public and therefore the standard required by the Consumer Protection Act 1987.

(f) Provide accurate instructions and warnings. These may make a product safe or allow a manufacturer to rely on defences such as contributory negligence or consent. Instructions and warnings should be clear and accurate, legible and securely attached to the product. Importers and exporters should ensure that instructions/warnings are accurately translated into the language of the country where the goods are to be marketed.

Warnings should:

    (i) identify the risk or danger in ordinary language;

    (ii) explain how the risk or danger can be avoided;

(iii)   advise of practical steps which may be taken (e.g) to combat injury caused (e.g: "May cause burning if comes into contact with bare skin; if the fluid does come into contact with bare skin, wash off immediately with plenty of cold water and seek medical advice".)

In some product sectors the content etc. of warnings is prescribed (e.g: for Asbestos Products: see regulations listed in this chapter). In addition the Department of Trade and Industry issues a booklet giving guidance on suitable warnings and warning symbols.

Where a product is to be supplied through an intermediary (e.g: drugs available on prescription) it may be enough to warn the intermediary and require him/her to pass on the warning.

(g) Keep records of any complaints, claims etc. Records should be monitored and if claims arise consider the need to:-

(i)   improve design;

(ii)   improve quality control, testing etc.;

(iii) issue warnings etc. through the press or otherwise;

(iv)   recall products: recall may minimise number of claims; failure to recall may amount to negligence.

(h) Keep up to date with relevant research and improved standards and modify product design/testing procedures/manufacturing systems in line with improving standards.

2. Steps to Transfer Loss

(a) Choose suppliers carefully, as above.

(b) Input testing, as above: promptly reject defective or substandard supplies.

(c) Keep accurate and comprehensive records.

(i)   All suppliers, whether direct to the public or to other businesses, should keep records which identify the business' own suppliers (1) to avoid "supplier" liability under the Consumer Protection Act and (2) to enable the business to seek contractual indemnities.

(ii)   Manufacturers' records should identify component suppliers, to allow contractual indemnities to be sought.

(iii) Manufacturers should keep records of requirements of/ instructions to component manufacturers. This may be relevant both to liability under the Consumer Protection Act and to the availability of an indemnity claim under s.14(3) of the Sale of Goods Act.

(iv)   Component manufacturers should keep records of customers' requirements.

(v)   Manufacturers should keep records of research, development and testing procedures.

(vi)   All suppliers should keep records of the date of supply of individual products.

(vii) Records should identify products to be identified and linked to (e.g.), manufacturing batches. This will facilitate identification of defects, identifying date of supply, identifying components etc. used and recalls of similar products affected. Products should be identified with batch numbers, etc.

Records should be kept for ten years from the date of supply of individual products. Records relating to the whole product line (e.g: research and development, testing etc.) should be kept for ten years from the end of the product line.

(d) Contracts should be carefully drafted. Contracts with customers should exclude liability for breach of contract etc. so far as permitted by the Unfair Contract Terms Act 1977. Contracts with suppliers should contain clear warranties and provision for indemnification against liability. Legal advice should be taken on contracts. Business procedures should be devised to ensure that standard terms of business are incorporated into contracts with customers/ suppliers.

The common law of negligence

The basis of liability

Negligence may be defined as the breach of duty of care, owed by the defendant to the plaintiff, which results in damage to the plaintiff.

The plaintiff must prove

- that the defendant owed him/her a duty of care.
- that the plaintiff was in breach of that duty.
- that the plaintiff has suffered forseeable damage as a result of that breach.

The fact that the plaintiff must have suffered damage in order to bring a claim means that there is normally no remedy in tort for goods that are simply shoddily made.

Because of the requirement of proving fault, a remedy in negligence will usually only be pursued where the consumer is unable to use statute-based remedies. For example, remedies under the Sale of Goods Act only apply to the purchaser of the goods, and claims for property damage are restricted under the Consumer Protection Act. In these circumstances, a claim may be brought in negligence.

Who is Liable

A manufacturer's liability in negligence for defective goods was established by the House of Lords decision in the case of *Donoghue v Stevenson 1932*. The appellant and a friend went to a cafe where the friend bought some ginger beer in a bottle made of dark opaque glass. After the appellant had consumed some of the ginger beer, the friend poured out the remainder which contained a decomposed snail. The appellant suffered shock and gastroenteritis as a result of the contaminated ginger beer. As the appellant was not the purchaser, she had no remedy against the cafe proprietor in contract. The House of Lords held the manufacturer was liable because: "a manufacturer of products, which he sells in such a form as to show that he intends to them to reach the ultimate consumer in the form which they left him with no reasonable possibility of intermediate examination, and with the knowledge that the absence of reasonable care in the preparation or putting up of the products will result in an injury to the consumer's life or property,owes a duty to the consumer to take reasonable care."

A manufacturer of an end-product is also under a duty of care regarding parts or components bought in from other manufacturers. In *Taylor v Rover Co Ltd*, the court agreed with the statement that "a manufacturer's duty is not limited to those parts of the product which he makes himself. It extends to component parts, supplied by his sub-manufacturers, or others".

Since *Donoghue v Stevenson*, liability has been extended to include virtually anyone involved in the production chain who is at fault including assemblers, packagers, sub-contractors, wholesalers, distributors, and – in limited circumstances – retailers. For example, in *Fisher v Harrods*, a retailer was held liable for supplying goods without first checking on the reputability of his supplier. The duty of care is an ongoing one, so that where a product defect comes to light some time after the product has been marketed, liability may exist if appropriate action, such as a product recall, is not taken to prevent damage.

What products are covered

In *Grant v Australian Knitting Machines*, the court rejected limiting the application of the principle in *Donoghue v Stevenson* to cases involving food and drink. The manufacturers of woollen underpants were held liable to the plaintiff who contracted dermatitis from an excess of bisulphite of soda in the garment. Since then, liability has been extended to cover a wide variety of goods, including cars, chisels, jewellery cleaning fluid, explosive chemicals, and lifts. Any product in domestic use would now be covered.

Who may sue

In *Donoghue v Stevenson*, Lord Atkinson said that a duty of care is owed to "persons who are so closely and directly affected by my act that I ought reasonably to have them in contemplation as being so affected when I am directing my mind to the acts or omissions which are called in question".

This extends the duty to include not only the user of the defective product, but all persons coming into contact with it. In *Vacwell Engineering Ltd V BDH Chemicals*, a duty was owed to employees handling a product and in *Stennett v Hancock*, a duty was owed to a pedestrian who was injured when a lorry wheel became detached, mounted the pavement, and struck him.

The Standard of Safety

In *Board v Thomas Hedley & Co Ltd*, Lord Denning stated that a product is dangerous "if it might affect normal users adversely, or even might adversely affect other users who had a higher degree of sensitivity than the normal, as long as they were not altogether exceptional". However, manufacturers will not be liable for a product which causes injury to an abnormally sensitive person. For example, where a woman with an abnormally sensitive skin contacted dermatitis after wearing a fur coat, the retailers were not liable.

A product may be dangerous due to

a) **Defective design or materials** In *Williams v Rock Quarries Ltd*, the manufacturers of a new type of drilling machine were held liable when the machine toppled over the edge of a quarry, killing an employee. Lord Denning said that "before sending a machine like this out for demonstration and putting it on the market, the toolmaker should have guarded against the possibility of its rising up and toppling over, and should have investigated these possible sources of danger.

b) **Defective assembly** In *Hill v James Crowe (Cases) Ltd*, the manufacturers of a packing case which collapsed when a lorry driver was standing on it were held to be liable for his injuries. The packing case was defective because it had been badly nailed. This case also illustrates the point that a product may be defective if it causes injury when used for a foreseeable purpose, even when it is not the intended purpose. It is foreseeable that a lorry driver may stand on a wooden packing case when loading his lorry, although that is not the intended purpose of the product.

c) **Inadequate Warnings or Instructions** The need for warning and directions for use generally depends on the likelihood and potential seriousness of damage. Both the wording and location of the warning or directions need to be adequate. However, a manufacturer need not always warn the ultimate consumer if the product is being supplied to an intermediary. For example, in *Holmes v Ashcroft*, a hair dye was supplied to hairdressers without the warning that it might be dangerous and that a patch test should be carried out. The manufacturers were not liable when the hairdresser ignored the warning and applied the dye to the plaintiff's hair without a patch test, and the plaintiff contracted dermatitis.

Damages

Consumers can recover compensation in cases of negligence for two types of damage:

a) death or personal injury resulting from a defective product including, where relevant, loss of earnings as well as non-pecuniary losses such as pain or suffering; and

b) property damage.

Defences

a) That the product defect was not the manufacturer's fault. Much will depend on the facts of the individual case. For example, the longer the period between putting the product into circulation and the subsequent damage, the less likely the claim is to succeed, because of the possibilities of wear and tear, misuse etc.

b) That the damage resulted from an abnormal or improper use of the product (but see above)

c) Contributory negligence. This is only a partial defence: the plaintiff's damages will be reduced in proportion to his responsibility for the damages suffered.

d) That the plaintiff is unusually sensitive.

e) That the defendant took all reasonable care.

f) Limitation Periods. Although all the other ingredients of a successful claim are present, the action will fail if it is not brought on time.

Transport

Paul Fawcett and John Hodgson

Name: The Transport Act 1968.

The two major provisions of this Act were the deregulation of Road Haulage (Part V) and the creation of Passenger Transport Authorities in major conurbations (Part II). Parts I, II and VII provided for a major restructuring of the State owned road haulage, passenger transport, and inland waterways operations respectively. The Railways Board's road haulage and passenger transport operations were transferred to the newly created operators.

The UK domestic Drivers' Hours regulations were amended (Part VI), as also was the Highways Act 1959 in so far as it related to Bridges and level crossings owned by either the Railways, London or Waterways Boards (Part VII) and the Road Traffic Regulation Act 1967 so as to extend and clarify the powers of the various authorities created by the principal Act to make traffic regulations. The Act comprises ten parts and eighteen schedules, some of which have been repealed, amended or expanded by later legislation. The following is a brief resume of those sections in force and directly applicable to the transport industry and to the transport operations of other industries.

PART I

The National Freight Corporation. (NFC) was created from the freight transport assets of the Transport Holding Company (including British Road Services) and the Railways Board (National Carriers). The Act provided that NFC was not to be regarded as a common carrier, ie. it was to have commercial freedom to contract to carry, or to decline to do so. (Part I).

NFC was disposed of, via an employee buy out, to National Freight Company, in 1980, under the privatisation provisions of the Transport Act 1980. The same Act also transferred NFC's majority share-holdings in Freightliner Ltd to the Railways Board, so that Freightliner is now a wholly owned subsidiary of BRB Passenger Transport Executives.

PART II

The Act enabled the Secretary of State for Transport to designate conurbations as Passenger Transport Areas, and to appoint, in conjunction with the Local Authorities concerned, Passenger Transport Authorities (PTAs). PTAs had a duty to secure the provision of a properly integrated and efficient system of public passenger transport to meet the needs of their area. They were empowered to establish a Passenger Transport Executive (PTE) to implement their policies, and the Secretary of State could provide by order for the transfer of the Local Authorities' passenger transport undertakings to the Executive. The Executive were empowered to precept councils in their area to meet any operating deficit. (Section 13). They could also, with the approval of the Authority, enter into agreements with BRB for the provision of passenger services in their area. (Section 16).

The Local Government Act 1972 created Metropolitan Counties, which then became the authorities responsible for the (by then) five PTAs. The Local Government (Scotland) Act 1973 created Strathclyde Metropolitan County which also became a PTA and the Transport (London) Act created the London Transport Executive of the Greater London County.

When, in 1986, the Metropolitan Counties were abolished by the Local Government Act 1985 the PTAs became joint authorities composed of elected members from the constituent District Councils. The

Transport Act 1985, which deregulated passenger transport outside of London, gave PTAs a new residual duty to secure, by tender, those services which the market did not provide to meet the "requirements" of their area. PTEs became "tendering authorities" retaining Section 16 powers to secure BRB services. PTE transport undertakings and municipal transport undertakings outside the PTAs became "arms length" companies in which the PTAs owned the assets (some have by now been disposed of by Employee Share Option Schemes (ESOPs). In London, the London Regional Transport Act transferred control of London Transport Executive, which it renamed London Regional Transport, to the Secretary of State for Transport.

The introduction of the Community Charge in 1990 meant that PTEs can no longer precept their District Councils under Section 13, but must agree with them the level of service they wish to be provided and invoice them for securing this. If the District councils wish, they may opt out of the PTAs and secure their own services.

PART III

Two public authorities, the National Bus Company and the Scottish Transport Group were created from the assets of the Transport Holding Company by the Act. The latter comprised the ferry services of Caledonian Steam Packet Company (owned by BRB) and David McBrayne and the Scottish Bus Company (both owned by the THC). Both authorities were given a duty to co operate with PTAs, BRB and London Transport Executive.

The Transport Act 1985 which deregulated bus services provided for the disposal of the NBC to the private sector. This has now been done by the Secretary of State for Transport. The Transport (Scotland) Act 1989 requires the Scottish Transport Group to formulate a policy for the disposal of its activities to the private sector Authorities and Boards.

PART IV

This part contains important provisions relating to the structure, powers and finance of the public Boards and Authorities concerned with transport. Of particular interest to industry are the provisions which allow the nationalised transport undertakings' workshops to manufacture or repair vehicles and rolling stock for outside customers as well as for themselves. (Section 48). The Secretary of State for Transport is empowered, with Treasury approval, to make grants towards the expenditure by any person of a capital nature for the provision, improvement or development of public passenger transport facilities in Great Britain. A local authority may similarly make payments where the facilities to be provided will benefit the community (Section 56) Section 56 grants, known as infrastructure grants, are the basis of the financing of bus stations, road/rail interchanges and light rapid transit schemes. The Department of Transport, in considering these, usually today requires a commensurate measure of private capital Regulation of the carriage of goods by road.

PART V

The Act deregulated road haulage by replacing the systems of quantity controls which had been in place since the Road and Rail Traffic Act 1933, with a system of quality control (Operator Licensing). Goods vehicles used on a road for hire or reward or in connection with the user's trade or business became subject to Operator Licensing. Exceptions were made for small goods vehicles of less than 3.5 tonnes gross vehicle weight (Section 60). Operator Licences were divided into two classes by subsequent regulations, a Standard Licence for Hire and Reward operation, and a Restricted Licence for Own Account operation.

Vehicles authorised under an Operator's Licence must be owned by the operator or in his possession, and the Operating Centre from which they are used must be specified and be within the area of the Licensing Authority granting the licence. The Licensing Authority (LA) is the Chairman of the Traffic Commissioners for each traffic area. Operator Licences are vehicle specific, and operators must inform the Licensing Authority within one month of the acquisition of a new vehicle, otherwise that vehicle ceases to be authorised, even if its acquisition does not result in the number of vehicles authorised in the licence being exceeded. This is known as "operating within the margin", the margin being the difference between the number of vehicles "in possession" and "authorised". There is provision for temporary detachment of vehicles to other traffic areas for a maximum period of three months (Section 61).

An operator may not hold more than one operator's licence in any traffic area. Applicants for an operator's licence are required to furnish the LA with specific particulars which in effect become statements of intent regarding such matters as the proper maintenance of their vehicles, the observance of drivers' hours regulations and weight limits. Applicants must notify the LA of any previous convictions and of any convictions received between the making of their application and its disposal by the LA. (Section 62). Applications must be published by the LA and certain prescribed trade unions and employers' associations, the police, relevant local authorities and planning authorities may make objections. (Section 64).

In considering an application the LA is required to have regard to whether the applicant appears to him to be a fit person, the arrangements for securing that his vehicles will be properly maintained and that his drivers will observe the drivers' hours and records regulations, and the financial standing of the operator. Except in the case where he is not satisfied on environmental grounds (see section 69 A below) he must grant the licence if he is satisfied about the above matters. In determining the operator's financial standing he may be assisted by a financial assessor. Conditions may be attached to a licence requiring the operator to inform the LA of any specified changes in the organisation, management or ownership of his business (Section 66).

An O licence, unless revoked or prematurely terminated, remains in force for five years , or until such later time as an application by the operator for a renewal of the licence (or any appeal under that application to the Transport Tribunal) is disposed of. An LA may grant an interim licence pending the determination of an application for a full licence. (Section 66). The Transport Tribunal has ruled that a "renewal" is to be treated as a new application, and that the grant of an interim licence does not amount to sanctioning any "material change" in advance of disposing of the substantive application *(Appeal 1986 No X29, Kirk Bros Ltd.).*

An LA may, on application by an operator, and (unless the variation sought is "trivial") having published this, vary his O licence by the addition or deletion of specified vehicles and trailers, altering any Section 66 condition (above) or converting the licence from a Restricted Licence to a Standard National or Standard International licence. (Section 68) An LA may revoke, suspend, prematurely terminate or curtail an operator's licence if during the preceding five years the holder has been convicted of prescribed "relevant" road transport offenses or has not complied with the statements of intent made when the licence was granted. Revocation is mandatory where the holder of a Restricted Operator's Licence has been convicted within five years of a second offence of using this for hire and reward. When an LA revokes an O licence, he may also disqualify the holder from obtaining or holding another O licence, either indefinitely or for such time as he thinks fit. He may direct that if whilst such a disqualification is in force the disqualified person controls or is a director of a company, or is a member of a partnership which holds an O licence, the licence in question shall be liable to revocation etc.

In *Appeal 1987 No Y37*, DCF International Ltd, the Transport Tribunal held that an LA cannot disqualify a director of a company unless the licence of that company is first revoked. An LA may not make an order of revocation, suspension, curtailment, termination or disqualification or attach a condition under section 66 without first holding a Public Inquiry if the operator requests this. He may direct that the order does not take effect until the time limit for any appeal to the Transport Tribunal has elapsed or any such appeal is disposed of. If he refuses such a stay the operator may apply to the Tribunal for a direction and the Tribunal must give its decision within fourteen days. (Section 69) Section 69 was extended by the Transport Act 1982 to impose environmental conditions on the operators of Goods Vehicles. The provisions of the following sections 69A–G are of vital importance to transport operators including industrialists with their own in house transport.

The Operating Centre from which the vehicles authorised in the O licence will be operated must be specified in the licence, and applicants may be required to give the LA particulars of the use which they propose to make of this. (Section 69A). A Statutory Objector (see section 63) may object to the grant of an O licence on the grounds that the operating centre is unsuitable on environmental grounds. Owners and occupiers of land in the vicinity of the operating centre may also make representations to the LA on the same grounds if the use of the operating centre could prejudicially affect their use of, or enjoyment, of their land. However, it is provided (s.69B(5)) that where there is no material change in the operating centre or the use made of this the LA may not refuse an application for a renewal of the licence on environmental grounds other than on the specific grounds that the parking of the authorised vehicles at the operating centre would cause adverse effects in the vicinity. An LA may instead of granting an O licence as applied, modify the grant by specifying on the licence only such places as are not unsuitable for use as operating centres. The grant of an interim licence is without prejudice to any subsequent grant of a substantive licence (Section 69B).

An LA may attach prescribed environmental conditions when granting an O licence regulating the number, type and size of vehicles to be authorised, the parking arrangements and the hours of operation. He may vary or remove these at any time. If he is precluded from refusing an application because there has been no material change in the operating centre or operations he may only attach such conditions if he first gives the operator the opportunity to make representations to him with respect to the effect of these on his business and he must then give special consideration to such representations. (Section 69C). An operator may apply to vary his operating centre or the environmental conditions on his licence but such an application will be published by the LA and could be subject to the same objections and representations as a substantive application. There is provision if the operator requests this for the LA to give an interim direction that his licence should continue in force until the application for the variation or any appeal arising out of his decision is disposed of (Section 69D).

An application for an O licence or for any variation (either the addition or deletion of specified vehicles or an environmental change) must be published by the applicant in a local newspaper circulating in the locality affected, otherwise it will automatically be refused by the LA. (Section 69E). An LA may revoke, suspend or prematurely terminate an O licence on the grounds that the operator has breached the conditions controlling the use of his operating centre, subject to the existing section 69 safeguards of Public Inquiry and continuance up to Appeal. (Section 69F).

Environmental objections and representations must be made within a prescribed period and in a prescribed manner. These, and the considerations which the LA is required to have regard to are set out in the Goods Vehicle (Qualifications and Fees) Regulations 1984, SI 176 regulation 22 and include, *inter alia*,

- the nature and use of the land in the vicinity;
- the extent to which the grant of an application would result in a material change in the operating centre or its use adversely affecting the environment in its vicinity;
- any planning permission relating to the land;
- the number, type and size of authorised vehicles and the arrangements for parking of these;
- the nature of the use of the land as an operating centre;
- the times of use; and
- the means and frequency of vehicle ingress and egress.

For the purpose of disposing of environmental objections an LA may consider an application for an O licence or a variation to an O licence in respect of each operating centre separately (ie. centre by centre). An applicant who is aggrieved by the refusal of an LA to grant an O licence, or by his decision to revoke, suspend, curtail or prematurely terminate this may appeal to the Transport Tribunal (Section 70). The Operator Licensing provisions in the Act have been considerably strengthened and amended for the purpose of enabling EC Directive 74/561 on "admission to the occupation of road haulage operator" to be implemented in Great Britain. The Goods Vehicle (Qualifications and Fees) Regulations 1984, SI 176 provides that O licences should be classified as:

- Standard, National;
- Standard, National and International;

- Restricted.

A standard licence is required by operators who carry for hire and reward (road hauliers) whilst a Restricted Licence is necessary for Own Account operation where only the operator's own goods are carried.

The qualifications required of applicants for an O licence are that they should be of:

- good repute
- appropriate financial standing
- professionally competent.

and an LA must refuse an application where the operator cannot meet these requirements, except that the requirement as to professional competence is not required of applicants for a Restricted Licence.

An applicant will meet the requirements for professional competence if he obtains by examination a Certificate of Professional Competence (examining body, Royal Society of Arts) or holds any other prescribed qualification recognised by the Secretary of State for this purpose.

It is now no longer possible to obtain a CPC by experience the so called "grandfather rights" lapsed in 1981.

PART VI

This part of the Act relates only to Domestic Hours Regulations. Drivers of most Goods Vehicles (other than small goods vehicles of less than 3.5 tonnes gross vehicle weight) now come within the scope of EC Directives 3820/85 (Driver's Hours of Work) and 3821/85 (Drivers' Records including tachographs). The Drivers' Hours (Harmonisation with Community Rules) Regulations 1986 SI 1458 repeals most of this part with the exception of the two limits of 10 hours driving and 11 hours work per day.

The requirement for drivers to return records to their employers within 21 days is retained in UK legislation, (Section 97A) although the EC Directive is silent on this matter.

PARTS VII to X

A brief resume of these parts was given in the introduction to the Act: they contain little of immediate relevance to industrialists, businesses or operators.

SCHEDULES 1–18

The same is in general true of these schedules. Schedule 9 dealing with Transport Manager's Licences was never implemented and was overtaken by EC Directive 74/561 which provided for Certificates of Professional Competence.

Name: Transport Act 1968 Part VI; EEC Regulations 3820/85 and 3821/85

These provisions deal with the use of tachographs and the requirements relating to drivers' hours and rest. There are still UK rules existing alongside the EEC ones but they are of little importance. Goods vehicles are required to be fitted with tachographs and the tachograph must be maintained in efficient order, regularly inspected and used. There is a list of exceptions; the only one of general importance relates to vehicles used for door-to-door deliveries. Although it is an offence to use a vehicle when there is any failure to comply with these requirements, it is regarded as the employer's responsibility to have the tachograph officially inspected and calibrated, and repaired or replaced if it malfunctions, and as the driver's responsibility to use the tachograph properly on a daily basis. Reg 3821/85 (The Community Recording Equipment Regulation) contains the detailed provisions relating to tachographs including annexes which define the types of tachograph which can be used. A vehicle operator is required to ensure that the tachograph fitted is an approved model, that there is a seal at either end of the drive cable from the gear-box to the tachograph, that the tachograph is inspected every two years and re-calibrated every six years (or on refitting) and that any defects are reported and rectified promptly. S97 of the Transport Act 1968 creates an offence of using a vehicle where there is no tachograph fitted, or where it is defective or otherwise not in compliance with the regulations. Care is required before putting into service a vehicle which has not been in orthodox commercial use, to ensure that it is fitted with a tachograph which complies with the rules.

Drivers are primarily responsible for complying with the drivers' hours rules, but an employer who causes or permits a breach of the rules will be guilty of an offence. There are a number of separate rules, and they are defined in a way which is designed to allow the greatest flexibility in operation consistent with safety; this does however lead to complexity and great care is necessary to avoid contravention of the rules. The detailed rules are contained in Reg 3820/85 and s97 (11A) of the Transport Act creates the offences.

Breaks from driving: (Art 4) The basic requirement is that the driver must have a rest of 45 minutes after not more than 41/2 hours driving. Up to three rests of at least 15 minutes each during the relevant driving period may be counted towards the total.

Daily driving: The basic rule is 10 hours driving in a working day. There are cases where this can be reduced.

Daily rest: (Art 8) The basic requirement is for a break of 11 hours. This can be reduced to 9 hours twice a week, and can also be taken as a break of 8 hours coupled with one of 4 hours taken during the following day. A driver must always be able to show that at any time when he is on duty he has taken a daily rest within the last 24 hours. If insufficient rest is taken the two periods of duty and the associated driving are aggregated.

Weekly rest: (Art 8) After six days on duty a weekly rest must be taken. This should be added on to a daily rest and give a total rest of 36 hours. If the weekly rest is taken away from base it can be reduced to 24 hours, but the difference must be made up as a single rest within two weeks.

The employer must arrange rosters and timetables so that these rules are not infringed (Art 15) but may also be liable under UK law for causing or permitting drivers to exceed hours or fail to take rests. Causing will usually involve a direct order to break the law, and is obvious; permitting is a little more complex. An employer who fails to carry out any check of the work its drivers are doing, whether by analyzing the tachograph charts or otherwise may be liable for permitting offences if it is clear that drivers are routinely breaching the rules and no warnings have been given. Also an employer who carries out checks, but takes no steps to discipline infringers or prevent repetition may be regarded as permitting, The burden is heavier in relation to weekly rests, which are part of the administration of the operation, as opposed to daily breaks and rests, where infractions can occur without fault or connivance on the part of the company.

Tachograph Records: (Art 14 Reg 3821/85) The driver must keep a record at all times. This applies even to double manned lorries. He must retain his charts for the remainder of the current week, and must also have the last chart of the previous week with him. This is to facilitate official checks. The employer is not entitled to have these charts, and if the information from them is required to calculate wages etc a photocopy must be taken. Subject to this tachograph sheets must be handed in within 21 days and then kept by the employer for a year. They must be produced for inspection by the police and Department of Transport inspectors. Failing to carry sheets, failing to return them and failing to produce them are all offences, and an employer who insists on holding records which he should not yet have, or fails to ensure records are handed in on time is also guilty of an offence.

Name: Road Traffic Act 1988

This is the principal legislation relating to the use of vehicles on the road. There are also many Regulations made under the Act which deal with matters of detail. It is impracticable to deal in detail with the Act and Regulations. Many of the provisions apply to all road users, and others are extremely specialised. It is assumed that those companies which are engaged in specialised transport operations will consult more specialised sources. This introduction is aimed at those whose transport operations are general in nature and subsidiary to their principal business activities.

In general it is the driver of a vehicle who is responsible for that vehicle. In relation to offences directly related to the driving of the vehicle (careless and reckless driving, non-compliance with traffic signs, reporting of accidents) liability rests solely with the driver. In other cases (basically insurance and construction and use regulations) the user will be equally liable with the driver, although where the driver is an employee the policy is to prosecute the user only unless the driver is actually to blame. In yet others the employer of the driver may be liable, e.g. where the driver does not hold the appropriate licence. In these cases the offence will normally be framed as "causing or permitting" the driver's offence.

Definition of "Using"

The person actually at the wheel clearly uses the vehicle, and where a company or firm employ someone to drive a vehicle for the purposes of the business the employer also uses the vehicle. The driver need not be a full-time permanent member of staff, casual employment or use of an agency driver will suffice, and the driver may even be self-employed as long as he is driving on the employer's orders and for the purposes of his business. The only exception to this rule is where the driver is himself a partner in the firm; in this case the driver only is liable. The employer will not be liable if the vehicle is being used for unauthorised purposes. The general policy of the prosecuting authorities is to proceed against the employer where the offence relates to the condition of the vehicle and against the driver only where he is actually at fault.

Definition of "Causing or permitting"

Causing an offence is fairly obvious. If the employer instructs an employee to drive a heavy goods vehicle when he knows that the employee only has an ordinary licence he causes the offence of driving without the appropriate licence. Permitting is a rather more nebulous concept. Some degree of fault is required. There may be a failure to take a necessary precaution; an employer who takes a new employee's word that he has a HGV licence, and doesn't require the licence itself to be produced may well be guilty of permitting an offence if the employee has deceived him. Other cases may be a matter of closing one's eyes to the obvious, as where an employer fails to check tachograph charts for evidence of hours and rest infringements, and has no proper system of checking hours worked. The area is a complex one and legal advice is necessary in relation to any given allegation.

It should be noted that some construction and use offences carry possible endorsement and disqualification where the charge is one of using a vehicle with dangerous defects (especially tyres, steering and brakes). The employee may escape endorsement where he can show that the defect was not apparent, and he was not responsible for maintenance, but an employer who is a sole trader, and all the partners in a firm, are liable to endorsement for using a vehicle in such condition.

Driving licences

Vehicles are divided into various classes, and a licence for the correct class of vehicle is required. An ordinary licence is all that is required for cars and light commercial vehicles. An additional HGV licence is required for larger vehicles. There are sub-groups comprising medium weight rigid vehicles, large rigid vehicles and articulated vehicles. There is an initial test of competence and a continual monitoring of medical fitness to drive. The criteria for HGV drivers are considerably more rigorous than for others.

Insurance

All vehicles must be insured against the compulsory risks, which are injury to any person other than the driver and damage to the property of any third party above a low threshold figure. It is theoretically possible to give a security for the settlement of claims by depositing a sum of money with the Supreme Court, but this is very rare. It is important to ensure that the cover afforded by the policy does actually extend to the use to which the vehicle is put. Common pitfalls relate to the driver; the policy may limit driving by reference to age etc, and will certainly only cover drivers who are licensed for the vehicle. It will normally be a condition of the policy that the vehicle is properly maintained and not overloaded or otherwise abused.

Name: The Road Vehicles (Construction and Use) Regulations 1987

As their name implies these regulations contain the detailed rules relating to the design construction and operation of vehicles of all types and their constituent systems such as brakes and steering gear. There is a similar set of regulations dealing specifically with lighting, and there are other UK and EEC regulations relating to design standards and type approval for vehicles and components. These regulations, and the construction aspect of the main regulations, are of interest primarily to vehicle manufacturers, but any vehicle user who requires specialised vehicles, or who wishes to rebuild or modify a vehicle will need to ensure that the contractor who undertakes this work is aware of, and complies with, the regulations. As noted earlier, liability for a defective vehicle rests with the user, and offences are absolute, in the sense that all that needs to be proved is that the vehicle was used when defective, and not that the user knew or ought to have known that it was defective. The penalty imposed by the court will of course reflect whether the court sees the offence as unintentional, as a careless oversight or as deliberate. There are specific provisions dealing with major components such as steering and brakes which must be in good working order properly maintained and adjusted, and tyres, where there are detailed requirements as to tread depth and integrity of the tyre's structure. There is also a general requirement that the vehicle must not be a danger to other road users by reason of its condition or load. All these matters are endorsable. There are also rules as to the permitted overall dimensions of vehicles, the marking of projections to front, side or rear, the use of trailers and as to permitted weights. These matters are not endorsable.

The regulations related to weight are complex, as they have to allow for a very wide range of vehicle types, including foreign vehicles which do not necessarily have permitted weights. Three types of weight are regulated, axle weights (including groups of compensating axles, which are treated as a single unit), the gross weight of each vehicle, and the overall or train weight of an articulated vehicle or lorry and trailer combination. There are general maxima fixed by law and which can be varied from time to time as a result of EEC legislation, eg 12000 kg for any one axle, 32520 kg train weight for a four-axled articulated vehicle and 38000 kg train weight for any vehicle under the general law. There is special provision for vehicles used for abnormal loads. Subject to these maxima each vehicle must be loaded within the individual permitted weights shown on its plate. Legal liability rests with the user, ie the vehicle operator, whether a haulier or one carrying his own goods. This is so even if the vehicle has been loaded by someone else. The loader can be prosecuted for assisting the commission of the offence, but this is in practice rare.

Plating and Testing

All vehicles are subject to periodic testing. In the case of semi-trailers and trailers the HGV test station issues a disc showing the period for which the current certificate is valid which must be affixed to the trailer. Goods vehicles and trailers are also plated to show their permitted weight. The manufacturer will attach a plate showing the design weights, which may exceed UK maxima, and are to that extent inapplicable. For vehicles an official certificate is issued showing the maxima for the type of vehicle and for vehicles and trailers a plate is issued by the Department of Transport giving those permitted weights.

The relevant plates must be displayed, and are used as the basis for calculating permitted weights in any weight check of the vehicle. It is possible to amend the Department plate, either by increasing the weights if there is a change in the general law, or the vehicle has been modified, or by reducing them to bring the vehicle into a lower Vehicle Excise Duty category.

Hazardous or sensitive cargoes

There are a number of sets of regulations which establish the rules for the carriage of different categories of cargo. There are regulations for petroleum products (under the Petroleum (Consolidation) Act 1928), nuclear products (Radioactive Substances (Carriage by Road) (Great Britain) Regs. SI 1974/1735) and hazardous chemicals generally (Dangerous Substances (Conveyance by Road in Road Tankers and Road Containers) Regs SI 1981/1059). The regulations cover crew training, hazard marking (to alert the emergency services in case of accident to necessary precautions) and physical conditions of carriage. In the case of the refrigerated transport of foodstuffs the emphasis is on public health rather than safety (The regulations are made under the Food Act 1984). It is the responsibility of vehicle operators whose activities fall within these categories to familiarise themselves with the regulations and comply with them.

Name: Vehicles (Excise) Act 1971

All mechanically propelled vehicles which are used or kept on a public road must be licensed. A vehicle may be kept off the road without a licence, but if it is then used without a licence, duty is payable back to the expiry or surrender of the earlier licence, or the date of acquisition by the current owner/keeper. There is a flat-rate licence for private and light goods vehicles, but there is a range of rates of duty for large goods vehicles. These vary with the permitted overall weight and the axle configuration of the vehicle, and there are special rates of duty for farmers and showmen; it is an offence to use a vehicle for a purpose or (in the case of an articulated vehicle, in a combination) which attracts a higher rate of duty. In addition to any penalty the higher rate of duty is payable retrospectively to the issue of the current licence. The current licence must be displayed, although there are 14 days of grace between licences where the new licence has been applied for, to cover administrative delays. Although legal liability rests with the user or keeper of the vehicle, in practice it is the operator who will be prosecuted.

Index

Post offices, 34
Power breakers, 60
Power stations, 31
Pregnancy
    Hours of work during, 56
Pressure systems, 64
Pressure Systems etc. Regs., 64
Pressure vessels, 64
Price fixing, 1, 18
Product Liability, 145–147, 150–154
    Defences, 147
Protective clothing, 64, 66
Protective equipment
    Personal, 71
Public Health Act 1936, 42
Public Lending Right Act 1979, 100
Public transport, 163–164
Purchasing agreements
    Exclusive, 8
Pushchairs, 150–151

R

Radioactive contamination, 30
Radioactive substances, 46
    Road Transport, 170
Radioactive Substances Act 1960, 46
Railway premises, 62
Recommended resale prices, 18
Records
    Health and safety, 57
Records keeping
    COSHH, 67
Refrigerated Vehicles, 170
Registered Designs Act 1949, 110
Rental rights
    Copyright material, 89
Repiratory protection
    See also Breathing apparatus
Reporting
    Health and safety, 56
Resale Price Maintenance, 19
Resale Prices Act 1976, 19
Research and Development
    Agreements, 9
    Planning permission, 34
Respiratory protection, 66
Rest rooms, 70
Restaurants, 34
Restrictive Practices, 18–19
Restrictive Practices Act 1973, 18
Restrictive Trading Agreements
    Registration of, 21
Retail Premises
    See also Shops
Retailing

See also Shops
Risk assessment
    Dangerous substances, 66
Road and Rail Traffic Act 1933, 164
Road haulage
    Operator's licence, 164, 166–167
Road Traffic Act 1988, 168
Road Vehicles Regulations 1987, 169
Roofs, 63
Ropes, 61

S

Safety committees, 55
Safety equipment, 62
Safety representatives, 55
    Training, time off, 55
Safety Signs Regulations 1980, 57
Sale of Goods Act 1979, 132
Sales, 132–137
    Samples, 135
Satellite Transmissions, 94
Scaffolding, 63
    Inspection of, 57
Scottish Transport Group, 164
Seating requirements, 59
Semiconductor Topographic Design
    Copyright, 99
Service Contracts, 141
Service Marks, 101
    Infringement, 102
Seveso, 30
Sewage, 44
Sex Discrimination Act 1989, 56
Shops, 34
    Health and safety, 62
Signs
    Hazard warning, 67
    Safety, 57
Single European Act 1986, 4, 27
Smoke, 45
Smoke control, 29
Sound rcordings, 89
Sound recordings, 85–86, 88–89
Stairs, 62
Standards
    For machinery guards, 60
State aids, 3
Statutory nuisance, 42
Steelworks, 31
Substance data sheets
    See Data sheets
Substances
    Work materials, safety, 53
Sulphur dioxide, 29
Sumps, 62